# LOVE AND THE EVOLUTION OF CONSCIOUSNESS

# Love *and the* Evolution *of* Consciousness

*A Study of the Transformation of the Human Soul, the Double, and the Spirit*

KAREN L. RIVERS

Lindisfarne Books | 2016

2016

LINDISFARNE BOOKS

An imprint of Anthroposophic Press / SteinerBooks

610 Main St., Great Barrington, MA 01230

www.steinerbooks.org



Cover art © Jorge Sanz-Cardona
Cover and book design by Jeanne DePrince Bowen

LIBRARY OF CONGRESS CONTROL NUMBER: 2016947090

Print ISBN: 978-1-58420-980-5
eBook ISBN: 978-1-58420-981-2

*To Chérie,*
*my beloved daughter*

# Contents

# List of Illustrations, Tables, and Diagrams

# Acknowledgments

> One can pay back the loan of gold, but one dies forever in debt to those who are kind.
>
> —Malayan Proverb

I wish to express my deep gratitude to the community of people whose kindness, generosity, and wisdom have supported me in one way or another during and preceding the research and writing of this book.

First and foremost I extend my deepest gratitude to Robert McDermott, for his steadfast support, rigorous guidance, astute intellectual direction, and warmth of heart. He has been a beacon of light that has kept my rudder on course. To Chérie Rivers Ndaliko, whose academic rigor challenged every idea and formulation, inspiring me to hone my thoughts and nuance my articulation of them. Her loving support and formidable questions raised the bar and lifted my sights.

I also extend my deepest gratitude for the generosity and intellectual guidance of Robert Powell, whose work and support have inspired my life's work. His vast and diverse contributions to world thought and creative expression, his steadfast devotion to the great work contributing to conscious evolution, and his meticulous attention to every request and question put to him, has been an enduring source of inspiration and strength for me. His life's work and personal support have been invaluable to this study.

I wish to thank Philip Mees for his kindness and generosity in transcribing the lectures I gave for the course "Exploring the Depths of the

Soul: Understanding the Human Double." His warm friendship and diligent support launched the initial stages of the writing of this book.

My heartfelt gratitude extends to the Sophia Foundation and all those who support it, for the presence of a community that seeks to uphold and promote the ideals presented herein.

I extend warmest gratitude to those friends who offered financial support during the final stages of my writing, enabling me to work part time for one semester: Jacob and Asha Blessing, Richard Bloedon, Nancy Calloway, Drude Clark, Michael Choy, Linda and Russell Delman, Mary Jane Di Piero, Wiene Frans, Betsyann Gallagher, Gale Gebstadt, Sharon and Scott Hamilton, Rosamond Hughes, Patricia Johnson, Susan Kirchhoff, Claudia Mclaren Lainson, Heidi Lazerson, Philip Mees, Davina Muse, Meg Pelose, Molly Rose, Tracy Saucier, Eileen Sullivan, Kelly Sutton, Henry Winogrond, and Katharina Woodman. To each and every one of you, I hold your kindness deeply in my heart.

Finally, I wish to express my gratitude to my family. To my father and mother, Roland and Jorna Hellman, whose strength and moral integrity laid a foundation for my life. My love and gratitude will always be with them. To my brother, David Hellman, for his loyal support and steadfast presence in my life. His noble character and loving support throughout my life has strengthened me and given me a sense of security. To my daughter, Chérie, for her presence in my life, her love and support as a daughter, her achievements that inspire me, her tenacious spirit, and her dedicated service in the world. To my son-in-law, Petna, for his loving support of my daughter and his devoted commitment to help bring justice and peace to the D. R. Congo. And to my most precious grandson, Mokozi, who brings joy and new insights to my life each day.

Very last, but not least, I wish to express my deepest gratitude to my husband, Michael, who has stood by me through this interminable process, with support, food, editing, encouragement, and love. He has lived every step of the way with me, and his partnership has brought comfort and joy to my work. My love and gratitude for him will always fill my heart.

# Introduction: Even Unto the Least of My Brothers . . .

> We have not understood yet that the discovery of the unconscious means an enormous spiritual task, which must be accomplished if we wish to preserve our civilization.
>
> —Carl Gustav Jung*

On March 2, 2008, seventeen pilgrims from the United States and Europe arrived in Bodhgaya, India, the place of Buddha's enlightenment. This was the fifteenth day of a twenty-five day pilgrimage sponsored by the Sophia Foundation. On this day I had a defining experience that catalyzed considerable reflection and self-scrutiny.

As our group was walking along the extensive sidewalks that led to the temple dedicated to Buddha's enlightenment, I reflected on Prince Siddhartha as a boy, growing up in a palace surrounded by a great wall that protected him from encountering the suffering of the world. When, as a young man, he ventured into the surrounding city, he was shocked to discover sickness, old age, and death. This awakened within him the desire to find a way to bring an end to suffering. This became his life's quest.

Our travels in India were colored by exposure to extreme poverty, suffering, and illness. I had the sense that my life as a privileged Westerner was analogous to living behind the protective walls of Siddhartha's childhood palace. In many ways, my experiences in India were akin to Siddhartha's

* Jung, 1973, p. 537. Letter of Sept. 23, 1949, to Dorothy Thompson.

venturing outside the palace walls: encountering a level of poverty unknown to me, experiencing sickness and deformity pressing in from all sides, and witnessing death in the streets and on the funeral pyres along the Ganges. My "palace of protection" afforded by privileged modern life crumbled, and the suffering I encountered penetrated to the core of my bones, stirring questions and thoughts not unlike Prince Siddhartha's.

As we approached the site of the Buddha's enlightenment, we were surrounded and assaulted by a throng of people whose lives were consumed in poverty, many of whom were crippled. A leper staggered forward, extending an oozing stump in supplication, gesturing toward her steel alms bowl, empty as her stomach. Her imploring eyes pierced my soul. Dozens of beggars pressed in upon us with outstretched arms and looks of anguish. Walking toward the entrance to the Bodhi tree something flopped onto my feet. The woman next to me gasped and leapt forward, hurrying away. Reflexively, I jumped over what I later discovered was the body of a crippled man whose legs were splayed. He was only able to move using his arms to pull himself along the ground on his belly. He chased me, flopping on my feet with imploring eyes and outstretched hands. Caught in the grip of shock and repulsion, I ran away. Confusion, horror, and shame swirled in the core of my being. The words of Jesus scourged my conscience:

> But I say to you, Love your enemies, do good to those who hate you, bless those who curse you, pray for those who abuse you. If anyone strikes you on the cheek, offer the other also; and from anyone who takes away your coat do not withhold even your shirt. Give to everyone who begs from you; and if anyone takes away your goods, do not ask for them again. Do to others as you would have them do unto you. Love your enemies, do good, and lend, expecting nothing in return. Be merciful, just as your Father is merciful. 'Do not judge, and you will not be judged; do not condemn, and you will not be condemned. Forgive, and you will be forgiven; give, and it will be given to you (Luke 6:27–31 and 35–38, Revised Standard Version).

This experience catalyzed a level of self-scrutiny that led me to realize the unmitigated presence of my reactive impulses, their power to override my values and beliefs, and my discomfort with this circumstance. I began a process of increased self-awareness, committed to bringing about the penetration of subconscious reflex responses with consciousness and self-direction, resulting in a new level of inner discipline. This process continues as a daily practice and lifelong commitment. The content of this book illumines a narrow passage through the corridors of the soul, leading to the portal of conscious love. I hope that this contribution may help you in your journey of inner development and your ever-growing capacity to love.

## Sources of Inspiration

As I have reflected on the arc of the journey that led to the undertaking of this inquiry, I realized that it was thirty-three years ago, now from the completion of this book, that I encountered the work of Rudolf Steiner. As Rudolf Steiner has been an extremely influential figure in my life, this seems a fitting interval—one of death and resurrection—to overlay on the completion of this work. Among the most significant occultists in the twentieth century, Rudolf Steiner (1861–1925) contributed to many fields of knowledge including evolution, history, psychology, philosophy, economics, Christology, comparative religion, education, science, agriculture, medicine, art, reincarnation and karma, life after death, social thought, and architecture. The complete edition of his published works numbers over 330 volumes, establishing him among the most prolific authors of all time.

As a highly developed clairvoyant and spiritual initiate, Steiner spoke from his direct cognition of the spiritual world. However, he did not see his work as religious or sectarian, but rather sought to found a universal *science of the spirit*. Rudolf Steiner called his spiritual philosophy *anthroposophy*,* which he defined as the *consciousness of one's humanity*, and the disciplined methods of studying this he termed *spiritual science*.

Steiner considered it his task to survey the spiritual realities at work within the realms of Nature and throughout the Universe. He explored the inner nature of the human soul and spirit and developed new methods

* For further information about Anthroposophy see: Steiner, R. (1976). *The Life, Nature, and Cultivation of Anthroposophy*. Great Britain: Rudolf Steiner Press.

of meditation for their potential growth. He investigated the experiences of human souls before birth and after death and made detailed studies of reincarnation and karma. He also looked back into the spiritual history and evolution of humanity and the Earth.

In 1918, Steiner presented suggestions for a conscious threefold differentiation of society, focusing on the development of freedom in the cultural sphere (art, education, religion), equality in the sphere of politics and legislation, and a globally oriented brotherhood in the sphere of economy. He believed that we can build a healthy social order only on the basis of insight into the material, soul, and spiritual needs of human beings. Those needs are characterized by a powerful tension between the search for community and the experience of the human I, or true individuality. As in independent thinking and free speech, the human I, or essential self, is the foundation of every creative endeavor and innovation, and crucial to the realization of human spirit. These ideas establish the foundation for this book.

Valentin Tomberg (1900–1973), a Russian Christian mystic, multilingual scholar, and hermeticist, contributed significantly to the fields of Christology, Sophiology,* inner development, and law. Strongly influenced by the Russian Sophiologist Vladimir Soloviev, in his youth Valentin Tomberg entered upon a serious study of Christian esotericism. As a student of Rudolf Steiner, he wrote and lectured on spiritual science (Anthroposophy), primarily addressing Christological themes.

While living in Amsterdam during the earlier part of World War II (1941–1942), Valentin Tomberg secretly met with a group of eight people on a weekly basis, giving a meditation course on the Lord's Prayer.** This effort to establish a spiritual counterforce to the power of National Socialism continued for two years until Tomberg was forced to leave Amsterdam for his safety. This unpublished meditation course, which I completed over a fourteen-year period, addresses the inner path of purification, illumination, and union, including sections on the ninefold double through Christology.

---

* Sophiology: the study of *Sophia*—the wisdom of creation.

** Valentin Tomberg's *Lord's Prayer Course* is an unpublished manuscript available in hand-written form through the Sophia Foundation: www.sophiafoundation.org.

Tomberg later moved to England, where he lived the remainder of his life in intense prayer, meditation, and esoteric study, while working for the BBC. It was here that he wrote in the spirit of the Egyptian Hermetic tradition, illumining the symbolism of Christian Hermeticism that draws upon many spiritual and mystical traditions. Tomberg was a person of intense spiritual discipline, practice, and dedication, of prayer and extraordinary meditative and esoteric accomplishment. He stands out as a leading Sophiologist, one of the great mystics of the twentieth century, and as the primary inspirer of Christian Hermeticism.* His writings have significantly inspired my life and the content of this work.

## Spiritual Context

I was raised in a Christian family, attending the Presbyterian Church every week of my life until I went to college. In high school as a student of Alan Barahal, a double PhD from Harvard University, I began investigating the common and uncommon themes in comparative religions. This influenced my university studies that culminated in a degree in comparative religions, philosophy, and world literature from the University of California, Berkeley. My studies of world religions deepened through active engagement in the Sufi Ruhaniat International. When encountering Rudolf Steiner's work through Waldorf education, many unanswered questions were met with breadth and depth that has engaged me in a lifelong study of anthroposophy and Christology.

Rudolf Steiner advocated a form of ethical individualism, to which he later brought a more explicitly spiritual component. In 1899, Steiner experienced what he described as a life-transforming inner encounter with the being of Christ. Previously he had little or no relation to Christianity. Thereafter his relationship to Christianity remained entirely founded upon personal experience, and was both non-denominational and strikingly different from conventional religious forms.

---

* For a more in-depth biography of Valentin Tomberg see Christopher Bamford's introduction to *Christ and Sophia* (Tomberg, 2006, pp. vii-xxxiv).

Steiner describes Christ's being and mission on Earth as having a central place in human evolution. This being unifies all religions as the central force in human evolution, not a particular religious faith. Rudolf Steiner maintained that Christ has been working on humanity's behalf since the very beginnings of its existence, long before the inception of the Christian religion. Steiner indicated that in both the ancient Mystery schools and in the miraculous events depicted in the Old Testament, the guiding hand of Christ shaped and developed peoples' cognition. Steiner stated that historical forms of Christianity need to be transformed continually in order to meet the evolution of humanity. He believed that Christ's incarnation into Jesus of Nazareth was a pivotal point in human history. In Steiner's esoteric cosmology, the spiritual development of humanity is interwoven in and inseparable from the cosmological development of the Universe. For Steiner, to be *Christian* is the ability to manifest love in freedom.

The name *Christ* is used here in the context described above, pointing toward a spiritual reality of the Christ that is universal among religions.

## Mapping the Course

*Love and the Evolution of Consciousness* offers a contribution to the essential need for humanity as individuals to transform their inner lives, to redirect the course of human interest from self-centered to community-centered (*community* being used here to indicate the larger world community of all living beings on the planet). This work presents insights and strategies to further the journey of self-development, to deepen the capacity for selfless love in its highest spiritual form, and thus affect world consciousness.

Chapter 1 ("Approaching the Inner Chamber of the Soul") introduces an interior map of the corridors of the human soul and the elusive nature of the ninefold double*—the shadowy impediment to human development—

* I first encountered the paradigm of the ninefold double in the *Our Mother Course* (the advanced part of the *Lord's Prayer Course*) by Valentin Tomberg. He introduced the nine aspects of the human double that form the skeleton for this work. He gave cryptic Christian esoteric indications of these dimensions of the inner spiritual life. His words have lived as seed thoughts working in me over the past twenty years as I have gradually formulated the content of this thesis.

with the object of cultivating a keenly awakened moral consciousness, independent spiritual cognition, and spiritual consciousness transcending materialism. Chapters 2 ("The Luciferic Double: The Crown of Glory"), 3 ("The Ahrimanic Double: The Claws of Fear"), and 4 ("The Karmic Double: The Web of Destiny") examine the thought patterns, default feeling responses, and subconsciously driven reactions of each of the three doubles, to offer the clarity needed to overcome them. Chapter 5 ("Karma and Forgiveness: Holding the Universe Together") concludes with insights into the dynamics of karma and the power of forgiveness to foster the mission of love.

I hope the reader will find this to be a transformative experience that bears many fruits.

# CHAPTER 1

# Approaching the Inner Chamber of the Soul

> What human beings will really give to the Earth is love, a love that will evolve from the most sensuous to the most spiritualized form. This is the mission of Earth evolution. Earth is the cosmos of love.
>
> —Rudolf Steiner*

I believe that love precedes all things, that it is the highest ideal in the Universe, and that it promotes compassion, forgiveness, and peace. Love always bears the possibilities that are yet to unfold, the potential that lives in the future. It holds the space for becoming. Love is to create, to enter selflessly into the current of time that ceaselessly flows toward us from the future. Many world religions, philosophies, and cultural values define the essential purpose of life in relation to the primacy of love. According to Rudolf Steiner, it is the task of human beings to transubstantiate the wisdom and very substance of the Earth into love (Steiner, 1998, p. 10).

In considering this ideology it is incumbent to ask: *What is love?* Throughout history, humanity has grappled with many perspectives on this primary question. The magnitude of love encompasses a diversity of meanings that exist in the lexicons of various cultures around the world. Indeed, despite cultural differences, some experiences are common to all humanity; one of these is love in its various manifestations.

---

* Steiner, 1998, pp. 68–69.

Love dominates the theme of many works from all historical periods and religious traditions around the world.* The question, *What is love?* occupies the thoughts central to the dialogue in Plato's *Symposium*, which I am choosing to foreground because it approaches the question from various perspectives leading to the highest human experience of divine love. Plato describes love as a dynamic, a flow of energy that operates throughout all levels of human awareness, uniting and transcending, or fragmenting and descending as it flows. Latent possibilities underlie different kinds of love—maternal and paternal love, brotherly and sisterly love, love of self, eros,** romantic love, love of life, love for humanity, agape, love of God—that can either lift us up to Socrates's unified and ultimate good in the world of Being,*** or drag us down into a dense, fragmented experience of the realm of forms**** (Plato, 1952, p. 163).

In *The Symposium*, Agathon hosts a party in which six characters discuss the meaning of love. After five guests deliver their arguments characterizing love, Socrates speaks. He recalls a conversation with Diotema, whose argument takes place solely within the framework of Socrates's memory; she is a step removed, by space and time, from the reality of the party and, by analogy, her argument is that much more evolved beyond the arguments that have gone before. To Socrates's question, "What then is Love?" Diotema answers: "He is a great spirit (daimon), and like all spirits he is intermediate between the divine and the mortal.... He is the mediator who

---

* Among many others, a few examples are: the Isha and Brihadaranyaka Upanishads; Bhagavagita chap. 4; The Four Immeasurables in Buddhism; John 4:7–21; Qur'an 2:177.

** Sexual love.

*** Plato developed a two-layer view of reality, the world of Becoming and the world of Being. The world of Becoming is the physical world we perceive through our senses. This world is always in movement, always changing. The world of Being is the world of forms, or ideas. It is absolute, independent, and transcendent. It never changes and yet causes the essential nature of things we perceive in the world of Becoming.

**** Plato's *forms* are archetypes; the forms are the perfect models upon which all material objects are based. The forms are not located in space and time. They are the ultimately real entities, not material objects. All material objects are copies or images of some collection of forms; their reality comes only from the forms.

spans the chasm which divides them, and therefore in him all is bound together" (Plato, 1952, p. 163).

Plato describes human beings as having a dual nature: existing in the world of matter with the potential for divine realization, a microcosm within the macrocosm. Love potentiates the longing to realize the Divine within our self and to help others realize their divine nature, as well. Love helps us build a relationship between the two worlds in which we live.

Diotema describes life as a process of ascent—a movement upward to a finer and finer understanding of love. Through love, which prompts our abilities to create, we ascend and come closer to God, first on the physical plane, then on correspondingly non-material planes such as the creation of works of art, which can range from a piece of literature, to a relationship, to one's self.

When Diotema asks Socrates what is it that one desires when one loves, he answers: "Immortality—union with the eternal" (Plato, 1952, p. 164). Love encompasses the potential to unite with the eternal, for in searching for and recognizing the Divine within the beloved, one also discovers the Divine within one's self, recognizing that in all its forms divinity is one. Love elevates consciousness; it is a process, not an end in itself, in which humans can touch the Divine and in this state of perception enter into a mystical experience, a union of the human spirit with God. Diotema's perspective on love, further developed by Socrates, describes the ultimate vision toward which this book leads.

Love is ultimately the most meaningful of human experiences. In all its various forms, love leads us to the fulfillment of human existence. Love has the power to unite us with our true self, to unite us with the spiritual essence in others, and it has the power to carry us on wings of selflessness to unite with the Divine.

Developing the capacity to love requires clarity regarding the impediments that obstruct our ability to choose love in response to every situation we encounter. The shadows that lurk within the human soul impede the ability to love. Exposing these shadows creates the possibility to overcome them and transform consciousness to cultivate love as a response to all the circumstances that present themselves in our lives.

A long history of investigation into the inner life of the human being has contributed vast resources for human development psychologically and spiritually. William James (1984), Sigmund Freud (1989), Carl Jung (1959), James Hillman (1997), Erik Erikson (Welchman, 2000), Abraham Maslow (2011), among many others in the field of psychology have contributed extensive research and theory on the development of the soul life. Likewise, in the field of spiritual consciousness, Sri Aurobindo (Ghose, and McDermott, 1988), Trungpa Rinpoche (2003), Suzuki Roshi (2011), Rudolf Steiner (1999), the Dalai Lama (2003), and many others, have presented spiritual teachings that address the purification of the human soul life and the development of spiritual consciousness.

Here the examination of the inner soul and spiritual life is approached from a foundation of Anthroposophy—the life work of Rudolf Steiner—and upon the esoteric writings of Valentin Tomberg, augmented by the inspiration of other eminent thinkers and spiritual leaders. This work contributes to spiritual literature within the fields of anthroposophy and spiritual psychology, foregrounding the development of a seminal, innovative inner path of consciousness aimed at preparing those interested to become forerunners of a future cultural age in which love and wisdom govern consciousness, in which the Spirit Self* within human beings comes to birth. This requires extensive knowledge of the human soul life.

When embarking upon the exploration of the inner realms of the soul, one can conjure up the image of Dante standing beneath the gate to the inferno, faced with the daunting reality of his fear and trepidation. Accompanied by Virgil, his guide, his passage through the inferno, purgatory, and paradise illumined his understanding of the trials of moral integrity and the journey the human soul experiences on its course of redemption. The process of internalizing a conscious understanding of this inner terrain and of the soul impediments we experience provides resources to transform and increase our ability to become self-realized and cultivate selfless love for others.

---

* *Spirit Self* is a term given by Rudolf Steiner to indicate the purified astral body, the astral body transformed by the forces of the ego (Steiner, 1979, p. 39). Defined in greater detail below.

Among the trials every individual encounters emerges the unfolding confrontation with one's *double*—the inner counter-evolutionary forces that work to undermine the development of one's consciousness. This encounter brings to the forefront questions of values and integrity, challenging the moral fiber of one's being. The struggle with the issues that arise and the decisions one faces often becomes a lonely process of confusion and isolation. For most people there has been no preparation, no warning, no educational support for this experience. If our educational systems taught children and adults about the landscape of inner life and the internal challenges that all human beings encounter, there would be quite a different potential for understanding, compassion, and love.

Knowledge of the inner realms creates the potential for those people with a commitment to self-development to: understand the needs behind destructive behaviors, give compassion to themselves and others, and choose love and forgiveness in times of adversity. The potential for conscious community that honors the integrity of humanity and Nature, guided by the spiritual forces of eternal love and divine wisdom, hangs on the collective efforts of those individuals willing to traverse the inner dimensions of the soul and work to expiate all obstacles hindering the path of love. A culture guided by the principles of love and wisdom can only arise through the requisite work of individual inner transformation.

As a result of cognizing the terrain of the human soul, understanding the intricacies of the human double, and engaging in conscious guidance of will forces and purification of soul forces, the human capacity for love will increase. This process seeds the potential for a new wisdom culture that will bear a moral quality of empathy and compassion, transforming self-interest into interest in the well-being of all, true inner freedom, and spiritual gnosis. Rudolf Steiner mentions a "golden rule" for those aspiring to the spiritual path: "For every one step that you take in the pursuit of higher knowledge, take three steps in the perfection of your own character" (Steiner, 1977, p. 57).

## Context

Rudolf Steiner described a future condition of humanity, referred to as the Sixth Cultural Epoch, as the age of brotherly and sisterly love, when a new consciousness will arise giving birth to the Spirit Self within human beings if, and only if, the transformation of soul forces occurs during our current cultural age, the Fifth Cultural Epoch.

> Our own epoch, throughout its duration, will develop and unfold the consciousness or spiritual soul. But what will give to external culture in the sixth epoch its content and character, must be prepared in advance. Many characteristics of the sixth epoch of culture will be entirely different from those of our age. Three characteristic traits can be mentioned, of which we must realize that they should be carried in our hearts for the sixth epoch of culture and that it is our task to prepare them for this sixth epoch (Steiner, 1915, p. 2).

Thus, according to Rudolf Steiner, building upon the spiritual achievements of the Fifth Epoch, humanity will have the potential to form communities arising out of individual freedom, around gnosis of Sophia, embodying a moral consciousness exceeding that of our current age.

Moral consciousness defines the essence of our own being; it encompasses the values we have, out of freedom, integrated into our being that determine our responses to life's encounters. A moral quality entails the ability to rise above personal preference or comfort to behold what is objectively important, to take interest in someone or something because of its intrinsic value as opposed to how it will benefit you, and to act accordingly. Mature moral consciousness grows through a deepening lifelong integration of moral motivation, agency, and critical discernment.

For example, two men witness an injustice about to be inflicted upon a third person. One man only asks whether anything about the situation is advantageous or disadvantageous to him; he will not be concerned about the injustice if he calculates that no personal damage to him can result from the other's injury. The second man is willing to take suffering upon himself rather than remain disinterested in the injustice which is about to be done to the third person. For the second man the preponderant question is not whether something is advantageous to him or not, but whether it is important in and of itself. The first man places his concern with himself. He is indifferent to others, indicating little moral consciousness. The second man bypasses the question of personal value and places higher importance on justice for everyone rather than on comfort, convenience, and interest in himself, exemplifying a developed moral consciousness. Moral consciousness necessitates seeing beyond one's own subjective horizon and, free from pride and concupiscence, does not always ask, *What is advantageous for me?* but focuses upon that which is important in and of itself—the true, the beautiful, the good—and serves it. Moral consciousness reflects a moral sense of identity, a sense of responsibility and agency, a deep sense of relatedness on all levels of living, and a sense of meaning and life purpose. This will be addressed in greater detail in chapter 5.

Goodness employs a dual role in the investigation of moral values. "Good" means moral value as such, and also the specific moral quality of goodness. Among the various virtues, goodness most completely embodies the entire canon of moral values, the inclusivity of all morality. Its central importance in the moral sphere consists, therefore, of a completely different type from that of other values. Other virtues are accepted as a presupposition for the moral life. Goodness, on the contrary, is not a presupposition, but the fruit of moral life. It is not a fruit among others—such as humility, patience, and generosity—but the fruit that culminates all morality in a unified way.

We say a person is good when disposed to help, when kind, just, ready to make sacrifices for others, able to pardon wrongs done, generous, and full of compassion. All these qualities express specific forms and manifestations of love. So here we see the close relationship that exists between love and goodness. Love expresses itself as flowing goodness, and goodness as the breath of love. Morality works to build up selfless love as a moral force in human consciousness.

The awakening of goodness and moral consciousness in the soul life will prepare individuals for a potential transition in consciousness—the birth of spiritual perception arising out of a mature, purified soul condition—making a culture of universal wisdom possible.

To seed the soil for the emergence of the Sixth Cultural Epoch three primary characteristics need preparation. The development of these characteristics requires an inner orientation that mandates: a keenly developed moral consciousness, independent spiritual cognition, and spiritual consciousness transcending materialism.

A keenly developed moral consciousness experiences the suffering and well-being of all of humanity as one's own. It constitutes a unifying fabric with all life, wherein our actions will be considered in relation to the effect on the whole of life. Rudolf Steiner describes the first characteristic in the following manner.

> One of the most significant characteristics of men living on the Earth at the peak of culture in the Sixth Epoch, will be a certain moral quality.... In the Sixth Epoch, the most highly cultured* will not only feel pain such as is caused today by the sight of poverty, suffering, and misery in the world, but such individuals will experience the suffering of another human being as their own suffering. If they see a hungry man they will feel the hunger right down into the physical, so acutely indeed that the hunger of the other man will be unendurable to them. The moral characteristic indicated here is that, unlike conditions in the Fifth Epoch, in the Sixth Epoch the well-being of the individual will depend entirely upon the well-being of the whole (Steiner, 1915, p. 2).

To achieve a moral consciousness that embraces the whole of humanity as one's own family, feeling the love toward every human being that one now feels toward one's own children and loved ones, will require a dramatic shift in inner orientation. The efforts of human will forces will be directed toward the well-being of all life on the Earth. This first preeminently moral trait that will characterize the Sixth Epoch can only come about through an overcoming of all notions of "the other" as the enemy, or insignificant, or unworthy. All judgments of others will have to dissolve. For those individuals who develop this level of moral acuteness, love will be the reflexive

* Here "the most highly cultured" indicates those people who have developed a refined sensitivity to the needs and feelings of others, experiencing the injustice, hunger, and indignation of others as if it is one's own.

response to all situations, for every person's condition will live within you as your own. Seeds of this transformed consciousness are already germinating in the Fifth Epoch.

A second characteristic intrinsic to the Sixth Epoch is the essential right for individual freedom in the sphere of beliefs and religious thought.

> In every sphere of religion in the Sixth Epoch, complete freedom of thought and a longing for it will so lay hold of men that what a man likes to believe, what religious convictions he holds, will rest wholly within the power of his own individuality. Collective beliefs that exist in so many forms today among the various communities will no longer influence those who constitute the civilized* portion of humanity in the Sixth Epoch of culture. Everyone will feel that complete freedom of thought in the domain of religion is a fundamental right of the human being (Steiner, 1915, p. 3).

The human soul will evolve to the condition wherein it experiences spiritual realities through personal inner activity, and will develop religious beliefs out of a free life of thought, independent of collective beliefs. The influence of institutional religious dictates will diminish as individual inner spiritual experiences increase, becoming the guiding inspiration for people in the Sixth Epoch. We see signs of this already as people increasingly express interest in spirituality outside the context of a religious tradition. But the spiritual freedom of the Sixth Epoch will arise out of inner spiritual experiences that will inform individuals, establishing a personal knowing or gnosis. This spiritual knowledge will inform people's beliefs, as well as scientific knowledge.

The third characteristic of the Sixth Epoch identified by Rudolf Steiner emphasizes the quintessential importance of uniting with the spiritual world in one's soul life, as well as in knowledge and in deeds.

---

* In this context Rudolf Steiner uses the work "civilized" to mean those people who carry the impulse to further the well-being of humanity as a whole and the Earth, who have developed the consciousness to act in integrity with their thoughts and values, working selflessly to advance evolution.

> The third characteristic will be that men in the sixth epoch will only be considered to have real knowledge when they recognize the spiritual, when they know that the spiritual pervades the world and that human souls must unite with the spiritual. What is known as science today with its materialistic trend will certainly not be honored by the name of science in the sixth post-Atlantean epoch. It will be regarded as antiquated superstition, able to pass muster only among those who have remained behind at the stage of the superseded fifth post-Atlantean epoch (Steiner, 1915, p. 3).

According to Rudolf Steiner, in the Sixth Epoch human consciousness will mature to a condition where the development of the consciousness soul,* central to the Fifth Epoch, will give birth to the Spirit Self. This will herald the infusion of spiritual awareness into all aspects of life. Human beings, as a matter of course, will only accept as science, forms of knowledge based upon spiritual research, upon pneumatology, as a result of widespread spiritual perception. This new phase of evolution bears the characteristics and values of a new wisdom culture. The attributes identified by Rudolf Steiner present a dynamic inner life that challenges the lifestyle of our time. Developing these conditions will only be possible with intentional preparation by individuals committed to deep personal inner transformation.

## The Mission of the Earth

We must consider the evolving human soul within the evolution of consciousness in light of the overarching mission or purpose of life on the Earth. Rudolf Steiner describes the cosmic development of humanity, the whole drama of the cosmic history of the Earth, as that of *love.*

> Divine creation is not simply a repetition of something already existing. Each planetary existence has a very definite mission. The mission of our Earth is the cultivation of the principle of love to its highest

* Consciousness soul (one of three aspects of the human soul, distinct from the sentient soul and intellectual soul) is the aspect of the soul that fathoms the ideal, that engages with consciousness beyond sensations, impulses and passions, the part of the soul in which values form. Described further below.

> degree by the beings evolving upon it. When the Earth has reached the end of its evolution, love should permeate it through and through.... The Earth is the planetary life condition for the evolution of love (Steiner, 1998, p. 66).

Steiner brought to consciousness that this highest form of love evolves in the unfolding realization of human freedom. Through full self-awareness and independence, one's love is purified of all unconscious elements and becomes a free gift from within. This love—in its highest form—is not a possession of the human being, but rather an expression of its true source, which a human being becomes capable of receiving and freely giving back through spiritual development. Rudolf Steiner emphasized the centrality of the human activity of receiving, transmuting through "I" consciousness, and giving spiritual love.

> Human beings exist so that they may take into themselves the warm love of the Divine, develop it, and return it to the Divine. But they can only do this by becoming self-aware I-beings. Only then will they be able to render back this love (Steiner, 1998, p. 72).

Amongst all the spiritual hierarchies, human beings experience the unique possibility to develop this capacity (Steiner, 1998, p. 72). The love given by spiritual beings is not free in the same sense as the love that is possible in the human being, because these beings have not experienced the painful separation from the Divine by incarnating fully into matter as a separate being. Love streams *through* spiritual beings from the Divine, but is not taken inwardly and developed *anew*; these beings *express* divine love, human beings *transform* divine love. With this understanding one comes to realize that the *whole purpose* of the drama of earthly evolution is the development of a being capable of consciously experiencing and developing the creative force of divine love.

This foundational premise underlies the development of the content in the following chapters. Conscious development of soul transformation lays the groundwork for the arising culture of brotherly and sisterly love, the Sixth Cultural Epoch, in which the Spirit Self will come to birth.

As individuals take up the essential work of inner transformation the human spirit will flower as an agent of love. If a sufficient number of people choose to prepare the soil of the future, to integrate transformative soul consciousness with spiritual striving, a radical, endemic shift in consciousness could take place, seeding the potential for a new wisdom culture, a culture of unity, a culture of brotherhood and sisterhood, arising out of selfless love for all peoples, and the kingdoms of Nature.

## The Ninefold Human Being

An archetypal matrix of the human being, based on the work of Rudolf Steiner, establishes an ordering principle for understanding the complexities of the human soul and the nature of the human double intrinsic to inner development. This vision of the human being consists of nine layers: three relating to the physical life—the physical body, the etheric body, and the astral body; three relating to the soul life—the sentient soul, intellectual soul, and consciousness soul; and three relating to the spirit life—Spirit Self, Life Spirit, and Spirit Human. Here the nine sheaths are introduced in their archetypal form. In chapter 2, the challenging forces that work within the various sheaths are described in the stages of the Fall. Ultimately, this book serves as a reference for understanding the negative forces within the human being and transforming them into vital forces of love.

Physical Body
Ether Body
Astral Body

---

Sentient Soul
Intellectual Soul
Consciousness Soul

---

Spirit Self (Manas—purified astral body)
Life Spirit (Buddhi—purified etheric body)
Spirit Human (Atma—purified physical body)

The three layers, or sheaths, relating to our physical existence establish the instrument through which we perceive the world through our senses. In the physical world we know life through sense experiences and we know ourselves as sense beings: seeing, hearing, touching, tasting, etc. Our senses interface between our bodily existence with the outer world.

The three soul sheaths exist in the inner realm of the human being, and cannot be perceived by the senses. These soul sheaths mediate the relationship of our physical existence and our spiritual nature. It is within the soul realm where the challenges arising from the human double are at play. The human soul is the stage upon which the inner drama and struggle for consciousness, transformation, and purification take place.

The three spirit sheaths exist in a dormant condition, for the most part, awaiting the preparation in the soul sheaths for their awakening. The three spirit sheaths are none other than the purified and spiritualized physical, etheric, and astral sheaths. The gestation period for the birth of the spirit sheaths of the human being is the period of transforming the human double, freeing the soul to give birth to the spirit within us. The content of this book addresses this process of transformation for the birth of the spirit.

The following descriptions of the nine sheaths of the human being culminate from years of my study and integration of numerous books and lectures by Rudolf Steiner.*

## Physical Body: Material Structure

The physical body is comprised of purely material substance, the same matter that constitutes the whole of physical nature—minerals, plants, and animals. The substance that lays in the coffin after death, separate from all vital life, comprises the physical body. Although it consists solely of matter, cosmic forces continually pour into the physical sheath imbuing it with life. Our physical body is the vehicle with which we live on the Earth, through which we observe and relate to objects and other beings in the outer world through the portals of our senses.

---

* For more about these terms see: Steiner, R. (1994). *Theosophy.* New York: SteinerBooks, or Steiner, R. (1997). *An Outline of Esoteric Science.* New York: SteinerBooks.

## Etheric Body: Life Processes

Beyond the physical body there exists a second sheath in the human organism: the etheric sheath, or life body. It is a body of vital life processes, permeated with streaming forces that continually build up the physical body. The etheric body is more or less luminous and fluidic. It consists of currents of diverse colors, surrounding the vortex of the heart. It is an organism that continually preserves the physical body from dissolution. The etheric sheath is known in Chinese medicine as Chi, and in Vedic medicine as prana.

The human body exists through propagation, and reaches its developed form through growth. Propagation and growth distinguish what is living from the lifeless mineral. The human species shares the characteristics of propagation and growth with plants and animals. Thus, the human being has the etheric body in common with the plant and animal kingdoms. The etheric sheath is most easily perceived in the plant kingdom, where one can identify the vitality or life force of a plant by its color, uprightness, and vibrancy. Etheric forces can also be perceived in the animal and human kingdoms by observing the presence of vitality, energy, and radiance of health.

All that lives has a permeating life organization that builds its physical form. A purely physical body, i.e., a crystal, builds its form by means of the physical formative forces dwelling within it. A living body, i.e., a plant, animal, or human being, does not have its form built up by means of these same forces. A living body grows by forces infused into it by the etheric body. We can see this when observing the moment in which death occurs. When life departs, the physical body is released from the etheric sheath and given over to physical (mineral) forces; it deteriorates and falls to pieces. The ether body is the organism that preserves the physical body from dissolution every moment during life. When a human being passes through the gate of death, the laws that govern the physical body lead to its decomposition. These physical forces are always present in the physical body; the living body does not submit to them during life, for the etheric or life body works in opposition to dissolution. After death the physical body dissolves into the mineral world, and the ether body into the etheric world.

The etheric body of the human being differs from that of plants and animals in that it is organized to serve the needs of the human thinking faculty. This is exemplified in part through the role that the etheric sheath plays in the capacity of memory. I recognize the significant body of work exploring human memory, and I suggest that Steiner's insights regarding memory contribute meaningfully to comprehending the depth and breadth of human memory. He describes that memory is the impression of a life experience that the etheric body engraves upon the physical body. When one remembers a past experience, the memory process becomes a subconscious act of reading (Steiner, 1919, p. 1).

> That which becomes a memory-picture goes through a considerable part of your entire organism, impresses itself on the etheric body and thrusts its way outward, so it can remain as an after-image for one's whole life. The point is that the impression must go deep enough and take hold of the etheric body, and that the etheric body does not retain it but transmits it to the outer ether of the Cosmos and inscribes it there (Steiner, 1919, p. 1).

Here we see how the vitality of the etheric sheath plays a significant role in the effectiveness of one's faculty of memory. It is our memory that establishes continuity in our life. Without memory, the human being would begin anew, every moment of life. In the context of memory research, Steiner uniquely identifies that it is through the activity of the etheric sheath that human beings develop the capacity of memory.

## Astral Body: Consciousness Body

A third sheath of the human organism, the astral body, contains the feeling life—instincts and impulses, desires and passions, everything we associate with the emotional activities of the soul. The feelings experienced in the astral sheath do not inhabit the etheric sheath or the physical sheath, but are specific to the astral body, which bears feelings of happiness and suffering, joy and pain, fear and hatred, jealousy and depression. The whole of the feeling life is anchored in the astral body.

The astral sheath has two dimensions: the subconscious-instinctive level, and the conscious, self-aware level. This distinction bears significance in comprehending the workings of the double and how the human being cultivates the capacity for self-transformation. The subconscious dimension of the astral sheath constitutes the realm of the instinctual feeling life: feelings of fear, self-preservation, survival, sexual desire, urges and impulses, etc. This dimension of the human astral sheath exists within the animal kingdom, as well as in humans, as animals also possess a form of instinctive astral consciousness.

The second dimension of the astral sheath, the conscious astral dimension, dwells singularly within the human being. This realm of the astral body constitutes conscience, feelings of a higher order that awaken an awareness of options. Here self-awareness infuses the instinctual feeling life, posing choices, based on feelings that are inspired by higher principles than pleasure or survival. Conscience, the operant characteristic of the conscious astral sheath, holds a place unique to the human experience.

The influence of the conscience upon the subconscious astral forces establishes the dynamics to overcome the human double. As the subconscious dimensions of the astral body are raised into consciousness, the forces of the conscience can initiate and propel the process of the birth of the spirit.

These first three sheaths of the human being provide the essential structure for physical life on Earth. As human beings, we build our bodies out of the materials in Nature in likeness to the minerals; as with the plants, we grow and propagate our species; and, like the animals, we perceive the objects around us through our senses, which, on the basis of the impressions we form, create our inner experiences.

## Sentient Soul: Feeling Soul Life

The fourth layer of the archetypal structure of the human being, and the first of three soul sheaths, bears the name *sentient soul*. The soul realm consists of an inner world that is unique to each person. The sentient soul provides the faculty to form sensations and impressions from experiences in the outer world. One perceives the external world through the senses, and the sensations that arise due to perceptions take place in the soul life. Perceptions enter from the outer world, sensations occur within one's inner world. No one can know if another person experiences even the simplest sensation in exactly the same way as one's self. Two people can perceive a red scarf with bodily senses, but one person cannot perceive the other's sensation of red because sensations originate in the soul, as an inner experience that cannot be perceived by another (Steiner, 1999, p. 86). With this example we can understand that sensations arise in the inner realm of the soul.

The first result of sensation is feeling. One sensation causes pleasure, another displeasure. Likes and dislikes, joy and pain, cannot be perceived with bodily senses; they are experiences of an inner soul realm. Although the soul experiences sensations that result in feelings, the soul realm is not solely predicated on physical sense perceptions of the outer world. We do not wander aimlessly from one sensation to another. We think about our perceptions and actions. By thinking about our perceptions we gain knowledge of things; by thinking about our actions we create a reasonable coherence in our life.

When ego consciousness works in the soul life, contemplating the external sensations that are taken in through the eyes, ears, and other sense organs, it fashions the ability to "feel" inwardly, resulting in sympathy or antipathy towards an external sensation. It can also acquire knowledge through "intuitions" from the ego concerning these inner feelings. When feelings of sympathy and antipathy expand to include concern for others, beyond the self, consciousness of one's relation to a greater existence begins to develop. When this awareness and concern grow into a longing for the well-being of the other, of community, of all peoples, the transformation or spiritualization of the sentient soul is in process. This longing can be experienced as a hungering and thirsting for justice and righteousness for all. This feeling arises in relation to thinking, which constitutes the essence of the next layer of the human being.

## Intellectual Soul: Thinking Soul Life

Just as the sentient soul interacts with the physical body—receiving perceptions, experiencing sensations, and developing likes and dislikes that affect our physical existence—it also interacts with the thinking realm of our being. Some people blindly follow their impulses, instincts, and passions, without the engagement of the intellect; this often leads to compromised situations. Thought creates the opportunity by which humans can determine their actions based on another level of consciousness, referred to here as the *intellectual soul.*

The activity of thinking serves the sentient soul. Thought-power has designed transportation systems, communication systems, political systems, medical services, educational systems, etc. The vast majority of all these developments serves to satisfy the desires and needs of the sentient soul. The force of thinking permeates the sentient soul in a similar way to that in which the etheric force permeates the physical body. The etheric sheath subjects the physical body to laws of propagation and growth different from the laws of the mineral body. In the same way, thought-force introduces the soul to conditions that it would not undergo as the sentient soul alone. Thinking influences the feeling soul life, and has the capacity to effect its transformation.

Thought life expresses human individuality through judgments, both positive and negative. The human intellect can be sharp and critical, cold and judgmental, condemning others and society. Thinking can be heartless and aloof, void of any moral factor, or it can be influenced by the forces of love to overcome personal egotism, and become an agent of compassion. When the intellectual soul transforms the egotistical nature of thinking with forces of love, infusing compassion and forgiveness into the feeling soul, it demonstrates the ennobled condition of its domain.

By thinking, we can transcend our personal life. We can engage in a process that extends beyond the soul, and beyond individuality. The human being can search for truth and seek the good or evil. Truth and goodness exist independent of the soul, as they are not ruled by desires and passions, but, on the contrary, direct them. Likes and dislikes, desire and loathing, belong to the personal soul, whereas moral values live beyond the realm of the soul. Human values develop through the activity of ennobled thoughts and feelings reaching beyond the sense world and uniting with a greater realm of consciousness, of truth and goodness that permeate the spiritual world. When this occurs, the soul is bathed in the light of the eternal, and forges values that become intrinsic to its essence. At times, values can be so strong that an individual will sacrifice his or her life for their sake. The strength of one's values, and the integrity to uphold them without compulsion or subjection, indicates the degree to which inclinations, likes and dislikes, have been ennobled. Truth and moral goodness work into the thought life, influencing the intellectual soul that then guides the sentient soul.

When the intellectual soul fully develops, it becomes capable of transcending personal thoughts, enabling one to contemplate thoughts of a supersensory nature. This higher level of thinking is called *Inspiration*—the capacity for spiritual hearing (Steiner, 1919, p. 1).

## Consciousness Soul: Will Soul Life

The sixth sheath of the human being (the third aspect of the soul) integrates the will forces into the thinking and feeling soul realms, infusing consciousness into human deeds. This dimension of the soul, called *consciousness soul*, works beyond all feelings of sympathy and antipathy, rises above personal desires or needs, and unites with the eternal, serving the true and the good. The consciousness within this sheath reflects full knowledge of the feeling and thinking soul nature, and guides them to their ennobled state.

The human soul engages with the outer world through the deeds of the will. The world of Nature works upon the sentient soul stimulating an effect in the feeling realm; in a like manner, the world of spirit (as well as the world of Nature) works upon the intellectual soul, stimulating an effect in the thinking realm. The actions that result from these experiences of the natural and spiritual worlds can be acts of consciousness soul if they arise from a motive of selflessness, if there is no self-interest or personal gain at stake. When the soul imbues itself with the true and the good, it becomes an instrument of higher consciousness and the eternal can work through it.

> In causing the self-existent true and good to come to life in his inner being, man raises himself above the mere sentient soul. The eternal spirit shines into this soul. A light is kindled in it that is imperishable. In so far as the soul lives in this light, it is a participant of the eternal. It unites its own existence with an eternal existence. What the soul

> carries within itself of the true and the good is immortal in it. That which shines forth in the soul as eternal is to be called here consciousness soul (Steiner, 1971, p. 25).

Consciousness soul reflects the eternal in the soul life. It becomes the prepared soil in which the spirit can take root.

According to the insights of Rudolf Steiner, the development of the consciousness soul is the task of our current cultural age, which will prepare the way for the Sixth Cultural Epoch described above. Uniting one's forces with the eternal, directing one's will to serve the true and the good, regardless of the biases of one's personal sympathies and antipathies, are the characteristics inherent in the consciousness soul; these are the qualities that indicate the ennoblement of the will soul. Through the development of this sheath, a bridge to the higher spiritual sheaths of the human being is established.

These three soul sheaths—the sentient soul, the intellectual soul, and the consciousness soul—make up the middle realm of the human being. As agents of feeling, thinking, and willing, respectively, these soul sheaths provide the vehicle that mediates between the physical aspect and the spiritual aspect of the human being. Without this soul realm, the body and spirit would have no way to interface with one another. The ennobled soul sheaths become the manger into which the first spirit sheath can be born.

## Ego: The Human "I"

Before continuing with the description of the three spirit sheaths of the human being, the Ego, or the "I," and its role in the evolving human odyssey, must be introduced. Self-consciousness leads the human being to know one's self as an independent being, separate from all others, describing one's self as "I." The "I" is the being of the self carried by the body and soul. When a human being says "I," there is an awareness of something within one's self that has nothing to do with any of the worlds from which the "sheaths" thus far mentioned arise.

The "I," or Ego, exists beyond the sense world, and is known through a capacity of perception that transcends the material world. When one sits and reflects on the question, *Who am I?* one enters a communion with the self, the Ego, the "I" of one's being. This "I" gradually establishes more and more influence over the body and soul. It is the "I" that initiates thoughts of truth and goodness to penetrate the soul sheaths.

The human "I" interfaces between the three soul sheaths—sentient soul, intellectual soul, and consciousness soul—and the three spirit sheaths—Spirit Self, Life Spirit, and Spirit Human. The body and soul serve the "I," but the "I" yields itself up to the spirit to become filled by it. The "I" lives in the physical body and soul realms, but the spirit, which is eternal, lives in the "I." It is most closely related to the intellectual soul and the consciousness soul, as they express the presence of the "I."

## Spirit Self: Purified Astral Body—Manas

The seventh sheath of the human organism, the Spirit Self, emerges as the astral body becomes transformed or purified through the influence of the "I." This aspect of the human spirit, also referred to by Rudolf Steiner as Manas (Steiner, 2008, p. 22), is the substance of the astral body metamorphosed to its purest essence, unaffected by the tides of human emotions and desires. This spiritual dimension of the human being bears the capacity for spiritual seeing, clairvoyant perception, referred to in Anthroposophy as Imagination.

In order for the Spirit Self to emerge from the spiritual world the "I" must prepare the three soul sheaths and the astral body. This preparation or transmutation of the soul brings consciousness to the inner life of the astral body. The astral body comprises impulses, instincts, desires, and feelings, in which anger, depression, greed, hatred, vengeance, sadness, jealousy, fear, etc., manifest. When the astral body is purified, these subconscious emotions no longer arise. The astral body becomes a vehicle for love and compassion, kindness and generosity, of interest in the well-being of the other. Impulses, emotions, and desires are brought under the influence of the consciousness soul guided by the Ego.

In its substance Spirit Self is identical with the astral body; there is merely a different ordering of what originally comprised the astral body, transformed through the "I" into Spirit Self. When the "I" has become strong enough to generate the purification of the astral sheath, it (the "I" or Ego) becomes the abode of the Spirit Self. Spirit Self lives in the "I."

## Life Spirit: Purified Etheric Body—Buddhi

The eighth sheath, Life Spirit, develops through the purification of the etheric body. When the human "I" works beyond the astral body, deeply into the etheric sheath, transforming the etheric forces to maintain radiant health without the presence of sickness or decay affecting the body, and establishing a flawless memory, the development of the Life Spirit body matures.

The etheric sheath establishes a medium for the temperament,* memory, and health. When the etheric sheath is purified, temperaments become balanced, so that no one temperament dominates. This balance permeates human physiology, establishing harmony in all the systems of the body. The etheric sheath also affects memory. Weak etheric forces result in a dull memory. When one strengthens memory out of Ego forces, the etheric sheath undergoes transmutation. Thirdly, the etheric sheath mediates health. When one overcomes health challenges through inner consciousness, this indicates the process of the purification of the etheric sheath. It is seldom that one quickly succeeds in fundamentally strengthening memory, overcoming a weakness in conscience, or developing the capacity to heal one's self. These are very slow processes.

> Transforming the etheric sheath leads to the development of inner occult powers.
>
> The essential characteristic of the pupil's Initiation is this: Learning is regarded as a mere preparation; much more is done for Initiation when the temperament itself is transformed. If a feeble memory has been changed into a strong one, if violence has been changed into gentleness, a melancholic temperament into serenity, more has been accomplished

* The four temperaments described by Rudolf Steiner, derived from the four Greek humors introduced by Hippocrates, express a dominance in the physiology resulting in tendencies in the personality. The four temperaments are: sanguine relating to the nervous system, choleric relating to the circulatory system, melancholic relating to the skeletal system, and phlegmatic relating to the digestive system. For more information see: Steiner, R. (1985) *Four Temperaments*. Forest Row, England: Rudolf Steiner Press.

> than the acquisition of great learning. Here lies the source of inner, occult powers, for this indicates that the Ego is working upon the etheric body, not only upon the astral body (Steiner, 1971, p. 30).

According to Steiner, the acquisition of great knowledge is merely a preliminary step that can prepare a ground for inner faculties to develop. Actual spiritual development does not result from knowledge; it requires Ego forces—the "I"—to work upon the astral and etheric sheaths. Transformation that occurs over time through disciplined inner work can bring about the soul development necessary to cultivate occult faculties. When the etheric forces strengthen the memory, conscience, and health, and balance the temperaments, they become penetrated with Life Spirit. This reveals that the life body has been restructured, transformed into something new. It has become the transmuted etheric body or Life Spirit. Then Buddhi or Life Spirit enters into the "I," empowering it with vital spiritual forces. This brings the capacity for spiritual hearing, clairaudience, referred to as Inspiration in Anthroposophy.

## Spirit Human: Purified Physical Body—Atma

After transubstantiating the astral and etheric bodies to develop Spirit Self and Life Spirit, the work of the Ego or "I" extends into the physical body. To achieve this one must learn to "control the breath and circulation, to follow consciously the activity of the nerves, and to regulate the processes underlying thought" (Steiner, 1993, p. 26). In the process of transubstantiating the physical body, the Ego unites with subtle forces that work within the physical body, bringing it into existence and allowing it to decay. The Ego purifies the physical body by transforming these forces of growth and decay into forces that sustain eternal life.

In normal life this occurs instinctively. A new level of consciousness arises when a human being, through spiritual insight, engages consciously in this inner working of the Ego upon the physical body. When this occurs, the ninth sheath, or third spiritual member of the human being, which Rudolf Steiner called Spirit Man, or Spirit Human, emerges. This new sheath of the human spirit develops out of the physical body through the work of the Ego.

> When the Ego becomes so strong that it is able not only to transform the astral and etheric bodies, but also the physical body—the densest of the principles in the human being and the forces of which extend into the very highest world—we say that a man is developing the very highest member of his being: Spirit Man, or Atma. The forces for the transformation of the physical body lie in the highest world of all. The transformation of the physical body begins with the transformation of the breathing process, for Atma is Atmen—breath. This transformation causes changes in the constitution of the blood that works upon the physical body; man is here functioning in the very highest worlds (Steiner, 1971, p. 30).

As the Ego works upon the physical substance of the human body—regulating the breath and circulation, controlling the nerve impulses from penetrating the circulatory system, transforming the constitution of the blood—the physical body becomes spiritualized. When it reaches the fulfillment of this process it becomes a resurrection body—Atma—the spiritual form Christ embodied during the forty days between Easter and the Ascension in the year 33 CE, during which He appeared to His disciples, and then disappeared again.

The purified physical body, Spirit Human (Atma), is the condition in which one can materialize spirit (bring spirit into form), and spiritualize matter (transform matter into spirit), at will. This is possible due to such a level of purification of the physical substance of one's body that one can densify light into form and dissolve form into light. The part of the physical body that has been spiritualized, that has become the Spirit Human, is not perceptible to the physical senses. To the degree to which the physical body has been spiritualized, it is only perceptible by spiritual faculties of perception. To the ordinary senses the spiritualized physical form will appear to be physical.

Humanity is now beginning to consciously transform the astral body. In the present phase of evolution human beings have begun to work consciously toward the development of Spirit Self (Manas). The Initiates, those individuals who are spiritually advanced, are consciously transforming the etheric body and in the future all human beings will consciously transform the etheric body and the physical body.

## The Interrelationships of the Nine Sheaths of the Human Being

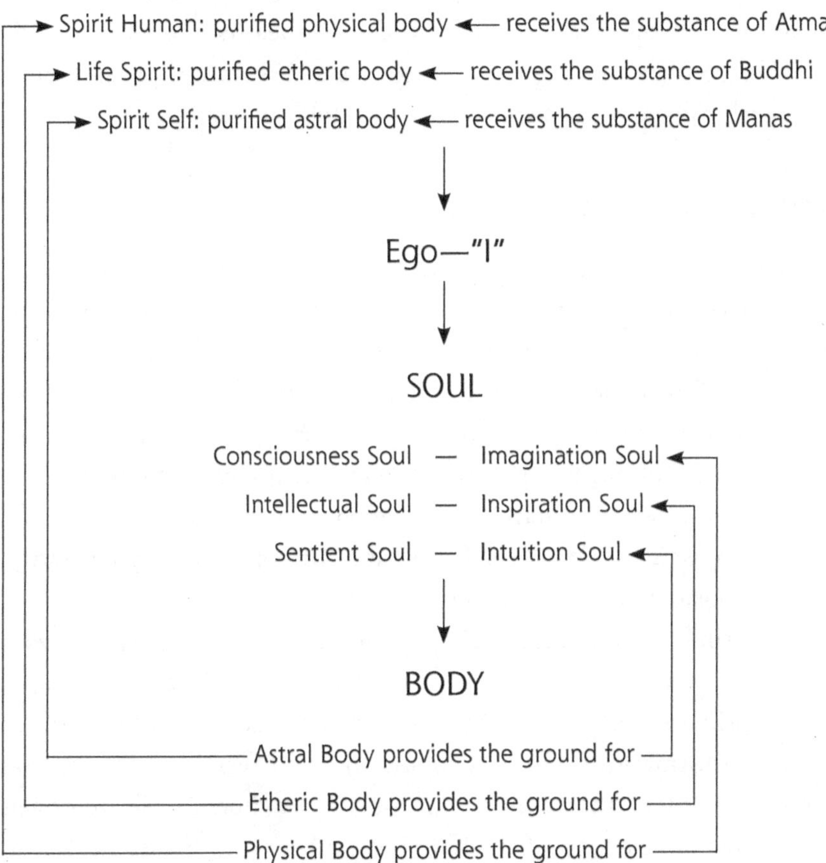


**Figure 1:** The above diagram illustrates the three sheaths of the body as foundational for the three soul sheaths and three spirit sheaths. The soul dwells within the body. The Ego or "I" dwells within the soul. The spirit comes to birth within the "I." The various sheaths nest within one another, the physical body providing the foundation for all the other sheaths to manifest upon Earth.

In addition to the evolutionary forces within the human being that seek truth and goodness, there also exists within the human being counter evolutionary forces, working to undermine the development of human consciousness. Rudolf Steiner refers to this influence as the *double*, or *döppleganger* in German (Steiner, 2004). Understanding this aspect of the human being establishes the conceptual picture of the challenge that lies before one in the endeavor to purify the soul sheaths and to create the potential for spiritual development. Below is a description of the double from the anthroposophical perspective of Rudolf Steiner.

## The Double: The Counter Image of the True Self

The above considers the human being as consisting of body, soul, and spirit. However, this image does not present a complete picture of the constitution of the human being. Alongside our existence as a being of body, soul, and spirit, we also incorporate into our being something that is contrary to our true nature, but integral to our life as an evolving being on Earth. I refer to this aspect of our being as the *double*. The double inhabits the subconscious realm of each human being. We have, in a sense, "another self" that exists alongside our "true self"; it is not our conscious higher nature, and is the opposite of our true birthright.

Through time we have acted in ways that are contrary to divine law, or the ordering principles of the Universe. Divine law constitutes unchanging organizing principles of the Universe—patterns observed to be invariant under all transformations. Human cognition of universal law results from distilling the wisdom that remains after state-dependent, culture-dependent, and time-dependent realities have been subtracted. Invariant denotes that which everyone can agree upon from different standpoints, that which is contra-disposed to transience, that which is ephemeral, natural, and subject to the cycles of birth and death, ebb and flow. All religions recognize a transcendent law, truth, or principle that governs the Universe and human affairs. They describe the Universe as an expression of the workings of a divine principle or natural law in both the realms of Nature and of human life. Human morality, in this context, is not solely explicable as the result of social and cultural conditioning. Morality and ethics are rooted not only in culture and social conditioning, but also in eternal principles that are as enduring as the laws of physics. Some of these laws manifest as the principle of reciprocity, the law of cause and effect, the law of karma, and the principle of divine justice through which each person reaps what he or she has sown. (See appendix A.)

Through actions that contraindicate the ordering principles of the Universe, we have built up this other part of our self, our double that is not who we truly are, but our "other self." The double evolves into a complex being with multiple facets. I will refer to the three primary facets of the double as the *luciferic* aspect of the double, the *ahrimanic* aspect of the double, and the *karmic* aspect of the double. An introduction to the three primary aspects of the human double follows. Each of these will be explored further in the following chapters.

## Lucifer in Hebrew Scripture

The name Lucifer means "light-bearer," derived from the Latin *lucem ferre.* In Hebrew scripture Lucifer was among the greatest of the angelic beings who served God in Heaven. Lucifer was considered second only to God in power and authority over the realm of the whole Kingdom. He was a being created by God to serve God as ruler of the Kingdom and leader of worship to God. But he was not satisfied with his glorious appointed station over all things in the Kingdom, and eventually he desired to be God himself.

> Your heart was proud because of your beauty; you corrupted your wisdom for the sake of your splendor. I cast you to the ground; I exposed you before kings, to feast their eyes on you (Ezek. 28:16–17, English Standard Version).

Lucifer felt his beauty and power. He became prideful and wanted to exalt himself above God. He rebelled against God and signified himself as the first being to transgress the divine order.

## Ahriman in Persian Mythology

According to Persian mythology two principles of eternity coexist. The first of these is Ahura-Mazda, or Ormuzd, the Creator Spirit of Good. Ahura-Mazda emanated from Primordial Light and from him came forth hierarchies of good and beautiful spirits, forming a pure and holy world. The second of these eternal principles is Ahriman, who, though born as pure as his brother, became jealous of him and marred everything in the Universe and on Earth, creating evil wherever he went. Ahriman became the Spirit of Evil, personified as Angra Mainya, "the destructive spirit," who introduced death into the world. From himself he brought forth a host of destructive creatures to overpower the goodness of Ahura-Mazda. According to Blavatsky, the "Two Brother-Powers," Ormuzd and Ahriman

> are inseparable on our present plane and at this stage of evolution, and would be meaningless, one without the other. They are, therefore, the two opposite poles of the one manifested creative Power, whether the latter is viewed as a universal cosmic Force which builds worlds, or under its anthropomorphic aspect when its vehicle is thinking man. For Ormuzd and Ahriman are the respective representatives of good and evil, of light and darkness, of the spiritual and the material elements in man, and also in the Universe and everything contained in it (Blavatsky, 1971, p. 1).

These two opposing forces live within each human being, sustaining the tension between spiritual reality and earthly reality. This tension drives us to integrate this dual existence in our consciousness. As citizens of Earth and of the Cosmos, we must, out of freedom, integrate both these realities, including death, through a process of choices and experiences that arise through these two opposing forces.

When Ahura-Mazda created the Earth, Ahriman entered into its grosser elements, so that whenever Ahura-Mazda did a good deed, Ahriman placed the principle of evil within it. When at last Ahura-Mazda created the human race, Ahriman became incarnate in the lower nature of man so that in each personality the Spirit of Good and the Spirit of Evil struggle for control. While Ahura-Mazda and Ahriman struggle for control of the human soul and for supremacy in Nature, Mithra, God of Intelligence, stands as mediator between the two (Grimal, 1965, p. 194–195). He works to harmonize the opposite poles of earthly and cosmic realities in human experience through our intelligence. The Avestan hymns describe Mithra as a God of heavenly light, all-seeing, guardian of oaths, protector of righteousness in this world and the next world, and above all, the arch-foe to forces of evil (Boyce, 1990, p. 28). Mithra, the messenger of Ahura-Mazda, mediated between the worlds of light and darkness, as humanity's ally in the struggle against evil, and as the soul's guide in its ascent to eternal life.

Correspondences have been delineated between Mithra and Christ, both having December 25 as their celebrated birth date. Steiner describes Ahura-Mazda as the pre-incarnatory manifestation of Christ.

> Although Christ appeared only later, he was always present in the spiritual sphere of the Earth. Already in the ancient Oracles of Atlantis, the priests of those Oracles spoke of the "Spirit of the Sun," of Christ. In the old Indian epoch of civilization the Holy Rishis spoke of "Vishva Karman"; Zarathustra in ancient Persia spoke of "Ahura Mazdao," Hermes [in Egypt spoke] of "Osiris"; and Moses spoke of the Power which, being eternal, brings about the harmonization of the temporal and natural, the Power living in the "Ehyeh asher Ehyeh" (I AM the I AM) as the harbinger of Christ. All spoke of the Christ (Steiner, 1909, p. 4).

Within this context Mithra of the Zoroastrian tradition aligns with the Archangel Michael in the Christian tradition.

## Lucifer and Ahriman in Anthroposophy

The spiritual beings of Lucifer, as described in Hebrew scriptures, and Ahriman in Zoroastrian scriptures of Ancient Persia, continue to influence life on the Earth and the realm of human consciousness. Their struggle for control of the human soul persists. Consciousness of their presence and subtle influence helps catalyze right thought, right speech, and right action in one's life. The crucial factor is that of understanding their role in human evolution, and knowing how to establish the conscious relationship with these beings.

In his book, *Secrets of the Threshold*, Rudolf Steiner addresses the cosmic authority of Lucifer and of Ahriman, describing their rightful tasks in the universal order, and illumining how each of them has become a force of opposition and rebellion against the cosmic order by overstepping their lawful power. He describes that it would be misguided to think that Lucifer and Ahriman are simply evil and harmful. They each have a purposeful sphere of activity that is essential during our current phase of evolution. They bring opposing forces that can balance each other within the human condition. They serve to help human beings orient themselves in the transmigration between the world of spirit and our earthly existence.

Ahriman holds the position of Lord of Death, as described in Persian cosmology; he regulates the destruction of life in a lawful way. His sovereign authority dominates the mineral kingdom, which is lifeless. The other kingdoms of Nature—the plants, animals, and humans—are subject to death, as they are permeated with minerals, and are under the lawful rule of Ahriman. We enter into a healthy relationship with the world of Nature when our interest in it does not demand eternal life of any of its physical forms. To be able to enjoy the things we experience in the sense world, and yet, not be so dependent on them as to wish to contradict the laws of death and decay, demonstrates an understanding of the lawful cycles of Nature under the dominion of Ahriman. The ability to establish a healthy relationship to death and decay indicates that the impulses of Ahriman are at work within the human being.

Beyond Ahriman's rightful authority as Lord of Death, he has overstepped his domain as the Lord of Death. According to Rudolf Steiner, Ahriman desires to take possession of human thinking, to detach human thinking from the brain (which is subject to decay and death), so that thinking will bypass destruction (Steiner, 1987, p. 25). This interference results in materialistic thought, directing thinking only toward the sense world. People who do not believe in the spiritual world, who only consider the sense perceptible world as real, may live under the influence of Ahriman's unlawful forces, permeating thinking with materialism.

Lucifer also has a lawful domain in accordance with the universal order. Lucifer works to disengage human beings and human soul activity from absorption exclusively in the physical-sensory world. When human beings create out of their imaginations, it is luciferic forces that disengage their soul life from the sense world, allowing it to rise into the imaginative sphere. The capacity for creative freedom makes possible original thinking, inspired culture, the burgeoning of new civilizations, and the possibility of human evolution.

Like Ahriman, Lucifer has also overstepped his domain of authority within the cosmic order. Whereas Ahriman works to contaminate the thinking capacities in human consciousness, the unlawful luciferic forces work into the human feeling life, contaminating the emotions, passions, impulses, and desires.

> Lucifer is lord over everything of soul feeling in the physical sense world. He has the tendency to detach and separate this feeling life of the soul from the physical world, to spiritualize it, and to set up, one can say, on a specially isolated island of spiritual existence, a luciferic kingdom composed of all the soul feeling he can seize and carry off from the sense world (Steiner, 1987, p. 25).

Lucifer entices human beings to feel the grandness of our being, infecting our thinking with egotism. He wishes to disengage the soul life from its earthly responsibilities and soar in the realm of egoistic fantasy. This can manifest in a variety of forms: arrogance, condescension, self-righteousness, narcissism, irresponsibility, deceit, falsification, anger, intolerance, etc. Lucifer seeks to permeate the feeling life with egotism, thus disengaging humanity from earthly responsibility, culpability, and humility.

On the one hand, Ahriman aims to wrest human beings away from any allegiance to, or even any awareness of the world of spirit, to chain humanity to the Earth and to immerse humanity in ease and materialism. He encourages apathy, indifference, cold intellect, inner stagnation, and hardness of heart. Steiner warns against spiritual cowardice—escaping from Ahriman by avoiding his many manifestations, pretending he is not there. In contrast to these forces, Lucifer encourages human beings to keep their heads in the clouds, to look down on everything and everyone, to escape from Earth into a world of illusion, to avoid material responsibility, to dream, to sleep, to foster the fanciful, the fanatical, the fantastic, and the formless, and to indulge in false and illusory mysticism. In order to be effective as human beings, we must achieve a dynamic balance between these two extremes: not a negotiated compromise, but a creative force that overcomes both.

## The Presence of Lucifer and Ahriman in the Human Soul

As indicated above, the forces of Lucifer and Ahriman have their rightful place in human life, and, beyond this, they seek to distort human consciousness to serve their own oppositional plan. How does this occur? In a lecture given on November 16, 1917, published in a collection of lectures entitled *Secret Brotherhoods and the Mystery of the Human Double*, Rudolf Steiner described that there are spiritual beings who want to conquer the Earth but do not have physical bodies of their own, and therefore seek to use human beings to enable them to live on Earth. Out of their own will, these beings decided that they did not want to live in the world in which they were destined by the wisdom of the spiritual hierarchies.

Steiner stated that as the human body develops, shortly before birth, these beings are able to enter into it, to permeate the unconscious part of our body and accompany us below the threshold of consciousness, alongside our soul (Steiner, 2004, p. 56).

> These beings lead their lives by making use of human beings to enable them to inhabit the sphere in which they wish to dwell. They have an exceptionally high degree of intelligence and a very significantly developed will, but no warmth of heart at all, no qualities of soul, nothing like what we would call the human qualities of soul and heart and mind. So we proceed through our life while having our souls and also a double, who is far cleverer than we are, who is very intelligent, but with a mephistophelian intelligence, and an ahrimanic intelligence, and in addition, also an ahrimanic will, a very strong will (Steiner, 2004, p. 56–57).

The forces of Lucifer and Ahriman work into human beings through the presence of spiritual agents—beings who wish they could have bodies—inhabiting the human soul and working to overtake human consciousness and establish dominion over the Earth. Their presence establishes the formative forces of the human double. Their keenly developed intelligence presents a force that human beings can only supersede with wisdom and the true power of love.

The presence of the luciferic and ahrimanic beings within us affects our physical and emotional health. Ahrimanic beings inhabit the etheric sheath, working to deteriorate physical health, leading to death. The presence of the ahrimanic double authors all physical illnesses that manifest from within, in contrast to outer injuries. The luciferic double inhabits the astral body and sentient soul sheaths, generating neurologically based illnesses: neurasthenia, neurosis, etc. They work to deteriorate emotional health. Accordingly, full understanding of the double provides a basis for cultivating organic medicine. Knowledge of these forces can enable us to prevent and heal illness by balancing and strengthening etheric and astral forces, displacing the efforts of these inhabiting forces.

These foreign beings that inhabit human bodies take delight in dwelling on Earth, but there is one thing they cannot endure in human life, and that is death. Therefore, they leave the human body in which they have established themselves before it gives way to death. They have not developed the ability to pass through the death process. According to Steiner, they want to be able to remain in human bodies beyond death, but thus far, are not able to do so. Therefore, as a person nears death, their double withdraws, and the true nature of that individuality shines forth, without the interference of the double.

## Karmic Double

It is becoming increasingly essential that human beings come to know that the presence of an ahrimanic and luciferic double exists within them, as it does intrinsically within all human beings. The influence of these beings varies within each soul, each aspect of the double having its own expression, but they are nevertheless universal to humanity. The individualization of these forces establishes a third aspect to the human double, the karmic double. The karmic facet of the double remains unique to each person, for it is simply an amalgamation of all the personal transgressions of universal law by a given individual, from all incarnations. Each human being bears a unique karmic double that is comprised of their luciferic and ahrimanic deeds. A more comprehensive exploration of the meaning and complexities of karma will be taken up in chapter 4.

Although this is but a brief introduction to the three primary aspects of the human double, let it suffice here to say that the human double plays a significant role in each human being's biography and in the evolution of humanity as a species. The greater consciousness that each individual has regarding his or her true inner life, the greater the possibility for human beings to develop the faculties of spiritual consciousness and establish a culture founded on wisdom and love.

# CHAPTER 2

# The Luciferic Double: The Crown of Glory

> You were the signet of perfection, full of wisdom and perfect in beauty. . . .
> You were an anointed guardian cherub. . . . You were on the holy mountain of God; in the midst of the stones of fire you walked.
>
> —Ezekiel*

Lucifer, the anointed cherub ordained by God to dwell among the stones of fire (Ezek. 28:14), plays a significant role in the life of the human psyche. He brings to the fore the dimension of *free will*, essential to human consciousness and evolution. Lucifer empowers human beings with intellectual independence, cognitive freedom, and spiritual inquiry, all of which are necessary to understand the "I" that dwells within us, and the fullness of the principle of divine love. Lucifer brings to consciousness what otherwise would remain in the unconscious.

In chapter 1, the context for an in-depth exploration of the various facets of the double was established. The work of inner development was introduced in consideration of the coming Sixth Cultural Epoch, the age of brotherly and sisterly love, when a new consciousness will arise giving birth to the Spirit Self within human beings if, and only if, the transformation of soul forces occurs during our current cultural age. The creation of a new wisdom culture of unity, embodying selfless love for all peoples and the

* Ezek. 28:12, 14, ESV.

kingdoms of Nature, necessitates individual inner transformation. To prepare the soil for this future epoch, inner development that integrates transformative soul consciousness with spiritual striving must occur. In chapter 1, the nine sheaths of the human being and the counter image of the human double were introduced as a working paradigm. The three primary aspects of the double—the luciferic, ahrimanic, and karmic aspects—were described as a general foundation for the following three chapters.

The complexities of each aspect of the double warrant extensive discussion. In this chapter the primary focus addresses the threefold luciferic double. The background of Lucifer, his rebellion in heaven, his role in the Paradise story, and the effects of his influence that have greatly contributed to the sculpting of human lives, history, and contemporary world conditions, set the stage for an understanding of how the luciferic double manifests in the human soul life. This chapter includes a discussion of the seven stages of the Fall from Paradise from the Genesis story, illumining a path of descent from spiritual union with God to isolation from the Divine. This matrix provides definition for the soul's progressive immersion into the workings of the double. The specific manifestations of luciferic forces in the thinking realm, the feeling realm, and the will realm constitute the central content of this chapter. In respect to the subtleties and complex unfolding of evolution, the noble and lawful attributes of Lucifer must be understood and honored, and the unlawful, ignoble traits and their resulting influence upon humanity and the Earth must be comprehended. Lucifer bears a complex, profound destiny that is worthy of deep consideration.

Lucifer was considered second only to God in power and authority over the realm of the whole Kingdom. His radiance outshone that of any other angel and his beauty was unmatched anywhere in Heaven (Ezek. 28:13–14). As the "anointed guardian Cherub" in the garden of God, he had great power and influence over the angelic host (Rev. 12:3–9).

Lucifer is described as "covered" in ten precious stones, similar to those described in the Book of Revelation adorning the Heavenly Jerusalem. But he was not satisfied with his glorious appointed station over all things in the Kingdom, and eventually he desired to be God himself.

> You were in Eden, the garden of God; every precious stone was your covering, sardius, topaz, and diamond, beryl, onyx, and jasper, sapphire, emerald, and carbuncle; and crafted in gold were your settings and your engravings. On the day that you were created they were prepared. You were an anointed guardian cherub. I placed you; you were on the holy mountain of God; in the midst of the stones of fire you walked. You were blameless in your ways from the day you were created, till unrighteousness was found in you. In the abundance of your trade you were filled with violence in your midst, and you sinned; so I cast you as a profane thing from the mountain of God, and I destroyed you, O guardian cherub, from the midst of the stones of fire. Your heart was proud because of your beauty; you corrupted your wisdom for the sake of your splendor. I cast you to the ground; I exposed you before kings, to feast their eyes on you (Ezek. 28:13–17, ESV).

Lucifer was not content to be a subordinate. As pride overtook Lucifer he turned away from servitude and exalted himself above God. After he secured the support of myriads of hosts of the angelic realms, he was cast out of heaven (Rev. 12:9, ESV).

> How art thou fallen from heaven, O Lucifer, son of the morning! Art thou cut down to the ground, which didst weaken the nations! For thou hast said in thine heart, I will ascend into heaven, I will exalt my throne above the stars of God: I will sit also upon the mount of the congregation, in the sides of the north: I will ascend above the heights of the clouds; I will be like the most High (Isa. 14:12–15, King James Version).

Lucifer's pride and self-aggrandizement, his dissatisfaction with his appointed authority, depicts the inception of disobedience. His rebellion against God and the cosmic order presents the archetypal seeding of egotism. Lucifer personifies egotistical, self-aggrandizing, prideful, self righteous, reckless effects in human soul forces.

On the other hand, Lucifer's work to disengage human beings and human soul activity from exclusive absorption in the physical-sensory world makes creative work possible (Steiner, 1987, p. 24). When human beings create out of their imaginations, it is luciferic forces that disengage their soul life from the sense world, allowing it to rise into the imaginative sphere.

> A large part of what is uplifting and liberating in the artistic development of [hu]mankind is inspired by Lucifer. We can designate something else as the inspiration of Lucifer: the human being has the chance through luciferic powers to free his thinking from a mere photograph-like copying of the sense world; he can raise himself above this in freedom, which he does, for instance, in his philosophy.... All creative work, in fact, that rises above the sense world we owe to Lucifer's rightful activities and powers (Steiner, 1987, p. 24).

The capacity for creative freedom plays an essential role in thinking, culture, civilization, and human evolution. The presence and influence of Lucifer inspires humanity in these ways through his rightful activities and powers.

As described in chapter 1, Lucifer also overstepped his lawful domain of authority by contaminating the human feeling life with egotism and self-aggrandizement. These forces disengage humanity from earthly responsibility, transparency, and humility.

A poignant legend depicting Lucifer's fall from heaven, referenced by Rudolf Steiner in the first lecture in the cycle *The East in the Light of the West*, describes that during the great battle in heaven a precious stone was loosened from Lucifer's crown and plummeted to Earth when he fell. The legend goes on to reveal that the stone from Lucifer's crown was lodged in the Earth, eventually mined, and formed into the cup* from which Christ and His disciples drank during the Last Supper. This same cup was also at

* The cup used in the enactment of the Last Supper is an archetypal symbol that can be considered on many levels. On the physical plane there was a vessel from which Christ shared wine with His disciples. This cup held the sacramental substance given by Christ to spiritualize human blood. It was a vessel that served an alchemical process. Another rendering of the Grail appears as a green stone in Wolfram von Eschenbach's *Parzival*. The Venus color green (the complementary color of blood) symbolizes the feminine principle of fecundity, and the stone represents the Earth as a chalice of spiritualized life forces, which received the blood of Christ on Golgotha. Another dimension of the Grail vessel can be understood as the human heart, a vessel that oxygenates human blood and participates in its spiritualization, the human heart that longs to receive the Christ.

the foot of the Cross and received Christ's blood when it flowed onto the Earth. This chalice became known as the Holy Grail,* and is sought by "those who wish to come to a true understanding of the Christ principle" (Steiner, 1986, p. 3). To find this precious stone in its transformed character—as the Grail—is to comprehend the *cross of the Christ in the star of Lucifer* (Steiner, 1986, p. 4), with the knowledge that the star of Lucifer and the precious stone from his crown were the same (Steiner, 1986, p. 6). This image of the *cross of the Christ in the star of Lucifer* depicts the principal archetype working through the content in this chapter.

Rudolf Steiner indicates that the precious stone from Lucifer's crown is nothing other than the power of the Ego, the true "I."

> Out of the stone, which fell from Lucifer's crown, was made the Holy Grail. This precious stone is in a certain respect nothing else than the full power of the Ego. In darkness this human Ego had to be prepared for a new and more intelligent beholding of the radiance of Lucifer's star. This Ego had to school itself by means of the Christ principle, it had to ripen by the aid of the stone fallen from Lucifer's crown in order to become capable once more of bearing the light which comes not from without. This light, which only shines in us when we ourselves have the power to do what is requisite for acquiring it, must shine again in the world (Steiner, 1954, p. 3).

The star of the light-bearer, the star of Lucifer, symbolized in the jewel fallen from his crown, radiates with the cross of light uniting the divine realm with the terrestrial realm. The cross of Christ—integrating the horizontal axis representing the redemption of the Earth, of human transgression, and of egotistical thinking, with the vertical axis of consciousness and deeds aligned with cosmic lawfulness—shines within the star of Lucifer since the event of

---

* The legend cited here stands among many Grail legends that have received considerable scholarship among which must be noted Arthur Waite's *The Hidden Church of the Holy Grail* (Waite, 1909), Emma Jung's *The Grail Legend* (Jung and Franz, 1998), Joseph Campbell's *Creative Mythology* (Campbell, 1991), John Matthews's *Sources of the Grail* (Matthews, 1997), Sylvia Francke and Thomas Cawthorne's *The Tree of Life and the Holy Grail* (Francke and Cawthorne, 1996), and Fr. Sergius Bulgakov's *The Holy Grail and the Eucharist* (Bulgakov, 1997).

Christ's crucifixion. This image will be discussed further after examining the influence Lucifer has wrought on humanity, his role in the evolution of human consciousness, and his karmic destiny as a spiritual being.

## The Fall from Paradise

The story of the Fall from Paradise in the book of Genesis describes the first interaction between Lucifer and human beings. Lucifer sought to entice the first humans to be free of God's authority, to be prideful and seek to be like God, to infect humanity with the forces that drove him out of heaven. Lucifer assumed the form of a serpent to beguile humanity through cunning.

> Now the serpent was more subtle than any other wild creature that the Lord God had made. He said to the woman, "Did God say, 'You shall not eat of any tree of the garden'?" And the woman said to the serpent, "We may eat of the fruit of the trees of the garden; but God said, 'You shall not eat of the fruit of the tree which is in the midst of the garden, neither shall you touch it, lest you die.'" But the serpent said to the woman, "You will not die. For God knows that when you eat of it your eyes will be opened, and you will be like God, knowing good and evil." So when the woman saw that the tree was good for food, and that it was a delight to the eyes, and that the tree was to be desired to make one wise, she took of its fruit and ate; and she also gave some to her husband, and he ate. Then the eyes of both were opened, and they knew that they were naked; and they sewed fig leaves together and made themselves aprons.
>
> And they heard the sound of the Lord God walking in the garden in the cool of the day, and the man and his wife hid themselves from the presence of the Lord God among the trees of the garden. But the Lord God called to the man, and said to him, "Where are you?" And he said, "I heard the sound of thee in the garden, and I was afraid, because I was naked; and I hid myself." He said, "Who told you that you were naked? Have you eaten of the tree of which I commanded you not to eat?" The man said, "The woman whom thou gavest to be with me, she gave me fruit of the tree, and I ate" (Gen. 3:1–13, ESV).
>
> The man called his wife's name Eve, because she was the mother of all living.

> And the Lord God made for Adam and for his wife garments of skins, and clothed them.
>
> Then the Lord God said, "Behold, the man has become like one of us, knowing good and evil; and now, lest he put forth his hand and take also of the tree of life, and eat, and live forever—" therefore the Lord God sent him forth from the garden of Eden, to till the ground from which he was taken. He drove out the man; and at the east of the garden of Eden he placed the cherubim, and a flaming sword which turned every way, to guard the way to the tree of life (Gen. 3:20–24, ESV).

This story of the Fall depicts an archetypal experience of the human soul and spirit, interwoven with subtle wisdom and hidden layers of content. At this point we will consider some of the less commonly understood aspects of this story—the seven stages of the Fall (Tomberg, 1941, p. 219).

When Eve encountered the serpent she was alone. One interpretation of this identifies Eve with the human soul and Adam with the human spirit, a traditional interpretation in myth and fairy tales associating the female character with the soul and the male character with the spirit. If we consider the soul as described in chapter 1, without the influence of the "I" or the spirit, in the initial encounter with the serpent Eve represents the sentient soul, the feeling life of sensations, sympathies, antipathies, and desire. When the serpent asks her, "Did God say, 'You shall not eat of any tree of the garden'?" (Gen. 3:1, ESV), Eve clearly knew God's instructions. She answered, "We may eat of the fruit of the trees of the garden; but God said, 'You shall not eat of the fruit of the tree which is in the midst of the garden, neither shall you touch it, lest you die'" (Gen. 3:2, ESV). The soul's intelligibility shone forth as steadfast. But when the serpent contradicted her saying, "You will not die. For God knows that when you eat of it your eyes will be opened, and you will be like God, knowing good and evil" (Gen. 3:3, ESV), Eve became confused. She did not know whom to believe. God had said to her, "If you eat from this tree you will surely die." The serpent said to her, "If you eat from this tree you will not die, but you will be like God." Soul consciousness entered the realm of doubt. Eve doubted God's word. *Doubt* fueled by confusion established the first stage of the Fall.

Secondly, Eve was intrigued by the notion that she could be like God; this sounded quite enticing. The tempter assured her that as soon as she ate of the fruit she would receive a new and superior knowledge that would make her equal with God. She witnessed the serpent eating from the tree of knowledge of good and evil and he did not die. Lucifer succeeded in seeding egotism within the human soul, for Eve desired to be like God. This shift from obedience to God, to desiring to be like God, designates the second stage of the Fall: *desire.*

Eve then plucked a fruit from the tree of knowledge of good and evil. She was emboldened because she did not feel the immediate signs of God's displeasure. She believed the words of the tempter to be all wise and correct. The act of taking the fruit depicts grasping for the unlawful substance, that which is not given in relation to one's position and worthiness. Eve was grasping for equality with God. This portrays the third stage of the Fall: *grasping.*

Then Eve ate of the fruit of the tree of knowledge of good and evil and was delighted, for she did not die. Eve sought Adam and related to him the wise discourse of the serpent and entreated him to eat of the fruit of the tree of knowledge of good and evil. She told him she had eaten of the fruit, and instead of feeling any sense of death, she now would be like God. Adam's love for Eve overruled his love of God. If she would die, he would die with her, for she was flesh of his flesh and bone of his bones. Adam took the fruit and ate of it. Now the deed was done, they could no longer change their minds. They disobeyed God and entered into communion with the serpent. The seeds of the fruit were now within them. Lucifer exulted in his success. He had now tempted the woman to distrust God, to question His wisdom, and to seek to penetrate His all-wise plans. And through her he had also caused the overthrow of Adam, who, in consequence of his love for Eve, disobeyed the command of God and fell with her. He fulfilled his plan; he enticed humanity to be prideful, to seek to be like God. Egotism arose within the human soul, establishing the fourth stage of the Fall: *egotism.*

The great wisdom Adam and Eve obtained was the knowledge of transgression and an inner sense of shame and guilt. The covering of light about them soon disappeared, a shivering seized them, and they tried to cover their exposed forms. This indicates the first appearance of karma in their light body. The light dimmed and was stained by the presence of a misdeed. Fear overtook them and they hid. They felt a dread of the future, a sense of want, a nakedness of soul. The peace and happiness they had always known seemed removed from them, and in its place a want of something came over them that they had never experienced before. The experience of *fear* signifies the fifth stage of the Fall.

For the first time they turned their attention to the external. They had not been clothed but were draped in light. The light that enshrouded them had now departed. To relieve their sense of lack and nakedness their attention was directed to seek a covering for their forms, so they sewed fig leaves together, for how could they meet the eye of God and angels unclothed? They now perceived their deed in its true light; their transgression of God's express command assumed a clearer character and shame arose. They sought to hide their nakedness, to deceive God of their transgression. *Deceit* constitutes the sixth stage of the Fall.

Then the Lord God visited Adam and Eve. As they heard God's majestic approach they sought to hide themselves from His inspection. While in their innocence and holiness they delighted to meet their God, but now they hid themselves in fear and shame.

> And the Lord God called unto Adam, and said unto him, "Where art thou?" And he said, "I heard the sound of thee in the garden, and I was afraid, because I was naked; and I hid myself." He said, "Who told you that you were naked? Have you eaten of the tree of which I commanded you not to eat?" (Gen. 3:9–11, KJV).

Adam acknowledged his transgression, not because he was penitent for his disobedience, but to cast reflection upon God (Gen. 3:12, KJV). The woman was then addressed: "What is this that thou hast done?" Eve answered, "The serpent beguiled me, and I did eat" (Gen. 3:13, KJV).

Then God effaced the pride of the serpent, relegating him to crawl on his belly in the dust, and assigned conditions for restoration upon Adam and Eve. A life of perpetual toil was appointed to Adam, instead of the joyous labor he had hitherto fulfilled; the human spirit must toil to regain its unity with the Divine. They would be subject to disappointment, grief, and pain; the soul must suffer to temper its desire. Finally they must come to dissolution. They were made of the dust of the Earth, and unto dust should they return; the body must die to return to the spiritual world anew. Therefore, to prevent Adam and Eve from eating of the tree of life, and perpetuating a life of disobedience, they had to be expelled from Paradise. Holy angels were sent to debar their way to the tree of life. Around these angels flashed beams of light on every side, which had the appearance of glittering swords. The consequence of death fulfills God's word and establishes the seventh stage of the Fall: *death.*

**Figure 2**

The Stages of the Fall

| Stage | Transgression | Rectification |
|---|---|---|
| first | doubt: seeing with the eyes of the serpent | allegiance to God: uniting the light of consciousness with life force |
| second | desire: the cause of all suffering and illness | live in harmony with the Divine: become an undistorted mirror of truth |
| third | grasping: false inspiration | listening to the voice of conscience: self-restraint |
| fourth | egotism: false intuition, concern only for one's self | humility: experiencing the true divine "I" |
| fifth | fear: loss of inner consciousness, paralysis | purification—Manas: integrate earthly and spirit consciousness |
| sixth | deceit: shame can lead to lying, self-beautification | honesty—Buddhi: shame can lead to repentance |
| seventh | death: consciousness and life are entirely separated | resurrection—Atma: live with full consciousness |

The seven stages of the Fall stand as a subtext to the story of Genesis 3. Another dimension of the story lies hidden within the text. If one considers this story from the perspective that Adam represents the human spirit and Eve the human soul, then Adam and Eve's presence in the Garden of Eden indicates that humanity only had a spirit and soul at this point in evolution. Once they partook of the forbidden fruit, they engendered karma—they acquired a misdeed that needed reconciliation. This required memory, which is developed through the activity of the etheric sheath. When Adam and Eve sewed together fig leaves, which are from the plant kingdom corresponding to the etheric world, they donned an etheric sheath. They then had a spirit, a soul, and an etheric body. When God sent them forth from Paradise he clothed them in a skin, "And the Lord God made for Adam and for his wife garments of skins, and clothed them" (Gen. 3:20). This symbolizes the incorporation of the physical body with the etheric, soul, and spirit sheaths. The human being then had the full capacity to grow and evolve on Earth.

The Genesis story of the Fall portrays an archetype of the descent of the human soul from a condition of innocence, purity, and unity with the Divine to a condition of inner conflict, suffering, and separation from the spiritual world. Lucifer enticed the human soul to taste freedom and journey beyond the bounds of obedience. This has empowered humanity with intellectual independence, creativity, cognitive freedom, a thirst to discover, creative power, and the accompanying trials of egotism, deceit, illusory thinking, irresponsibility, and pride.

The metaphor of Eve tasting the forbidden fruit depicts the inception of the human double, the entrance of luciferic forces into the human soul. The forces of egotism introduced by Lucifer live in every human soul. All of humanity shares this condition, each individual to a greater or lesser degree. In some human beings the luciferic forces dominate the soul life, in others they play a less prominent role, but these forces dwell in every human soul. If one comprehends the complexity of Lucifer's influence over human consciousness, one will discern that luciferic forces infiltrated the *feeling* life—desiring to be like God, the *thinking* life—believing I won't die, and the *will* life—taking the fruit and eating it. This distinction delineates the three facets of the luciferic double: the realms of luciferic thinking, luciferic feeling, and luciferic will.

The transformation of the luciferic double requires establishing a right relationship with luciferic impulses—understanding the positive aspects of luciferic influences that empower human thinking and creativity, and the negative aspects of luciferic forces that lead humanity into false relationship to the Divine, to others, and to one's self. The luciferic forces addressed here in relation to luciferic thinking, feeling, and willing constitute the negative aspects that entice human beings into actions that arise out of self-interest and personal advancement at the expense of others.

Luciferic forces alienate: 1) they alienate us from the spiritual world—from God; 2) they alienate us from our fellow human beings; 3) they alienate our higher consciousness from our subconscious realm (Tomberg, 1941, p. 33).* Luciferic impulses divide and separate; they oppose the conditions of love, compassion, forgiveness, kindness, peace, and unity:

| | | |
|---|---|---|
| luciferic thinking | separates | human beings from the spirit world |
| luciferic feeling | separates | human beings from one another |
| luciferic will | separates | higher consciousness from the subconscious |

## Luciferic Thinking

The operant orientation under the influence of luciferic thinking claims a platform of authority and power: I come in my own name, out of my own power. This orientation reflects the archetypal question Lucifer posed, "Why do I have to be subservient to God? I want to be master of my own existence." The luciferic principle in thinking establishes authority through one's own light. "Lucifer shines but does not let the light [of God] shine through him" (Tomberg, 1941, p. 34). Separation from God denied the possibility of divine light working through him. Christ spoke the words, "I come in my Father's name, not in my own name" (John 5:43, ESV). His

* Valentin Tomberg's *Our Mother Course* is an unpublished manuscript available in hand-written form through the Sophia Foundation: www.sophiafoundation.org.

orientation permitted Him to work in union with the spirit world, to allow divine light and wisdom to stream through His being. What does it mean to come in service to a higher power, to humble one's self in service to a greater cause than one's self? This matter lies at the heart of the ability to overcome luciferic thinking.

Luciferic thinking manifests when objectivity is lacking; surmising, presuming, supposing, living with thoughts that are not objective but in the realm of fantasy. In the luciferic realm one does not know whether these thoughts are true or not. Whenever we speak or act out of presumption, we do so from a luciferic orientation. This easily leads to deceit, lies concerning one's self and/or others. Whenever one forgets the creator and acts out of self-interest and self-serving thought patterns, rather than remembering divine presence and the needs of others, one engages in luciferic thinking.

Judgments about other people occur when we elevate ourselves to a position of judge or authority not deemed by public position. Judgments of another lack omnipotent understanding of the circumstances, lack knowledge of karmic background, lack humility and personal culpability. Judging and condemning others constitutes the most common capitulation to luciferic thinking.

The building of the tower of Babel in Shinar, under the command of Nimrod, was an attempt to establish a kingdom that reached to the heights of heaven, procuring the power of the almighty. This stratagem resulted in the division of peoples into tribes and nations that could no longer speak the same language—separating human beings from one another. The Jewish-Roman historian Flavius Josephus (circa 37–100 CE) wrote a comprehensive *History of the Jews* for the Romans. In *Antiquities of the Jews* (94 CE), he recounted the history of the building of the Tower of Babel.

> Now it was Nimrod who excited them to such an affront and contempt of God.... He persuaded them not to ascribe it to God, as if it were through his means they were happy, but to believe that it was their own courage which procured that happiness. He also gradually changed the government into tyranny, seeing no other way of turning men from the fear of God, but to bring them into a constant dependence on his power. He also said he would be revenged on God, if he

> should have a mind to drown the world again; for that he would build a tower too high for the waters to reach. And that he would avenge himself on God for destroying their forefathers.
>
> Now the multitude were very ready to follow the determination of Nimrod, and to esteem it a piece of cowardice to submit to God; and they built a tower, neither sparing any pains, nor being in any degree negligent about the work: and, by reason of the multitude of hands employed in it, it grew very high, sooner than any one could expect. It was built of burnt brick, cemented together with mortar, made of bitumen, that it might not be liable to admit water. When God saw that they acted so madly, he did not resolve to destroy them utterly, since they were not grown wiser by the destruction of the former sinners; but he caused a tumult among them, by producing in them diverse languages, and causing that, through the multitude of those languages, they should not be able to understand one another. The place wherein they built the tower is now called Babylon, because of the confusion of that language which they readily understood before; for the Hebrews mean by the word Babel, confusion (Josephus, 94, chap. 4).

The intention of Nimrod, manifested in the building of the tower of Babel, defied the preeminence of God. In the course of time, this posture will meet its demise with consequence to humanity. One who comes in his or her own name, or who builds a "tower" to replace the presence of the Divine by what he or she has fabricated, will undergo the humiliation of being reduced to his or her own subjectivity and to terrestrial reality. The tower was struck by lightning and the people dispersed and divided into tribes and nations, no longer united as one people of the Earth.

Luciferic thinking can lead to inflation, superiority complex, or megalomania. Friedrich Nietzsche (1844–1900), a brilliant yet tragic German philosopher, personified luciferic thinking in *The Gay Science*, first published in 1887, in which he first proclaimed, "God is dead" (Nietzsche, 1974, p. 167). Two years later he also made this claim in *Thus Spoke Zarathustra*. Nietzsche not only stated, "God is dead," but also that we must banish even his shadow from the caves of our minds (Nietzsche, 1974, p. 167).

This concept appeared in a graphic depiction in Section 125, under the title of "The Madman." The madman, a portrayal of Nietzsche himself, appeared in the image of a new Diogenes. The following is an extract.

> Have you not heard of that madman who lit a lantern in the bright morning hours, ran to the market place, and cried incessantly: "I seek God! I seek God!"... The madman jumped into their midst and pierced them with his eyes. "Whither is God?" he cried; "I will tell you. We have killed him—you and I. All of us are his murderers. But how did we do this? How could we drink up the sea? Who gave us the sponge to wipe away the entire horizon? What were we doing when we unchained the earth from its sun? Whither is it moving now? Whither are we moving? Away from all suns?" He continues: "God is dead. God remains dead. And we have killed him. How shall we comfort ourselves, the murderers of all murderers? What was holiest and mightiest of all that the world has yet owned, has bled to death under our knives: who will wipe this blood off us? What water is there for us to clean ourselves?... Is not the greatness of this deed too great for us? Must we ourselves not become gods simply to appear worthy of it?" (Nietzsche, 1974, p. 181).

Nietzsche's madman revealed the consequences of "God is dead": "Must we ourselves not become gods?" This idea led to his concept of the *superman*. Nietzsche established the absence of the Divine in his worldview, and replaced God with his ideal of the superman, demonstrating luciferic thinking at its apogee. In January 1889, at the age of forty-four, Nietzsche suffered a mental breakdown in Turin, Italy. Nietzsche spent his last decade in mental darkness and died in Weimar on August 25, 1900.

## Humility: The Antidote for Luciferic Thinking

> He who exalts himself will be abased, and he who humbles himself will be exalted (Luke 14:11, ESV).

Humility transforms luciferic thinking. The root of humility is reverence for God, an inward bowing down or prostrating of the heart and conscience before God's transcendent worth. It opposes pride and vainglory, which urge one to do great things beyond one's station and capacity. Humility establishes a modest estimate of one's own worth, and submits to others. "The virtue of humility consists in keeping one's self within one's own bounds, not reaching out to things above one, but submitting to one's superior" (Aquinas, *Summa Contra Gentiles*, bk. IV, chap. lv). Unpretentious and modest, a humble person does not think one's self better or more important than others.

Silencing the ego in the realm of thinking stills the continuous rationale that validates and perpetuates luciferic thought patterns. Bringing one's thoughts to stillness and peace—relinquishing one's egotistical thinking—can, in the silence of one's mind, allow cosmic wisdom to flow in and reveal truths that illumine one's understanding. Remembering God in every thought, word, and deed counters the tendency toward luciferic thoughts, dissolving egotistic thought patterns. If through inner quiet we learn to hear the thoughts of God, then we can also speak them and live them.

Self-knowledge is central to the virtue of humility. Recognition of one's own state of spiritual imperfection and personal limitations opens the portal to the inner condition of humility. If you know yourself well, truly see and admit your weaknesses and faults, welcome others' recognition of them, and do not glory in any praise that others may give, you practice humility. Honesty and truthfulness are essential elements of humility. They manifest as one's ability to honestly assess one's self, to recognize and admit one's own faults and defects, and to admit the truth of one's compromised situation. Sadly, many people try to create false images of themselves, both to posture, to convince themselves of their own greatness, and to manipulate others into believing that they are great. Only through internal honesty can one begin to make real progress in spiritual life. To clean out the conditioning that has accumulated in the soul over many lifetimes, one has to first recognize these habitual patterns, to admit that they are there, and then to remove them in all earnestness. Without such truthfulness, one cannot make tangible progress in developing humility.

Humility does not preclude the pursuit of great things. God gives us gifts in the hope that we'll use them in worthy ways. "Of him to whom much is given, much is expected" (Luke 12:48, ESV). Our social responsibility mandates that we contribute to the community with the full strength that we are given, that we fulfill our potential. One can accomplish great things with different motives. Prideful individuals may do impressive things with their talents, using them for their own glory, crediting themselves with their accomplishments, whereas, individuals of a humble nature credit God for their talents and attempt great things to bring glory to God.

Knowledge that one lives within a greater context of a divine order, designed and created by forces far beyond any individual capacity, supports the cultivation of humility. Reverence for God, self-knowledge and honesty to acknowledge one's faults and mistakes, and honoring our fellow human beings—these characteristics form the bedrock of humility and the essential disposition to overcome luciferic thinking.

## Luciferic Feeling

Luciferic thinking creates alienation between the human being and the spiritual world, while luciferic forces work in the feeling life to disrupt harmony in human relations. Luciferic feeling constructs a wall that separates one from one's fellow human beings. Self-righteousness, self-assertion, blame, the desire for power, and the assertion of self-interest by projecting one's self out into the world to gain or maintain personal power, exemplify luciferic feeling. This is often cloaked in the disguise of human rights: it is our "right" to do this. We can go so far as to say that any feeling of partisanship that pits one person or group against another personifies luciferic feeling.

The following incident described in the Gospel of John reveals the motives at work within luciferic feeling.

> The scribes and the Pharisees brought a woman who had been caught in adultery, and placing her in the midst they said to him, "Teacher, this woman has been caught in the act of adultery. Now in the Law Moses commanded us to stone such women. So what do you say?" This they said to test him, that they might have some charge to bring against him. Jesus bent down and wrote with his finger on the ground. And as they continued to ask him, he stood up and said to them, "Let him who is without sin among you cast the first stone." And once more he bent down and wrote on the ground. But when they heard it, they

> went away one by one, beginning with the older ones, and Jesus was left alone with the woman standing before him. Jesus stood up and said to her, "Woman, where are they? Has no one condemned you?" She said, "No one, Lord." And Jesus said, "Neither do I condemn you; go, and from now on sin no more" (John 8:3–11, ESV).

A vociferous group of scribes and Pharisees brought a woman to Jesus, claiming she had been caught in the act of adultery and that it was the law of Moses that an adulteress was to be stoned to death. Their righteous indignation warranted investigation. Why did they want her put to death? Why was she condemned alone without the man with whom she was caught? The novel, *The Remnant*, by Mary Lacroix, offers a possible background to this forceful demand for execution. Within the genre of historic fiction, the unfolding events in this sequence in the novel portray the persona of luciferic feeling. The scribes and Pharisees dragged the woman before the Roman officials, who would not sanction her execution, but told them to bring her before a rabbi to be judged, for it is the law of Moses that condemns adultery to the penalty of death.

Lacroix describes that the woman's accusers who then brought her before Jesus of Nazareth were hiding their true motives under the guise of upholding the law. They had enjoyed the pleasure of her company and in their intimacy with her had confided their secrets to her. When they realized that she had been visited by some of their enemies they were afraid she would reveal their secrets to them. The scribes and Pharisees came with the ulterior motive of wanting her silenced by death so she could not reveal any of the information they had told her. To protect themselves they brought her to be judged and condemned to death by stoning, according to the law of Moses (Lacroix, 1981, p. 395–396).

Their personal desire to hide the truth and maintain power was veiled by their claim that according to Moses this was the lawful punishment for the woman. They asserted their own power under veiled pretenses. They created a disguise to protect their personal interests and avoid having the truth about them exposed. The accusers had no concern for the woman; her death was inconsequential to them to protect their pride. Luciferic feeling divides human beings from each other. It expresses self-interest, covering over one's own misdeeds, and disregarding others.

Jesus remained silent. He bent down and with his finger wrote upon the Earth. Rudolf Steiner indicates that Jesus drew a symbol that depicted the law of karma.

> What did He write? He inscribed the sin in the spiritual world. And that sin will find its adjustment from out the spiritual world. But he reminded the others if perchance they themselves were conscious of no sin. For unless they themselves had nothing for which to make amends, they could not feel free from participation in the woman's sin and were unfit to judge her.... Everything is written in the book of Karma. Jesus wrote in the Earth, which He had already permeated with his spiritual light; that is, He confided to the Earth what should lie in the Karma of the adulteress. He meant to say: "Follow the path which I now mark out for you. Learn to say: We judge not; we leave that which is in the human being to the adjustment of Karma" (Steiner, 1944, p. 188).

Jesus, in silence and with gesture, called upon the conscience of the accusers. He awakened in them awareness of the law of karma—that one's deeds determine the future; karma will be fulfilled in the course of earthly evolution. Then Jesus stood up and said, "Let him who is without sin among you, cast the first stone" (John 8:7, ESV). The accusers fell silent, convicted by their own conscience. Their fiery countenance paled and one by one they retreated into the dark of the night until they were all gone.

The woman was left standing there. Jesus wrote in the dirt again, looked up and said: "Woman, where are they? Has no one condemned you?" (John 8:10, ESV). He said this to turn her thoughts away from outer judgment and point to her inner karma (Steiner, 1988, p. 121). When she answered, "No man, Lord," she was left to her karma. She no longer had to concern herself with outer punishment, but could turn her focus inward, to change her life. Then Jesus said to her, "Neither do I condemn thee. Go and sin no more" (John 8:11, ESV).

A personal experience in the life of environmentalist Tom Brown provides another example of luciferic feeling. He was out hiking in the wilderness when he heard a motor and then saw a man drive up in a truck. The man proceeded to get out of his truck and change the engine oil, dumping the old oil in the soil right by the river. After he put new oil into the engine he took out a fishing pole and began fishing. Tom was horrified and outraged that this man had dumped his engine oil right beside the river. He "fought back the anger that consumed his every thought" (Brown, 2000, p. 155). There were used oilcans and his old oil filter thrown on the ground. Filled with anger, Tom judged this man for his ignorance and lack of environmental consciousness, separating him from his fellow human being.

Tom approached the fisherman, startling him with the greeting: "Nice truck." In the ensuing conversation, Tom realized that the man did not mean to pollute the Earth, he just did not know any better. Tom's anger subsided as he taught the man about the woods and fishing. He helped him catch the largest fish he ever caught. Then Tom told him that if he liked to fish he should catch as many fish as he possibly could, because the ponds and rivers were being polluted and would not be producing fish much longer. So, he should enjoy it while he could. He explained that people are pouring poisonous things in the soil right near the rivers and ponds and it is all leaching into the water and killing the fish.

> I had no idea where the words were coming from, for it was like my body and mind were moved with a force outside of myself (Brown, 2000, p. 156).

Tom Brown allowed inspiration to flow through him, as he was able to set aside his judgments and righteous indignation. As abruptly as he appeared he said goodbye and disappeared down the trail. After some time Tom looked back to see what the fisherman was doing. He saw the man digging the oil-soaked soil with a shovel, dumping it into a bucket and putting the bucket into his truck. He cleaned up the empty oilcans and the used filter and went to a grove of pine trees and dug up a sapling and transplanted it in the spot where he had cleaned up his oil, as if he were planting a garden.

Tom initially experienced anger, judgment, and righteous indignation. He was able to transform these luciferic feelings toward another human being into interest in the other, generously educating him without condemnation. As a result, the fisherman changed his relationship to the environment. Had he not looked back Tom might never have known what the man did. That being the more common occurrence, most often we do not know the results of our deeds. If we are serving a higher principle we can leave the fruits to God.

## Silence and Questioning: The Antidote for Luciferic Feeling

Here we have two examples of luciferic feeling: the first demonstrates having one's own interest at heart, one's own personal power and gain without caring about the well-being of others. The second appears to have the well-being of all at heart, but in truth the offender is excluded; he is subject to judgment. The process of transforming luciferic feeling requires developing a concern for the well-being of others, and eventually all beings, so that our feelings embrace the whole of life on Earth. One's feelings can be turned outwards to encompass all of humanity and all of Nature. This applies to both examples above. The ingredients for transforming luciferic feeling are twofold: silence and questions. That was the medicine that Jesus used; he became very silent and drew a symbol for karma upon the Earth to remember divine law, the law of karma, the law of reciprocity. In silence—rather than speaking of "my rights"—and in questions, one can come to an inner orientation that takes to heart the interests of all. These principles also apply to the encounter between Tom Brown and the fisherman. In his inner silence a greater wisdom was able to speak through him that honored the fisherman, the offender.

Silence and questioning can lead to an awakened conscience that can transform the desire for power and self-assertion to serve one's own ends, to concern for the well-being of all, transforming self-interest to magnanimity, greatness of heart. The self-righteous stance demanding personal rights can become a truly righteous stance for the rights of all humanity and the Earth.

## Luciferic Will

We have seen how luciferic thinking alienates human beings from the spiritual world, and luciferic feeling divides human beings from one another. The luciferic will constructs a wall that separates one's consciousness from one's subconscious. Either the conscious mind suppresses the subconscious, or the subconscious rules the conscious mind. With this orientation, personal will supersedes divine will, opposing the third petition of the Lord's Prayer: "Thy will be done." There is a desire to hide the truth, to cover over the subconscious (covering over with the fig leaf in Paradise), a desire for self-beautification or false image—all of which are forms of deceit.

The story of King Saul and David in the first book of Samuel exemplifies luciferic will. After David slew Goliath, his fame and reputation grew. It was said, "Saul has slain his thousands, and David his ten thousands" (1 Sam. 18:7, ESV). Saul became jealous and sought David's death. When searching with his soldiers in the mountains of Engedi, Saul entered a cave to rest for the night. Not knowing that David was in the back of the cave hiding with his men, Saul and his soldiers slept. Thus, according to the promise of the Lord, David's enemy was delivered unto him. "Behold, I will deliver your enemy into your hand, that you may do to him as it shall seem good to you" (1 Sam. 24:4, ESV).

Although prompted by his men to kill Saul, David chose instead to cut the skirt off Saul's robe as it lay beside him where he was sleeping. In cutting the length of the king's robe to that of a page, symbolically David diminished Saul's dignity and importance in the affairs of men. In those times a dignitary in a short skirt had little authority among his subjects.

David could have justified killing Saul by right of several arguments: *It is self-defense; Saul is out to kill me. I am in the right; God promised me the throne. God has delivered him into my hands; it is a God-given opportunity and I should take it. I'm so tired of running, hiding, and fighting Saul; this can put an end to it.* But David refused to justify violence against his king. Instead, he demonstrated a radical, obedient trust in God.

David awaited the fulfillment of God's promise: "You will inherit the throne of Israel" (Ezek. 34:23, ESV). Saul, in his jealousy, sought to prevent

God's promise from being fulfilled. As God had placed Saul in a position of authority, David knew it was disobedient to kill Saul so he deferred to God's omnipotence to execute jurisdiction over Saul. David refused to use personal power to fulfill God's promise.

Saul employed a luciferic will, hunting human souls to take them. In his case it was ruled by jealousy. Saul strove to assert his will for personal power and glory. David, in cutting the skirt off Saul's robe, deprived the luciferic will of its authority and power, exposing it in its true light, and subjugating it to a higher will, that of the Divine.

After Saul left the cave, David went out and called after Saul, "My lord the king!" (1 Sam. 24:8, ESV). And when Saul looked behind him, David bowed with his face to the earth and paid homage to Saul. David then told Saul that he sought him no harm; even though he was delivered into his hands, he spared his life. David then expressed his desire to live in peace, with no intention of overthrowing Saul, to which Saul replied:

> "Is this your voice, my son David?" And Saul lifted up his voice and wept. He said to David, "You are more righteous than I, for you have repaid me good, whereas I have repaid you evil (1 Sam. 24:16–17, ESV).

David did not let luciferic thoughts or feelings govern his will, even though he was being hunted. His wisdom empowered his "I"—higher Self—to govern his subconscious thoughts and feelings. In the end, David's magnanimity disarmed Saul's egotism.

The Salem witch trials depicted in Arthur Miller's *The Crucible* expose the kind of inhumane events that occur when the luciferic subconscious impulses override the higher nature of the human being—the "I"—that transforms subconscious forces. In *The Crucible*, the townsfolk engage in a hysterical climate of accusations and executions of innocent people out of religious piety and because it gives them a chance to express repressed sentiments and to act on long-held grudges. These all exemplify the influence of the luciferic double.

The witch trials insidiously thrive on accusations, projection of guilt onto innocent people. As the play begins, Reverend Parris fears his daughter Abigail's increasingly questionable actions, including hints of witchcraft surrounding her coma, will threaten his reputation and force him from the pulpit. Parris accuses Abigail of dishonoring him, and he then makes a series of accusations against his parishioners, making scapegoats of people like John Proctor who question his authority (act 3, scene 1).

Giles Corey, Proctor, and Putnam respond in kind, creating a chorus of indictments before Reverend Hale, the expert on witchcraft, even arrives. The wealthy, ambitious Thomas Putnam gains revenge on Francis Nurse by getting Rebecca, Francis's virtuous wife, convicted of the supernatural murders of Ann Putnam's babies (act 3, scene 2). Hysteria suspended the rules of daily life and allowed the acting out of deceitful, sinister desires and hateful motives under the cover of righteousness.

Early in the play, Proctor (the protagonist), has a chance to put a stop to the girls' accusations of witchcraft, but his desire to preserve his reputation, an impetus of luciferic deceit, keeps him from testifying against Abigail, hiding an affair he had with her in the past. Abigail and her group achieve an extremely unusual level of power and authority for young, unmarried girls in a Puritan community. They established the power to destroy the lives of others with a mere accusation; even the wealthy and influential were not safe. In her jealousy, Abigail exploits the escalating hysteria by accusing Proctor's wife, Elizabeth, of witchcraft and has her sent to jail (act 2, scene 4, p. 73).

Proctor's sense of guilt begins to eat away at him. He knows that he can bring down Abigail and end her reign of terror, but he fears for his good name if his hidden sin of adultery is revealed. The pressing knowledge of his own guilt makes him feel judged, but Elizabeth points out that the judge who pursues him so mercilessly is himself. Proctor has a great loathing for hypocrisy, and, here, he judges his own hypocrisy no less harshly than that of others.

Eventually Proctor attempts to break this cycle by confessing to having had an affair with Abigail, but his confession is trumped by the accusation of witchcraft against him, which in turn demands a confession. At the end of the play, Proctor's desire to keep his good name leads him to make the heroic choice not to make a false confession and to go to his death without signing his name to an untrue statement. "I have given you my soul; leave me my name!" he cries to Danforth (act 4, scene 4, p. 133). Proctor's decision to die, rather than confess to a sin that he did not commit, finally breaks the cycle. The court collapses shortly afterward, undone by the refusal of its victims to propagate lies. Honesty in the face of shame and guilt overcomes the luciferic double.

A more subtle example of luciferic will, portrayed through Peter's denial of Christ, described in the Gospel of Matthew, brings a different perspective to this dimension of the psyche. In the previous two examples both Saul and the Salem accusers acted out of an impulse to destroy others—who were perceived as enemies—to cover up their own guilt or inadequacy. Their subconscious impulses overruled their higher nature. In this next example, Peter's subconscious overrules his conscious will by betraying his most beloved friend and teacher.

After the Last Supper, Jesus spoke to his disciples and Peter declared to Jesus:

> "Though they all fall away because of you, I will never fall away." Jesus said to him, "Truly, I say to you, this very night, before the cock crows, you will deny me three times." Peter said to him, "Even if I must die with you, I will not deny you." And so said all the disciples.
>
> Then Jesus went with them to a place called Gethsemane, and he said to his disciples, "Sit here, while I go yonder and pray." And taking with him Peter and the two sons of Zebedee, he began to be sorrowful and troubled. Then he said to them, "My soul is very sorrowful, even to death; remain here, and watch with me." And going a little farther he fell on his face and prayed, "My Father, if it be possible, let this cup pass from me; nevertheless, not as I will, but as thou wilt." And he came to the disciples and found them sleeping; and he said to Peter, "So could you not watch with me one hour? Watch and pray that you may not enter into temptation; the spirit indeed is willing, but the flesh is weak." Again, for the second time, he went away and prayed, "My Father, if this cannot pass unless I drink it, thy will be done." And again he came and found them sleeping, for their eyes

> were heavy. So leaving them again, he went away and prayed for the third time, saying the same words. Then he came to the disciples and said to them, "Are you still sleeping and taking your rest? Behold, the hour is at hand, and the Son of man is betrayed into the hands of sinners. Rise, let us be going; see, my betrayer is at hand." While he was still speaking, Judas came, one of the twelve, and with him a great crowd with swords and clubs, from the chief priests and the elders of the people (Matt. 26:33–47).
>
> Then all the disciples forsook him and fled. Then those who had seized Jesus led him to Caiaphas the high priest, where the scribes and the elders had gathered. But Peter followed him at a distance, as far as the courtyard of the high priest, and going inside he sat with the guards to see the end... (Matt. 26:56–58).
>
> Now Peter was sitting outside in the courtyard. And a maid came up to him, and said, "You also were with Jesus the Galilean." But he denied it before them all, saying, "I do not know what you mean." And when he went out to the porch, another maid saw him, and she said to the bystanders, "This man was with Jesus of Nazareth." And again he denied it with an oath, "I do not know the man." After a little while the bystanders came up and said to Peter, "Certainly you are also one of them, for your accent betrays you." Then he began to invoke a curse on himself and to swear, "I do not know the man." And immediately the cock crowed. And Peter remembered the saying of Jesus, "Before the cock crows, you will deny me three times." And he went out and wept bitterly (Matt. 26:69–75).

Overrun by fear for his life, Peter denied knowing his most beloved friend and teacher. His subconscious instinct for survival overpowered his conscious devotion to Christ. His realization of his failure to be faithful to Jesus awakened deep shame and remorse within him. He wept to wash away his grief and guilt. Shame uncovers what is false; deceit can be transformed into spiritual realism through the awakening forces of shame. In the ideal, subconscious impulses will be raised into consciousness and come under the guiding influence of the higher Self, in which case nothing needs to be hidden. Meditation creates the means for consciousness to penetrate the subconscious.

## Honesty and Shame: The Antidote for Luciferic Willing

The luciferic principle in the will seeks to create false glory by covering over the truth. We cover over our subconscious to create an illusion of beauty. We "clothe" ourselves. The archetype of this impulse occurred in the Paradise story when Adam and Eve covered themselves with fig leaves to hide their transgression. Saul covered his lower self and glorified his person with a kingly garment. The accusers in the Crucible covered their own guilt by directing blame on others. Peter covered his conscious love of Christ with his subconscious fear of death. In each instance, the subconscious forces governed behavior.

When deceit or blame dominates behavior, uncovering the truth inevitably leads to shame—the agent that transformed each of the circumstances cited above. I am using the word "shame" to indicate a natural feeling that arises within every human being when we act or speak in a way that is out of integrity with our own values. We know we have transgressed our own sense of goodness or moral integrity when a sensation of inner discomfort arises. This feeling arises as a beacon of light to bring our attention to a schism in our soul. Our conscience bears the weight of disintegration. Shame calls us to awaken and reintegrate our deeds with our values. Establishing a healthy attentiveness to shame strengthens the fiber of our moral development. Healthy shame lays the psychological ground for humility.

Rigorous, candid honesty (admitting the unadulterated truth) and shame (stimulating moral courage for impartial justice) create the antidote for luciferic will impulses. Honesty frees the soul of guilt, compromise, and moral degeneration. Shame awakens consciousness which when heeded leads to self-knowledge and potential progress on the path of inner purification. When King Saul experienced David's magnanimity, eventually shame brought him to the awareness that his intention to kill David was maligned. Shame activated his conscience, leading to reconciliation and peace. In *The Crucible*, Proctor's shame activated his longing for integrity and justice. His shame strengthened his courage to reveal his own infidelity as a necessary step to expose the false accusations and moral injustice that was prevailing in the Salem community. When the truth came out, the witch trials came to an end. In a similar manner, when Peter heard the cock crow and he met the gaze of Christ, he experienced deep shame. This awakened in him the awareness of the power of his subconscious forces to override his conscious intention, setting him on a path of inner inquiry and purification.

The luciferic double in its threefold expression seeks to dominate the soul life with egotism, self-aggrandizement, and false glory, through judging, blaming, projecting, accusing, over-powering, deceiving, covering over, protecting, and hiding. The transformation of the luciferic double requires humility, silence and questioning, honesty and shame.

**Figure 3**

The Transformation of the Luciferic Double

| | Luciferic Thinking | Luciferic Feeling | Luciferic Will |
|---|---|---|---|
| Separates: | us from the spirit world | us from one another | higher consciousness from subconscious |
| Remedy: | humility | silence and questioning | honesty and shame |

## The Redemption of Lucifer

Lucifer, who was the signet of perfection, full of wisdom and perfect in beauty, dwelling upon the holy mountain of God (Ezek. 28:12, 14, ESV), initiated rebellion in heaven, catalyzing the formation of the legion of fallen angels, and he tempted humanity to follow his example of defiance and independent thinking. Lucifer tempted Eve—the soul—to take "into herself" the substance of the Ego or consciousness. Lucifer led humanity away from the divine spiritual world and into the world of senses thereby enabling humanity to develop freedom and individuality.

Lucifer seeded positive characteristics of independent thinking, creativity, and conscious freedom. Humanity would be drowned in a sea of materialism, would persist in the belief that nothing exists except the outer world of matter, if we did not experience inspiration through the luciferic principle. The luciferic principle intensifies and develops spiritual faculties.

Luciferic spirits also slipped into the human astral body, thereby subjecting the human soul to the temptation of evil. The negative luciferic forces working in human consciousness prevail on Earth in expressions of egotism, arrogance, self-righteousness, vanity, speculation, judgment, and numerous other manifestations in the human double. Lucifer's radiance governs a domain of lawful influence upon the Earth, and oversteps this realm, influencing humanity to experience the fullness of knowledge of good and evil.

When considering the conundrum of humanity's relationship to Lucifer, we must come to know that a turning point in the stratagem for luciferic power took place at the time of the Crucifixion of Jesus of Nazareth, the bearer of the Christ Being. Several esotericists—Rudolf Steiner, Valentin Tomberg, and Anne Catherine Emmerich among them—perceived that Lucifer was present and bore witness to the Crucifixion. At this time Lucifer had the penetrating insight that he was responsible for the condition of human consciousness that brought about this event and that it was he who should have borne the suffering on the cross. This monumental realization catalyzed an inner experience of conversion (Tomberg, 1985, p. 173).

> Pierced by that pain, there arose in Lucifer at that hour a ceaseless longing for suffering and humiliation. To the proud spirit—to the shining spirit of beauty personified—nothing thenceforward has become more hateful than the incense of admiration for his character—it burns him like fire—and nothing more desirable than the recognition of his wrongdoing and the humiliation of his spirits—this is as balm to him, soothing his pain. And he is filled with a passionate hope that at some time in the Cosmos he may be allowed to experience a martyrdom equaling that of the Other.... For the Spirit of Self-conscious Beauty had recognized that the true and highest beauty is in sacrifice.... This inward conversion of Lucifer was the beginning of the retrieval of the whole luciferic territory for the work of Goodness (Tomberg, 1985, p. 174).

Witnessing the Crucifixion of Christ, Lucifer experienced shame and humility to an intense degree equivalent to his deeds of unlawful rebellion. He grasped the reality of his culpability in the unfolding of this cosmic injustice. He took the guilt upon himself. Initiated by this horrifying realization, he began a process of transformation. He experienced the true power of sacrifice, as he felt the power of Christ's sacrifice infusing his being with shame, remorse, and love. Lucifer began the inner process of realigning with the will of God, in service to the Christ impulse of love and the redemption of humanity. He underwent a profound metamorphosis.

This conversion took place only within him, however, not within the legions of fallen angels who allied with him. He changed his course out of a deep inner experience. Those angelic hosts who followed Lucifer, as well as all of humanity, having incorporated luciferic forces, still live under the influence of the unlawful impulses of Lucifer. Each angel and each human being must go through his or her own experience of conversion to transform the luciferic forces within. But now we have before us the guiding light of Lucifer who has blazed a path of redemption.

Golgotha marked a significant transformation in the relationship between Lucifer and Christ, and Lucifer and humanity. Since the Fall, Lucifer was ever-present within the human soul life, enticing human beings toward freedom, on the one hand, and egotism, on the other hand. Since the Crucifixion, Lucifer longs for Christ to become ever more apparent as an indwelling reality within human soul life, while he assumes ever-greater radiance in the outer world (Steiner, 1986, pp. 6–7). Steiner states that Lucifer will increasingly become the soul's guide in our inner journey to penetrate the mystery and reality of Christ within us.

> The healing of future humanity will be accomplished by the fact that within the union of the two streams, the mighty Christ Being, guiding as He does the evolution of the Universe and of man, is understood through the light received by the soul from within, out of the kingdom of Lucifer. Christ will give the substance, Lucifer the form, and from their union will arise impulses which shall permeate the spiritual evolution of [hu]mankind, and bring about what the future has in store for the healing and the blessing of the peoples (Steiner, 1986, p. 137).

Steiner foresaw an eventual marriage of these two worlds, Lucifer and Christ, as they "unite themselves in love" (Steiner, 1986, p. 137) as an agapé of Logos—Christ, and Light-Bearer—Lucifer. Through Lucifer's inspiration we will be able to comprehend the meaning and significance of Christ's incarnation for the Earth. Their union will herald the essential kernel of a new spiritual stream that needs to flow through the world (Steiner, 1986, p. 136).

We can see that Lucifer's destiny serves to guide humanity not only through the Fall to the knowledge of good and evil, seeding all the luciferic aspects of the double, not only to freedom and independent cognition, giving rise to spiritual and creative inspiration, but also to an understanding and experience of the Mystical Christ—of the ultimate power of love and sacrifice in the course of evolution for the Earth and humanity. As legend foretold, the star of Lucifer—the stone that fell from Lucifer's crown when he was cast out of heaven—transformed into the Holy Grail. Here we begin to understand the meaning of the cross of Christ in the star of Lucifer (Steiner, 1986, p. 4): Christ's sacrifice and all that it wrought for the Earth and humanity will come to be understood through the radiant light of Lucifer. Lucifer has regained the brilliance of light he originally had when he walked among the fiery stones, but now at the center of his radiance shines the cross of Christ—devotion to redemption through love. Humanity followed Lucifer through the Fall in search of freedom and knowledge. Now can we follow him to a humbling experience of the mystical Christ in quest of redemption through love?

# CHAPTER 3

# The Ahrimanic Double: The Claws of Fear

> One must not say that the world is imperfect because it contains evil. Far rather is it perfect precisely on that account. The creators of the world needed evil in order to bring the good to development. A good must first be broken on the rock of evil. The All-Love can only be brought to its highest blossoming through self-love.
>
> —Rudolf Steiner*

The profound mystery of evil has occupied the thoughts of many great philosophers and theologians. The exploration of the origin and meaning of evil under consideration here derives from the spiritual research of Rudolf Steiner who in his lecture, "The Origin of Evil," states that evil arises in conjunction with free will, and is therefore isolated to the human kingdom (Steiner, 1906, Berlin). Human beings choose to love or to hate, to be self-serving or selfless in their actions, to be warm and interested or to be cold and calculating. This polar condition of choice not only makes evil possible, but Steiner indicates that without evil there would be no freedom. Freedom and evil originate from the same source: Lucifer, who enticed humanity to know good and evil through free will.

The primary relationship between freedom, good, and evil involves a fundamental inquiry into the meaning of Earth evolution. As free human

* Steiner, 1906, Berlin.

beings, we experience the world in duality or multiplicity. Contrast clarifies definition. In order to know "good" we must also have "evil" before us as an option. Why do people choose evil? Steiner asserts that evil "dwells within us as the force of self-love"* (Steiner, 1906, Berlin). This brings a unique perspective to the meaning of evil. According to this point of view, evil arises as a distortion of love. Or one could say, it arises as an immature form of love. Recalling the original premise in chapter 1—that the mission of life is to transubstantiate the very substance of the Earth into love—brings light to the essential presence of evil as a developmental stage in humanity's learning to love in the most spiritualized sense. "Love must turn to the self only in order to set the self in the service of the world" (Steiner, 1906, Berlin). The process of maturing love constitutes the substance of each human biography and the evolution of humanity.

Chapter 2 recounts the Paradise story from Genesis at the moment when the origin of freedom, good, and evil were introduced into the stream of human consciousness. Within the context of Lucifer's rebellion in heaven and his role in the Paradise story, the threefold nature of the luciferic double establishes a platform for Lucifer's influence sculpting human lives, history, and contemporary world conditions. The concluding section of chapter 2 introduced the poignant redemption of Lucifer, initiating his role as guide on our inner journey to penetrate within us the mystery and reality of Christ—the cosmic being of eternal love—demonstrating an evolutionary progression of love.

In this chapter, the diabolic figure of Ahriman assumes the central focus. Ahriman is recognized in many cultures: in Persia as the god of darkness; among the Hebrew people as Mephistopheles;** and in biblical references as Satan, the personification of evil. The mythological background to Ahriman introduced in chapter 1 lays the foundation for understanding the nature of

* Self-love here means complete focus on the self, giving no value to others: self-absorption, narcissism, egotism. This does not suggest that one should not have a strong sense of self, and care for one's self.

** Mephistopheles: The name, originally Hebrew, is derived from "mephiz" meaning destroyer, and "tophel" meaning liar. Mephistopheles is a fallen archangel, one of the seven great princes of Hell (one of the maskim, q.v.). Davidson, G. (1994) *The Dictionary of Angels*. New York: Free Press.

the ahrimanic double. As the Lord of Death, Ahriman lawfully regulates the destruction of life, and concomitantly he unlawfully seeks to take possession of human thinking. This chapter explores the intricacies of the threefold nature of the ahrimanic double from the perspective that evil results from self-love. The balance of these weighty ahrimanic forces dwells within us.

The ahrimanic influence in the Western world has escalated to epic proportions in the present Fifth Cultural Epoch. The modern scientific revolution, beginning in the fifteenth century with the advent of the Copernican Revolution, until the present burgeoning electronic era, reflects the immense influence of Ahriman. He promotes intelligence and materialistic scientific thinking but opposes increased consciousness. Ahriman inspires amoral, atheistic, mechanistic materialism, and related cleverness. He aims to wrest human beings away from any allegiance to, or even any awareness of the world of spirit, to chain humanity to Earth and to immerse us in ease and materialism. He encourages apathy, indifference, cold intellect, inner stagnation, and alienation.

Contrary to the servants of Lucifer—the fallen angels of light who create a kingdom of illusory enticement—the immensely powerful servants of Ahriman strive to blind human beings to the spirit, to the existence or presence of spirit. These servants seek to convince us to behold the Universe merely as a machine, and to entice us to believe that only things that can be measured, weighed, and quantified constitute reality. Ahrimanic spirits of materialism seek to turn humanity into lifeless matter and forget its spiritual ancestry and destiny. By contrast, luciferic spirits would amplify spiritual life so abundantly that humanity might forget that its destiny concerns the responsible and loving regeneration of Earth, upon which we must remain sure-footed.

According to Steiner, if Ahriman succeeds in immersing humanity in excessive materialism, he will nearly have taken possession of human thinking. His interference in human consciousness results in materialistic thinking—thinking directed only toward the sense world. As a result, people who do not recognize the spiritual world as a reality, who only consider the sense perceptible world as real, can come to live under the influence of Ahriman's unlawful forces, permeating thinking with materialism.

Ahrimanic forces seek to eradicate all possibility of free, individualized human consciousness. On the emotional level, they arouse fear, hatred, lust for power, and destructive sexual impulses in our subconscious instincts. On the mental level they inspire rigid, automatic thinking empty of genuine thoughts, but fixated in literalistic interpretation, leading to falsehood. This "abstract" thinking, devoid of any conscious, inner activity and devoid of any real connection to living experience, creates a lifeless consciousness without light, color, or image.

The forces of Ahriman not only work within the human double but as a result permeate human culture. In the social-cultural sphere ahrimanic influences saturate society. We see this in trends such as: antagonistic nationalism based on ethnicity; dogmatic party politics that engender hatred and bitterness arising from the refusal to acknowledge other points of view; religious fundamentalism; the subjugation of cultural life (e.g., medicine, education, research, criminal jurisprudence) to political and economic power; and mechanization of the political state, bound by rigid laws, with little place for free human initiative. In everyday life these forces appear as tedium, alienation, lack of interest in one's work, and disinterest in intellectual work.

Ahriman works to make knowledge devoid of warm human interest and personal connection, to be stored in unread books rather than to live in human souls. This cold, impersonal knowledge appears in many aspects of post-modern civilization. In medicine we experience materialistic, mechanistic experimentalism and treatment, without an adequate understanding of the living human individual. In social science and economics this appears as blind acceptance of statistics and the belief that the satisfaction of economic needs by itself will secure human welfare. In capitalism it manifests in the impersonal mechanism of profit seeking that leads to the subjugation of all living and human interests to the inhuman, to the "artificial person" of the corporation. In religion this appears as narrow, simplistic interpretation of the sacred texts without appreciation for the occult wisdom needed for an approach to the deep mysteries of these scriptures. In industrial production there are cold, mechanistic developments, albeit refined, directed only at satisfying animal needs, promoting human immersion in the sense-world to the exclusion of the supersensible. This condition also lives in beliefs such as: humans are animals, animals (and all living things) are mechanisms, soul and spirit do not exist, and the denial of morality. The ahrimanic "Mammon" archetypally promotes the power of money over life.

Ahrimanic beings inhabit the etheric sheath—the body of formative forces where memory resides—working to deteriorate physical health, leading to death. The existence of these beings in our etheric body leads to illnesses of our organs. In the astral body these forces manifest in psychological disorders and nerve illnesses. Illnesses that arise within the body (as opposed to ingesting poisonous substances) derive from these forces working within us.

To counter these forces, each human being must engage in practices to overcome egotism, the root cause of the activity of the double. In a lecture given January 15, 1914, entitled "Evil Illumined through the Science of the Spirit," Rudolf Steiner stated that evil arises from egotism.

> Basically, human evil proceeds from what we call egotism. In the whole scope and range of "wrongs," from the smallest oversight to the most serious crime, whether the imperfection or evil originates more in the body or in the soul, egotism is the fundamental trait that underlies it all. We can ascertain the real meaning of evil by connecting it in our minds with human egotism, and all striving to reach beyond imperfection and evil involves a struggle with egotism (Steiner, 2003, p. 25).

Progress in the struggle with egotism requires developing a strong sense of self that bares the mark of humility. This struggle constitutes the transformation of self-love into love that extends out, initially to one person, and eventually includes the love of all life.

To encounter evil effectively in the outer world, beyond our inner struggle with our own double, we must first achieve a heightened degree of self-knowledge that instills both humility and the compassion to confront evil in a morally transformative and redemptive manner. An example of this morally transformative stance follows. A man approached Martin Luther King Jr. and asked him, "Are you Dr. King Jr.?" Dr. King answered, "Yes, I am." The man then spat on him. Dr. King stopped, pulled out a handkerchief, wiped off the spittle, folded the handkerchief neatly, and handed it to the man saying, "I think this belongs to you" (Cousineau, 2011, p. 15). Dr. King exhibited the capacity to override anger and retribution with dignity and compassion, an example of a morally transformative deed.

Confrontation with the forces of evil ripens the "I," bringing it to a higher degree of maturity. As indicated before, evil exists to make the good stronger. Evil exists to bring the "I" to its full development. Like the fire in a kiln that brings clay to perfection in the finished pottery, evil transmutes the "I." We need the confrontation with evil in order to bring to realization the divine love within us. For example, exposure to the facts and personal stories of the holocaust precipitates an inescapable awareness of, and identification with, the people who experienced the horrors of that world event, intensifying our commitment to justice and human rights, and to the well-being of all people.

In chapter 2, we considered the confrontation with evil within the dynamics of the threefold luciferic double. Luciferic thoughts, feelings, and actions establish a platform for ahrimanic forces to enter. The growing power of egotism breeds fear and the desire to control. Metaphorically speaking, Ahriman waits patiently for Lucifer to establish a foothold in the human soul, and then creeps in to entangle our feelings with fear and gravity. Lucifer incites anger; then Ahriman activates fear. Ahriman breeds a cold, calculated, mechanistic, isolated orientation in which materialism reigns.

Ahrimanic forces infiltrate the thinking life, the feeling life, and the will life, promoting dry, prosaic, philistine, materialistic people, hardening what would be healthily mobile, supple thoughts, feelings, and even bodies. Cold-hearted, calculating strategies for power, asserting domination in a godless world, personify ahrimanic thinking. Indifference, weariness of life, heaviness, boredom, coldness, rigidity, loneliness, and emotional paralysis through fear and depression, characterize ahrimanic feeling. People become viewed as spiritless objects in an amoral game of materialistic gain. Ahrimanic will manifests in actions that serve one's own purposes, regardless of the impact on others, including, for example, murder, child pornography, and sadomasochism. The three aspects of the ahrimanic double erect barriers that lead to isolation and loneliness. Ahrimanic thinking separates our true thought nature from the spiritual world. Ahrimanic feeling separates our true soul nature from our fellow human beings. Ahrimanic will separates our conscious impulse to act in the world from our subconscious impulses (Tomberg, 1941). A clear understanding of these aspects of our subconscious nature can activate great progress in inner transformation.

## Ahrimanic Thinking

As mentioned in chapter 1, according to Rudolf Steiner, Ahriman desires to take possession of human thinking, resulting in materialistic thought, directing thinking only toward the outer world, perceived by the senses. People who do not believe in the spiritual world, who only consider the sense perceptible world as real, live under the influence of Ahriman's unlawful forces, permeating thinking with materialism. The effect deepens as Ahriman wishes to harden the etheric sheath to the degree that it becomes a vehicle of automatic, intellectual thinking devoid of will, and thus make it possible (after a person's death) to keep human etheric bodies permanently in the region of the Earth (Steiner, 1987, p. 25). This restriction of the etheric would harden the vitality of the Earth so that it would not support further evolution. Humanity would become clever, animalistic, ghostly, Earth-bound creatures, aborting the fulfillment of the mission of love.

Ahrimanic thinking generates diabolical actions. In Shakespeare's *Othello*, he exposed the nature of ahrimanic thinking in the character Iago, servant to Othello. Endowed with an almost superhuman intellect, a creative genius, unrestrained by any moral law, Iago enacts a heart-wrenching portrayal of ahrimanic forces at work in human behavior. He effortlessly manipulates all those around him to do his bidding—to kill Cassio, destroy Othello, discredit Desdemona's virtue—by taking advantage of their trust and using their motivations and weaknesses to achieve his ends.

In act 1, scene 1, Iago expresses his hatred for Othello for choosing Cassio as his lieutenant rather than himself, as he expected. In retribution Iago suggests to Othello that Cassio and Desdemona are having an affair, which earns Iago Othello's trust and, eventually, the position as lieutenant. Although Iago achieved his coveted position, his thirst for power and manipulation increases. His acute intellect accompanies a hard and callous heart, demonstrating perfect indifference to moral good or evil. His joy arises from the success of his treachery where suffering is inflicted on others.

Iago expresses his cold, calculated thoughts at various points in the play. In act 1, after discovering that Othello has wed Desdemona, Iago converses with Roderigo:

**Roderigo**
What a full fortune does the thick lips owe,
If lie can carry her thus!

**Iago**
Call up her father:
Rouse him (Othello) make after him, poison his delight,
Proclaim him in the streets, incense her kinsmen,
And tho' he in a fertile climate dwell,
Plague him with flies: tho' that his joy be joy,
Yet throw such changes of vexation on it,
As it may lose some color (act 1, scene 1, lines 66–73).

Iago wishes to steal Othello's joy, to taint his happiness, and take pleasure in his demise. We witness ahrimanic thinking in act 2 when alone Iago speaks his most insidious monologue.

**Iago**
. . . Divinity of hell!
When devils will their blackest sins put on,
They do suggest at first with heavenly shows,
As I do now; for while this honest fool
Plies Desdemona to repair his fortunes
And she for him pleads strongly to the Moor,
I'll pour this pestilence into his ear
That she repels him for her body's lust;
And, by how much she strives to do him good
She shall undo her credit with the Moor.
So will I turn her virtue into pitch,
And out of her own goodness make the net
That shall enmesh them all (act 2, scene 3, lines 350–362).

Iago identifies himself with the divinity of hell. The essence of Ahriman, bent on destroying goodness and life, is embodied in Iago.

In act 3, as Iago begins to work Othello to his purpose, he ingeniously treads a guarded, insidious path. His dexterous artifice crafts his words as he enters upon the execution of his plan.

**Iago**
My noble lord.

**Othello**
What dost thou say, Iago?

**Iago**
Did Michael Cassio,
When you woo'd my lady, know of your love?

**Othello**
He did from first to last.
Why dost thou-ask?

**Iago**
But for a satisfaction of my thought,
No further harm.

**Othello**
Why of thy thought, Iago?

**Iago**
I did not think he had been acquainted with it.

**Othello**
O yes, and went between us very oft—

**Iago**
Indeed!

**Othello**
Indeed? Ay, indeed. Discern'st thou aught of that?
Is he not honest?

**Iago**
Honest, my lord?

**Othello**
Honest? Ay, honest.

**Iago**
My lord, for aught I know.

**Othello**
What do'st thou think?

**Iago**
Think, my lord!

**Othello**
Think, my lord! Alas, thou echo'st me,
As if there was some monster in thy thought
Too hideous to be shewn. Thou dost mean something:
I heard thee say even now, thou likedst not that,
When Cassio left my wife: what didst not like?
And when I told thee he was of my counsel
In my whole course of wooing, thou criedst "Indeed!"
And didst contract and purse thy brow together,
As if thou then hadst shut up in thy brain
Some horrible conceit. If thou dost love me,
Show me thy thought.

**Iago**
My lord, you know I love you.

**Othello**
I think thou dost;
And, for I know thou'rt full of love and honesty,
And weigh'st thy words before thou givest them breath,
Therefore these stops of thine fright me the more;
For such things in a false disloyal knave
Are tricks of custom, but in a man that's just
They are close dilations, working from the heart
That passion cannot rule (act 3, scene 3, lines 93–124).

Extraordinary powers of will and intellect designed Iago's evil machinations. The deep workings of treachery under the mask of love and honesty, the anxious watchfulness, the cool earnestness, and the passion of hypocrisy, marked in every line, reach their height in the inconceivable burst of pretended indignation when Othello doubts his sincerity. This dialogue sets in motion Iago's plan that culminates in his killing Roderigo, and Othello smothering Desdemona based on false accusations of infidelity. Emilia professes the truth; Othello tries to kill Iago but is disarmed. Iago kills Emilia (his wife) and flees. Othello then takes his own life. Iago, left standing to witness the devastation from his ploy, is sentenced to execution.

In the end, ahrimanic thinking often defeats itself because it overreaches. The thirst for satisfying self-interest does not know when to stop. In *Othello*, Iago failed to take into account that real events do not happen entirely according to cold calculation alone. Other influences such as his own wife's remorse and Othello's hot temper—emotions that fall outside the scope of cold ahrimanic thinking—often interfere with and destroy its objectives.

It is difficult to conceive that the human soul capacity can encompass the extremes of love embodied by Christ and the hatred and wickedness of Iago. Iago expresses jealousy and anger for his evil designs. To Iago, the ruination of Othello is a game: "Let us be conjunctive against him. If thou canst cuckold him, thou dost thyself a pleasure, me a sport" (act 1, scene 3, line 363). Honor, loyalty, honesty, and fidelity hold no value in Iago's paradigm. Rather, ingratitude and cruelty guide his actions. Iago exhibits no conscience; he feels no guilt or concern over his behavior. He does not see the goodness in anyone or anything. He is driven by a tantalizing intrigue for evil. We experience in Iago the most evil of all of Shakespeare's characters, absolute and unequivocal egotism—a condition of all-consuming self-love that denies the worth of others.

We see less extreme versions of this same orientation prevalent in contemporary society: how can I manipulate people to get what I want? This can be expressed in as simple a manner as a child trying to manipulate her parent to give her a treat. Or it can emerge in strategies to manipulate employees, spouses, the consumer public—or the general populace about terrorism or homeland security. Calculated plots to use others for one's own gain conceal a gradation of ahrimanic thinking.

In the largest fraudulent financial scheme in U.S. history, Bernard Madoff, Wall Street financier, defrauded thousands of investors of over $64.8 billion in investments (New York Times, 2011). Madoff seems to epitomize the ahrimanic thought paradigm of deifying money and devaluing fellow human beings. On March 12, 2009, Madoff pled guilty to eleven federal felonies, including securities fraud, wire fraud, mail fraud, money laundering, making false statements, perjury, theft from an employee benefit plan, and making false filings with the SEC (Voreacos, 2009). He was sentenced to 150 years in prison.

Two years after Madoff's arrest his son, Mark Madoff, committed suicide. Bernard's wife made two suicide attempts. Similarly French hedge fund manager, Thierry de la Villehuchet, whose company, Access International Advisers, lost $1.4 billion of its clients' money in Madoff's scam, was found dead in an apparent suicide on December 28, 2008. One of Madoff's fraud victims, William Foxton, at age sixty-five, killed himself amid claims he was unable to face the shame of losing his family savings through Madoff's Ponzi scheme. As in *Othello*, the cold, calculated deceit of one man led to numerous deaths, and horror in the hearts of the victims and witnesses of his ingenious, amoral, self-serving scheme.

The devastating results of ahrimanic thinking plague the world in overt and less directly visible forms. Historically, in wartime, soldiers strategically rape women as a coordinated, deliberate, en masse weapon of terror. Systematic rape numbers in the hundreds of thousands of women reported in Europe and Nanking during the Second World War (Brownmiller, 1975, p. 472), Bangladesh (Brownmiller, 1975, p. 472), Rwanda (United Nations Security Council, 1999), and the former Yugoslavia (United Nations Security Council, 1999). In both Rwanda (Prosecutor v. Furundzija, 1995) and Yugoslavia, the International Criminal Tribunal recognized rape as a strategy for ethnic cleansing and genocide (Prosecutor v. Jean Paul Akayesu, 1996).

Currently, the Democratic Republic of the Congo sets the stage for the most sinister en masse sexual atrocities, designated as rape with extreme violence—including gang rape, genital mutilation, and intentional transmission of sexually transmitted diseases (Schnurr and Swatuk, 2010, ch. 7, p. 6). The strategists behind this calculated tactic intend not only to terrorize, displace, and demoralize communities, but also to destroy social cohesion and the identity of women—the upholders of family structure, culture, and societal potential for future generations. The impact of sexual violence, exacerbated when rape is committed in public, sears impotence and debasement into the collective memory of the community. The far-reaching effects of military rape on the population as a whole ultimately undermine national, political, and cultural solidarity; it confuses the loyalties of the survivors and the identities of subsequent generations. The thinking behind these strategies reflects no moral conscience, no value of human life and dignity, and encompasses no consciousness of spiritual existence or spiritual law: i.e., karma or reciprocity. These cold, calculated, amoral, masterminding war strategies are fixated on power and monetary gain.

A less obvious aspect of the war strategies employing sexual violence in the Democratic Republic of the Congo links the implicit collusion by multinational corporations whose products include laptop computers, cell phones, digital cameras, mp3 players, video games, and pace-makers (Adbelkader, Dec. 28, 2011). These products require the natural metallic ore, columbite-tantalite (known as coltan), or cassiterite, mined in D.R. Congo, which, when refined, store an electric charge in a capacitor used in electronic devices. Terrorizing communities through sexual violence against Congolese women in regions rich in these minerals enables the illicit exploitation of these natural resources in Eastern D.R. Congo (Adbelkader, Dec. 28, 2011). Rebel soldiers from neighboring countries use mass rape as biological warfare to take control of mining regions to exploit the natural resources. Most consumers do not understand the complex chain of events that ties widespread sexual violence in D.R. Congo with the minerals that power their cell phones, laptops, mp3 players, video games, and digital cameras. The consumers of all electronic devices benefit from the atrocities committed to secure the necessary resources. We are all implicated in this web of human rights violations.*

* For information about projects dedicated to informing and creating transnational legislation to protect human rights see: www.friendsofthecongo.org

When ahrimanic thinking is witnessed in world conditions or in other people it is easy to judge it and denounce it with antipathy. If we take this stance we enter into luciferic feeling based on the subtext: *I am superior to them.* If we can recognize this condition with the realization that *I, too, am capable of doing such deeds or complying consciously or unconsciously with these forces that in some way ultimately benefit me,* we begin a process of self-awareness that can lead to overcoming ahrimanic thinking.

The subtleties of ahrimanic thinking pervade individual, community, national, and international engagement throughout the world. If we ask ourselves the following questions, we further the process of eradicating ahrimanic forces from our life: *How do I choose to live with this reality? How can I recognize this force, whether overt or subtle, to prevent my thinking from being cold and calculating or disassociated and indifferent toward faceless, unknown people who suffer so that I may prosper? How can we free ourselves and the world from the web of human denigration, the complicit violation of human justice, and overcome the perpetration of heartless atrocities designed for personal gain?*

## Warmth: Transformed Love—The Antidote for Ahrimanic Thinking

Love imbues the human soul with the power to dispel ahrimanic forces. Through freedom we can choose to transform self-love—which in the extremes propagates evil—into selfless-love that encompasses interest in and concern for the well-being of all. Mercy, compassion, and forgiveness defeat ahrimanic thinking. Warmth transmutes cold thinking as light illumines the darkness. The true impulse of selfless love transcends all temptations, insults, mockery, and suffering. It singularly possesses the power to disarm ahrimanic forces.

Selfless love grows out of a sense of gratitude seeded in childhood, compassion and empathy cultivated during one's youth, and the capacity to forgive and sacrifice for others which matures in adulthood. The emotional capacities of empathy and compassion for the suffering of others form a cornerstone of social interconnection and humanism founded on a keen awareness of the interdependence of all things.

Compassion requires that we dethrone ourselves from the center of our world and place others in our stead. We demonstrate selflessness when we honor the inviolable sanctity of every single human being by treating each one—without exception—with justice, equity, and respect. Like turning a sock right-side out, self-focused love can be redirected from an inward orientation of self-interest to an outward concern for others. Rooted in a principled resolve to transcend selfishness, compassion can break down political, dogmatic, ideological, and religious boundaries. It is indispensable to the creation of healthy personal relationships, a just economy, and a peaceful global community.

## Ahrimanic Feeling

Ahrimanic forces work insatiably to disconnect human beings from one another and debilitate our inclination to love. These forces appear in our feeling life as fear, greed, hatred, despair, cowardliness, callousness, cynicism, resignation, confusion, doubt, depersonalization, insecurity, and the need to control. The ahrimanic double instills a deep source of intemperance in our astral body, precipitating a condition of weariness, heaviness, boredom, coldness, depression, and loneliness. Ahrimanic impulses and desires tend to overly incarnate and entrap us in the material world, disconnecting us from spiritual consciousness and human community.

The main character in Albert Camus's novel, *The Stranger*, serves as a magnification of a disaffected, amoral young man afflicted with aimless inertia. In a fragmentary account of a segment of the life of a clerk from a small-time establishment in Algiers, Meursault seeks meaning in his life. Embroiled in the petty intrigues of a local pimp, one day while walking on the beach Meursault inexplicably kills an Arab man. When imprisoned and eventually brought to trial he remains dispassionate, cynical, and disengaged from his own emotions.

Why does Meursault murder the man on the beach? He has the power to kill or not to kill. In the absence of any spiritual presence or moral canon, no outside influences affect him other than the beating sun and the drunkenness of his senses. Removed from reality and social context he squeezes the trigger without intent. "Then I fired four more times at the motionless body where the bullets lodged without leaving a trace. And it was like knocking four quick times on the door of unhappiness" (Camus, 1989, p. 119). His description makes the act of murder seem trivial, magnifying his disconnection to reality, his lack of moral conscience, and any sense of remorse.

When in prison, against Meursault's wishes, the chaplain visits and asks why Meursault has refused to see him. Meursault reasserts his denial of God's existence. When the chaplain states that Meursault's attitude results from "extreme despair," Meursault says he is afraid, not desperate. The chaplain insists that all the condemned men he has known have eventually turned to God for comfort. Meursault becomes irritated by the chaplain's insistence that he spend the rest of his life thinking about God. He feels he has no time to waste with God. The chaplain tells Meursault that his "heart is blind." Meursault suddenly becomes enraged. He shouts that nothing matters and that nothing in the chaplain's beliefs is as certain as the chaplain thinks. The only certainty Meursault perceives in the whole of human existence is death.

Camus then articulates the ultimate expression of existential alienation, demonstrating a victory of ahrimanic forces, through his hero, Meursault.

> And I felt ready to live it all again, too. As if that blind rage had washed me clean, rid me of hope; for the first time, in that night alive with signs and stars, I opened myself to the benign indifference of the world. Finding it so much like myself—so like a brother, really—I felt that I had been happy and that I was happy still. For all to be accomplished, for me to feel less lonely, I had only to wish that on the day of my execution there should be a huge crowd of spectators and that they should shout hatred at me (Camus, 1989, p. 123).

Meursault wanted to be free from hope because in his mind hope meant that there was a disparity between who he should attain to be and who he actually was. He just wanted to blend into his environment and no longer have to bear the burden of proving to the rest of the world he existed on their terms. He wanted to define the world on his terms without consideration of a cosmic order, a social order, or a moral order within the human soul. The last line, “I had only to wish that on the day of my execution there should be a huge crowd of spectators and that they should shout hatred at me,” underscores Meursault’s fierce indifference to society and to human life. By suffering final judgment from the world he realizes that he is no longer bound to conform to the standards of others. With death he believes he will be free. At his execution the “cries of hate” would be proof that he did not exist for the acceptance of others but rather was content to be alone in a world of his own creation.

Meursault exhibits a stark inability to love. His indifference and callousness reveal entrenched ahrimanic forces disconnecting him from any spiritual consciousness and from human community. His amoral, disaffected capacity to murder without conscience indicates the extreme depth of ahrimanic feeling at work in his soul. He thought that death, the realm of Ahriman, became his gate to freedom. Anti-life forces gained victory over Meursault.

Ahrimanic feelings pervade contemporary life. The omnipresence of fear infects the post-modern human soul as governments promote war on terrorism, environmentalists fervently proclaim anticipated cataclysmic effects of global warming, and individuals struggle with increasing trauma, health threats, and financial insecurity. Fear dominates the human psyche in pathological proportions as sales of pharmaceuticals designed to alleviate fear skyrocket.

The most primal form of fear arises in the reptilian lobe of the brain as a survival instinct when danger is present (Pearce, 2002, p. 25). This form of fear heightens the senses and alertness to enable one to meet unexpected, threatening circumstances. It is considered, for the most part, a beneficial mechanism in the human psyche heightening instinctive survival capacities.

It is useful to highlight a distinction between the fear and adrenalin that arise when, for example, in one instance a person is walking across a road and a truck comes barreling toward them, the driver unaware of the pedestrian, and in a second instance a person is walking in a forest and a lion comes down the path toward him. In the first instance the obvious strategy is to get out of the way of the truck. The truck, being an inanimate object, does not pose a relational threat; the situation requires immediate removal from the path of the truck. In the second instance the lion poses a relational threat, an interaction that requires a different response than merely getting out of the path of a moving object. This situation incorporates beliefs and feelings that arise about wild animals and the dangerous nature of lions. These feelings and beliefs will intensify or alleviate the initial surprise and fear depending on one's inner orientation toward, in this case, lions.

An experience in the life of Laurens Van der Post demonstrates the powerful dichotomy in the dynamic between fear and love. On a military patrol in Java, accompanied by a Badoeis guide, Van der Post encountered a predatory feline. Walking through a narrow track in the jungle lined with tall bamboo on each side, obstructing any possible escape, he came face to face with a tiger. As the tiger stopped in front of him, snarling angrily, Van der Post believed this was his end. His Badoeis guide went down on his knees in a gesture of prayer and repeated the phrase, "Tuan Tiger" (Lord Tiger). The tiger gradually grew quiet, his tail stopped thrashing, and the look of aggression left the tiger's face that "became filled with light" (Van der Post, 1978, p. 9). The great cat turned back and ambled away into the distance.

This incident demonstrates the power of love to affect circumstances in which fear would likely be self-fulfilling. After surviving this encounter with possible death, Van der Post concluded that

> it is possible out of a true wilderness awareness to communicate with animals and get a mutual recognition of kinship ... an awareness that encloses and protects people as helpless as the two of us were that morning in the face of the tiger, more effectively than any contrived armor can (Van der Post, 1978, p. 9).

Van der Post's guide entered a state of reverent honor for the tiger, in contrast to the fear many people would experience in this situation. This inner state of reverent honor expresses love and respect for the lion. Animals sense fear and commonly attack a fearful animal or person. The tiger received the energy of the Badoeis's prayer. He became peaceful and non-aggressive, feeling no hint of threat. Many other incidents like this have been recorded, one of which I recommend is recounted in the first chapter of Linda Tucker's book, *Mystery of the White Lions: Children of the Sun God.*

The foregoing example considers human fear in relation to the animal kingdom—living beings of a different species. Let us now consider an example of human fear in relation to another human being—our own species. Jane Addams (1860–1935), founder of the Hull House in Chicago, pioneered social work in America as a feminist and internationalist, and was the first American woman to receive the Nobel Peace Prize (1931).

One night Jane awoke to the noise of a burglar in her room. Her movement alerted the burglar that she had awakened. He turned on her with a weapon. Jane spoke to the man explaining that he was welcome to take her money and possessions, but if he sold them it would only feed him for a short time. She told him if he wanted to come back to her office downstairs at 9:00 AM, she would see to getting him a job so that he would be able to feed his family for the rest of their lives. He left and returned the next morning to attain employment at the Hull House that lasted many years (Weber Linn and Firor Scott, 2000, p. 114). We can see the acute disparity between fear and love. Fear leads to death; love to renewed life.

Jane Addams's courage fueled her social activism. Opposed to America's entry into World War I, she was attacked in the press and expelled from the Daughters of the American Revolution. But she found an outlet for her humanitarian impulses as an assistant to Herbert Hoover in providing relief supplies of food to the women and children of the enemy nations. She wrote of this in her book, *Peace and Bread in Time of War*, in 1922.

The examples above derive from encounters with external circumstances, both in relation to animals and human beings. A fundamentally different aspect of fear arises out of our conscience in response to deeds that contradict our values or the conventions of our parents, school, employment agency, government, religion, etc. These fears haunt us because we live with an uncertainty of our misdeed being discovered. In this case the fear grows from a sense of cause and effect, a conscious or unconscious sense of the universal law of reciprocity. I have violated someone, and either I will be punished or, in the long run, have to compensate for my misdeed.

This type of fear can be alleviated if one is willing to tell the truth. Here the dynamic of deceit underlies the fear, as described in chapter 1 in the story of the Fall when, after eating the fruit from the tree of knowledge of good and evil, Adam and Eve were afraid and hid. They awaited discovery and fear of the results of their disobedience. This type of fear can be overcome with the courage to live in truthfulness, to have the humility to admit one's transgression and seek to redeem it, establishing inner peace. Honesty dispels fear.

Fear also arises without direct external threat or sense of transgression. This category of fear manifests as inner projections based on memories, stories, or fantasies. These inner imaginations of negative future events express a soul condition trapped in a belief that negativity will occur: *I am going to fail; We are all going to die; No one will ever love me; I am going to lose my financial footing and become homeless; I may have a terminal illness and die.* These fears paralyze the will. Usually an experience backgrounds these fears. The fear can dominate a person's consciousness and render him or her incapable of action. This paralysis of the will feeds depression and cynicism. The antidote lives in coming to an understanding that meaning and purpose underlie all human experience. A willingness to embrace the future, to accept what comes with equanimity and interest in the meaning of the experience, dissolves fear of life and transforms it into a love of life.

Fear can arise in resistance to spiritual insight. In "The Human Soul in Courage and Fear," an essay published in *On the Life of the Soul*, Rudolf Steiner describes that

> fear meets one at the threshold to spirit knowledge. And fear causes one to recoil from this knowledge. One now becomes creative in recoiling instead of in pressing forward. One does not allow the spirit to shape creative knowledge in oneself; one invents for oneself a sham logic for disputing the justification of spirit knowledge. Every possible sham reason is brought forward to spare one from acknowledging the spiritual, because one retreats trembling in fear of it (Steiner, 1985, p. 20).

Here Steiner identifies fear as a subconscious strategy to obstruct a person from gaining spiritual insight into self-knowledge, illumining the situation at hand. This fear leads to doubt and fallacious reasoning that refutes all spiritual reality as illusory. "The denial of the spiritual world is a desire to run away from one's own soul" (Steiner, 1985, p. 21). Steiner likens this attempt to that of a cataract on the eye which hampers vision. In like manner, one who denies spirit knowledge darkens the soul through illusive reasoning born of fear. Spiritual strength of soul can mature gradually if one overcomes the soul's fear of the unknown. Through spiritual practice spirit presence empowers the creative will that otherwise remains paralyzed.

Depression, a close ally of fear, also plagues post-modern consciousness. The overwhelming exposure to tragic, seemingly irreconcilable conditions of hatred, war, political leverage that disregards human rights, natural disasters, personal loss, and an inner sense of ineffectiveness and isolation contribute to depression. I only mention the vast subject of depression here in brief, positing it as a condition infused with ahrimanic forces weighing the feeling soul down to a level of disengagement with life. Depression overpowers the feeling life to the degree that it debilitates the will. One becomes so heavy in the feeling realm that engagement with other people becomes undesirable, leading to isolation and loneliness. Depression separates human beings from one another, preventing the experience of love.

Other ahrimanic feelings commonly arise as boredom, greed, hatred, covetousness, anxiety, insecurity, criticality, condemnation, hopelessness, cynicism, alienation, loneliness, sinister behavior, etc. Every one of these feelings separates us from one another, excludes us from relationship, focuses on self-interest, and exposes the absence of love. Continual awareness and consideration of others with interest, warmth, and compassion is required to eradicate these tendencies. Relating with others in truth, integrity, trust, cooperation, consideration, and care dissolves ahrimanic feelings which otherwise lead to isolation and despair.

## Love: The Antidote for Ahrimanic Feeling

To transform ahrimanic feeling we must first recognize it and name it. When this feeling or tendency is exposed, it generates hatred in an effort to overpower the intruding consciousness. This has the potential to lead to even greater alienation from others. Instead of nourishing reactivity to this force, it can be brought into servitude and eventually cast out. One must grant this aspect of the double no nourishment to sustain its power.

By perceiving it and recognizing it the ahrimanic double recoils. It must be overcome or dissolved through love, as a lit candle dispels the darkness.

Self-love, self-absorption, and self-interest characterize aspects of immature love—love that values self over others. The task of humanity, as described in chapter 1, calls us to transubstantiate the wisdom and substance of the Earth into love, to transubstantiate the very love in our being into spiritual love that knows and upholds the unity and value of all life. Love, the greatest power of all powers, transmutes indifference, fear, hatred, depression, and all ahrimanic impulses, and thereby enliven us.

The figure below represents an imagination of the heart chakra with twelve petals. The first image depicts self-love, where the forces of the heart flow inward toward the self. The second image depicts mature, selfless love, where the forces of the heart stream outward into the world. Our evolutionary task is to invert the heart of self-love into a heart that serves the world. A version of the two images below can be found in Valentin Tomberg's *Anthroposophical Studies of the New Testament*, pp. 56–57, where he discusses the twelve cosmic currents flowing from the constellations of the zodiac streaming to the center point of the heart as part of the spiritual *Trial by Air*.

**Figure 4**

The Metamorphosis of Love in the Heart Chakra

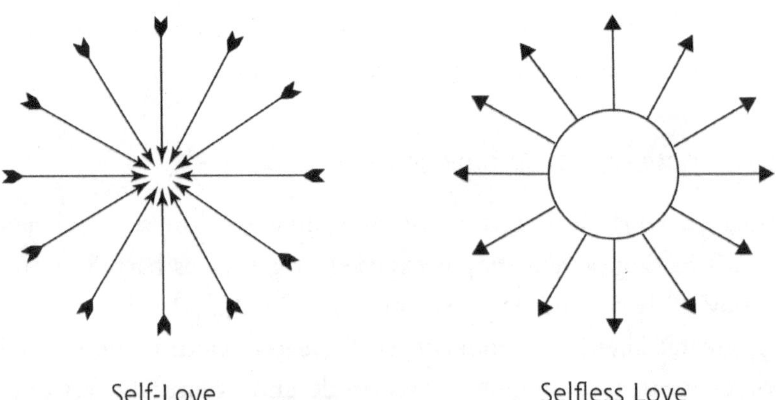

Self-Love
*heart forces directed inward*

Selfless Love
*heart forces directed outward*

## Ahrimanic Will

Ahrimanic will motivates actions devoid of conscience, leading people to treat others and Nature as material objects without spiritual essence. When driven by ahrimanic will forces, one takes whatever actions suit his or her desires without any regard for the impact on others. King Herod's slaughter of the innocents (Matt. 2:16–17), King Leopold's tyranny in the Congo, the National Socialist movement resulting in the holocaust, child pornography, and sadomasochism all exemplify ahrimanic will.

Quantifying human life as in a census or reports of war deaths given as numbers of people lost rather than names of people who died bears the stamp of ahrimanic will. "Thirty soldiers died today in a skirmish." "Fifty troupes are missing in action." Rather than naming the people, honoring their personal lives and their families, they are reduced to numbers to alleviate the guilt and culpability of the decision makers behind the war machine. News reports tainted by ahrimanic forces dehumanize and mechanize tragic information to veil the true source of culpability.

Scientists engaging in research and inventions that disregard human conscience, that treat life as mere matter devoid of spiritual essence, bring ahrimanic will forces into their work life. Robert Oppenheimer, a brilliant nuclear physicist, cultivated scholar, and humanist known as the father of the atomic bomb, engaged in thinking that created the power capable of destroying the world. Appointed director of the Manhattan Project in 1943, Oppenheimer worked with Edward Teller, Enrico Fermi, David Bohm, James Franck, Emilio Segre, Felix Bloch, Rudolf Peierls, James Chadwick, Otto Frisch, Eugene Wigner, Leo Szilard and Klaus Fuchs in developing the atom bombs dropped on Hiroshima and Nagasaki (Hoddeson et al., 1993, pp. 42–44).

At 5:29:45 (Mountain War Time) on July 16, 1945, in a white blaze that stretched across the basin of the Jemez Mountains in northern New Mexico, "The Gadget" ushered in the atomic age. The light of the explosion then turned orange as the atomic fireball began shooting upwards at 360 feet per second, reddening and pulsing as it cooled. The characteristic mushroom cloud of radioactive vapor materialized at 30,000 feet. Beneath the cloud, all that remained of the soil at the blast site were fragments of jade green radioactive glass created by the heat of the reaction, to say nothing of eighty thousand people dead and hundreds of thousands infected with radioactive sickness (Bird and Sherwin, 2009, p. 307).

Upon witnessing the explosion, its creators had mixed reactions. Robert Oppenheimer, though ecstatic about the success of the project, quoted a fragment from the Bhagavad Gita: "I am become Death," he said, "the destroyer of worlds" (Bird and Sherwin, 2009, p. 309). In the *Bhagavad Gita*, chapter 11, verse 32, Krishna speaks these words—*I am the destroyer of worlds*—to Arjuna describing one dimension of his power as a creator-destroyer god. At the sight of the explosion, Oppenheimer realized the magnitude of power unleashed by his creation, and knew he had stepped into the realm of the "Lord of Death," Ahriman. He crossed a boundary into a domain outside the rightful relationship of human beings to creation. He became the "destroyer of worlds."

Later in 1945, in an address to the American Philosophical Society, Oppenheimer lamented the subservience of science to human cruelty:

> We have made a thing, a most terrible weapon, that has altered abruptly and profoundly the nature of the world. We have made a thing that, by all standards of the world we grew up in, is an evil thing. And by doing so ... we have raised again the question of whether science is good for man (Valiunas, 2006, p. 94).

This public admission of personal despair at the moral collapse of the world's leading scientific enterprise reveals a transparent contrition. The heartbreak of everlasting loss unmistakably haunted his conscience. Modern science had permanently altered the nature of moral and political life. He also remarked to Harry S. Truman: "Mr. President, I feel I have blood on my hands" (Bird and Sherwin, 2009, p. 332).

Oppenheimer felt the ominous destructive power that now exists through his contribution to physics. He knew the responsibility he bore for the deaths of innocent people in Japan, and its potential impact throughout the world. He knew he had overstepped his rightful relationship to powers of destruction and death. He had served the agency of Ahriman. Ten years after Robert Oppenheimer's death from cancer in 1967, his daughter, Toni, plagued by the defamation of her father, hanged herself in the beach cottage her father had built on Hawksnest Bay (Bird and Sherwin, 2009, p. 591). Death proclaimed victory.

Scientific research devoid of spirit addresses the natural world, including human beings, as objects that can be known through empirical research. Bill Engdahl, a distinguished Research Associate of the Centre for Research on Globalization, authored *Seeds of Destruction: The Hidden Agenda of Genetic Manipulation*. It uncovers a chilling story exposing the U.S. government and the plans of four giant Anglo-American agribusinesses to achieve world domination by patenting life forms to gain worldwide control of the food supply.

The question looms: when do the fruits of science serve vital life forces and when do they serve material greed and/or destructive death forces? Engdahl's investigation focuses on the development of a variety of genetically modified seeds designed to have specific capabilities. One strand of the research explicated by Engdahl describes Terminator technology that refers to plants that have been injected with a terminator gene to render the seeds sterile at harvest. The inbuilt gene produces a toxin just before the seed ripens whereby in every seed the plant embryo will self-destruct. Developed by the multinational seed/agrochemical industry and the U.S. government to prevent farmers from saving and re-planting harvested seed, Terminator technology has not yet been commercialized or field-tested, but tests are currently being conducted in greenhouses in the United States.

Genetic Use Restriction Technology (GURTs) is the official name used at the United Nations and by scientists for Terminator technology. It refers to technologies that in their design provide a mechanism to switch introduced genes on or off using external inducers like chemicals or physical stimuli such as heat shock. This mechanism allows for restricted use or performance of transgenes. There are two types of GURTs technologies that rely on the same mechanism: variety-related (V-GURTs) and trait-related (T-GURTs). V-GURTs aim to control reproductive processes to result in seed sterility, thus affecting the viability of the whole variety; T-GURTs aim to control the use of traits such as insect resistance, stress tolerance, or production of nutrients.

In San Diego, a small, privately owned biotech company, Epicyte, reported that they had successfully created the ultimate GMO crop: contraceptive corn. They had taken antibodies from women with a rare condition known as immune infertility, isolated the genes that regulated the manufacture of those infertility antibodies and, using genetic engineering techniques, inserted the genes into ordinary corn seeds used to produce infertile corn plants (Engdahl, 2007, p. 270).

One ethical consideration regarding Terminator technology concerns the farmers' inability to plant their harvested seeds the following season, leaving them cropless and/or wholly dependent upon the seed companies for new seeds. This establishes a means for agribusiness giants to control food availability in the world. A second ethical consideration concerns the effects on consumers of foods that contain infertility genes. What will be the effects on human health of consuming seeds with the life generating force removed and sterilization genes injected?

Dr. Arpad Pusztai, biochemist, formerly of the Rowett Research Institute, Scotland, at the invitation of the Scottish Agriculture Office, implemented and published the first independent scientific study on the safety of gene-modified food in the world in 1995–1998. He expected his study would confirm the safety of GMO technology. The results of his study showed rats fed GMO potatoes had smaller livers, hearts, testicles, and brains, damaged immune systems, and showed structural changes in their white blood cells making them more vulnerable to infection and disease when compared to other rats fed non-GMO potatoes. The rats fed GMO potatoes had thymus and spleen damage, and enlarged tissues including the pancreas and intestines. There were cases of liver atrophy as well as significant proliferation of stomach and intestines cells that suggested greater future risk of cancer. These results occurred after 10 days of testing and the changes persisted after 110 days—the human equivalent of 10 years (Engdahl, 2007, p. 23). Dr. Pusztai was fired and defamed for his findings (Engdahl, 2007, p. 24).

Research published in 2009 in the *International Journal of Biological Sciences* comparing two control groups of rats, one feeding on non-GMO corn and the other on three varieties of GMO corn, showed negative effects mostly concentrated in kidney and liver function—the two major diet detoxification organs—in the rats fed with GMO corn. The details of the results differed with each GM type. In addition, some effects on heart, adrenal, spleen, and blood cells were also frequently noted. The study concluded that the data strongly suggests that these GM maize varieties induce a state of hepatorenal toxicity (Vendômois, Roullier, Cellier, Séralini, 2009, pp. 706–726).

Science in the hands of self-interest can become a tool of extreme self-love. In the case of genetic engineering, also known as a means of biological warfare, the subjects of experimentation no longer remain isolated in a control group. In his review of Jeffrey Smith's *Seeds of Deception*, Stephen Lendman stated:

> Today we're all lab rats in an uncontrolled, unregulated mass human experiment, the results of which are as yet unknown. The risks from it are beyond measure, it will take many years to learn them, and when they're finally revealed it will be too late to reverse the damage (Lendman, 2008, p. 11).

Although humanistic ideals form the foundation of our civilization, in our current age of "free markets," science, commerce, agriculture, and even seeds have become tools of destruction and power in the hands of those focused on money and power at the risk and expense of humanity as a species.

The omnipresence of modern materialistic science and technology in the twenty-first century creates a perilous gulf between the inner experience of human consciousness and the external scientific investigation of the physical world. In chapter 1, I introduced three potential characteristics of the future Sixth Cultural Epoch of brotherly and sisterly love. Rudolf Steiner indicated that modern science, with its materialistic presuppositions and methods, will not be considered science in the Sixth Cultural Epoch but regarded as antiquated superstition (Steiner, 1915, p. 3). According to Steiner, human consciousness will mature beyond our current belief in science to a condition in which, as a matter of course, we will only accept as science forms of knowledge inclusive of spiritual research, upon pneumatology, as a result of widespread spiritual perception. Developing these conditions will only be possible with intentional preparation by individuals committed to deep personal inner transformation.

How do we get from here to there? How do we transform the ahrimanic impulses that drive the destructive forces of materialistic science or the destructive forces within our own souls? What awakens human consciousness to want to overcome these impulses and redirect our lives?

## Starving the Impulse: The Antidote for Ahrimanic Willing

To overcome ahrimanic will forces necessitates holding in consciousness the divine essence that indwells everyone and everything. When we acknowledge the divine nature of every aspect of creation, and act with this consciousness, our will forces become immune to ahrimanic impulses. We cannot transform ahrimanic forces; we cannot tame ahrimanic forces; we must starve them by giving them no energy. When recognized through Ego consciousness these forces lose power. When we turn away from self-interest, from cold-hearted acts designed for personal gain, and redirect our thoughts and deeds to benefit the whole, we dissolve ahrimanic forces within us. A Cherokee legend supports this principle.

> One evening an old Cherokee told his grandson about a battle that goes on inside people. He said, "My son, the battle is between two 'wolves' inside us all. One is Evil. It is anger, envy, jealousy, greed, and arrogance. The other is Good. It is peace, love, hope, humility, compassion, and faith." The grandson thought about this for a while and then asked his grandfather, "Which wolf wins?" To which the old Cherokee simply replied, "The one you feed" (Rosen, 1998, p. 15).

We choose which wolf we feed. We can raise our consciousness to name the wolves, to identify the ahrimanic driven wolf within us, acknowledge it, and turn away.

When we identify and uncover ahrimanic forces at work in others, hatred pours forth. Ahriman hates to be recognized; he likes to remain hidden and invisibly sow hatred, fear, and greed. For example, Dr. Arpad Pusztai was fired and defamed when his research was published. After years of litigation he discovered that Monsanto backed the assault on him (Engdahl, 2007, p. 23).

In order to overcome these forces we must know the territory. We must develop vigilant self-awareness and self-scrutiny. We must build the spiritual maturity to be immune to personal temptations. We must have the courage to withstand opposition in various forms. We must not be surprised by intensely cold and aggressive attacks. Love in the face of hatred and all adversity overcomes ahrimanic forces.

The figure below recapitulates strategies to dissolve ahrimanic forces:

**Figure 5**

| The Transformation of the Ahrimanic Double | |
|---|---|
| Consciousness | Recognize the presence of ahrimanic forces through Ego consciousness and name them. |
| Thinking | Raise thinking up from material consciousness to spirit-filled wisdom. Order thoughts; infuse warmth—heart forces—into thinking. Meditate on spiritual truths warmed with feeling. |
| Feeling | Cultivate love for all of creation. Take selfless interest in others. Transform self-love into selfless love for Earth and humanity. |
| Willing | Immobilize ahrimanic will forces through lack of nourishment. Bring consciousness and warmth of feeling into deeds in service to others. |

Here we can see that the dissolution of ahrimanic forces requires infusing thinking with feeling and will; infusing feeling with thinking and will; and infusing will with thinking and feeling. We must harmonize our thoughts, feelings, and deeds to diminish these forces.

## The Crucifixion and Resurrection of Love through Ahriman

Ahrimanic forces play an essential, dynamic role in the evolution of Earth and humanity. Evil must oppose the good to bring consciousness to the existence of both, to confront humanity with a choice, to develop our true "I" nature. Rudolf Steiner's words, "A good must first be broken on the rock of evil" (Steiner, 1906) express an evolutionary process through which the possibility exists for goodness to prevail. The shattering of the good exposes the nature and motivation of good and evil.

The Crucifixion of Christ was a breaking of the good on the rock of evil. This pivotal event in world history demonstrated the power of insight that can be attained through breaking the vessel of goodness. The anonymous author of *Meditations on the Tarot* writes:

> There is nothing mechanical or automatic at the foundation of world existence. Take away the mechanical appearances and you will find that the world is something moral—crucified love. Yes, mercenaries took His clothes and divided them into four parts, one for each mercenary, and they drew lots for His tunic; whereas the heart of the world—naked—is love crucified in the middle of two other crucified ones, on His right and on His left (Anonymous, 1991, p. 457).

Here the anonymous author states that the world is moral. World existence is crucified love—crucified between one criminal on His right representing luciferic forces, and the other on His left representing ahrimanic forces. To the criminal representing luciferic forces He speaks the words, "Today you shall be with me in Paradise." To the criminal representing ahrimanic forces He does not respond. The image of the redemption of Lucifer lives in the words He spoke to the criminal on His right. He portrays the necessity to ignore ahrimanic forces by not responding to the criminal on His left.

The words "crucified love" touch a very deep place in the human soul. In the above passage from *Meditations on the Tarot*, these words directly speak of Christ as the great teacher of love, crucified by humanity, love broken on the rock of evil. When thinking of this world event within the context of Rudolf Steiner's words that evil "dwells within us as the force of self-love" (Steiner, 1906, Berlin), we can consider the thought that love was broken on the rock of self-love, that love was crucified by self-love.

Christ laid a path for humanity to achieve the purification of all nine sheaths culminating in a purified physical body, a resurrection body. The necessary work to develop a purified astral body through the force of our consciousness soul is described here. It lays the ground for all further levels of spiritual development. For the purification of the astral body to be achieved, an inner crucifixion is required. There must be a death and resurrection of love; self-love must be crucified and resurrected as spiritual selfless love.

The mystery of evil lies in its gift to unveil the true nature of love. The forces of Ahriman within us perpetuate self-love that must experience a death and resurrection. The Lord of Death must travel the path of his dominion in order that we transubstantiate ourselves and the substance of Earth into love.

# CHAPTER 4

# The Karmic Double: The Web of Destiny

> There is a law of compensation in the Universe, meaning that all evil-doing has its own retribution by Nature's own act. Leave it therefore to the gods to avenge you if you have suffered, and suffered wrongly. Give justice when you receive injustice. Ally yourselves with the gods, with your own inner god. Requite never hate with hate, for thus you but add fuel to an unholy flame. Requite hatred with compassion and justice. This is the ancient law. Thus also you make no evil Karma for yourself; thus you ally yourself with Nature's own spiritual procedures and you become a child of the cosmic life, which thereafter will beat in your own heart with its undying pulses.
>
> —Gottfried de Purucker*

## The Weaving of Karma

The journey of self-transformation unfolds in relation to the law of karma, concurrent with the luciferic and ahrimanic characteristics seeded within the human soul. Chapter 3 focused on the role of evil as a presence in the world that is necessary to enable humanity to perceive and choose the good. It describes the ahrimanic double in its threefold nature, demonstrating how death forces infiltrate human consciousness, science, and our current world conditions. In the concluding section of chapter 3, a crucial step in

* Purucker, 2000.

the process of inner development is described, namely that the forces of Ahriman can catalyze an inner realization to a personal inner crucifixion and resurrection of love on our path of self-development.

The luciferic forces described in chapter 2 and the ahrimanic forces described in chapter 3 interweave within each individual to form the third primary aspect of the human double—the karmic double—the central theme of this chapter. As luciferic and ahrimanic forces emerge and commingle within each individual biography, the personal karmic double develops in accordance with the law of karma.

The Sanskrit word *karma* expresses the principle of action and reaction, or the law of consequences. This unerring law of justice governs existence from the microcosmic dimension of the atom to the outermost cosmic spaces. The law of karma establishes that every thought and deed sets up a chain of causation that acts on every plane to which that chain of causation reaches. Constantly and progressively, every human being becomes the result of her or his thoughts, emotions, and actions. We stand at every moment as our own autobiographer with the tools of destiny in hand to carve our own life as a work of art, and compelled under the laws of being, to carve and carve until the outer becomes a worthy temple for the god within us. Life then becomes the highest art.

Each day every person co-participates in creation by way of thoughts, feelings, and actions. In the Epistle to the Galatians, Paul formulates the law of karma in the well-known words: "For whatsoever a man soweth, that shall he also reap" (Gal. 6:7, KJV). In the Buddhist canon, the Law of Cause and Effect is stated as: Effect follows cause as the wheel of the cart follows the foot of the oxen.* When we think, speak, or act, we initiate a force that will produce a reaction accordingly. Every action must be balanced before the end of human evolution. Each act of deceit, error, or illusion creates a

* The Dhammapada, verses 1–2. The complete verses are: "Our life is shaped by our mind; we become what we think. Suffering follows an evil thought as the wheels of the cart follow the oxen that draw it. Our life is shaped by our mind; we become what we think. If one speaks or acts with a pure thought, happiness follows one, like a shadow that never leaves." The Dhammapada is an anthology of Buddhist verses belonging to the part of the Theravada Pali Canon of scriptures known as the Khuddaka Nikaya, which consists of 423 verses arranged in 26 chapters.

hindrance in a person's progress. Every harmful deed results in a step backward in soul development. Through the law of karma, each error requires restoration of balance. Expunged errors result in a step forward. Resistance to rectify misdeeds impedes progress in our personal soul development or toward humanity's evolutionary goal. Without the forces of karma, it would be impossible to attain this goal (Steiner, 1976, p. 8).

The elemental karmic energies urging individuals into this or that pathway of action, thought, or emotion work through a physical organ in the brain. This organ, the pineal gland, expresses and carries over into the physical body the karmic urges that will impel us to follow a given course of action, eventuating in either blessing or anguish (Blavatsky, 1978, vol. 2, p. 302).

The true nature of karma consists of flexible, complex possibilities that integrate human freedom. When misunderstood as an iron law that the past determines the present, the concept of karma disregards free will. Self-determination and accountability in each individual soul rests on its capacity for free choice. In each moment every human being can choose, in freedom, to act in a way that serves the well-being of another or harms another's well-being. To choose a harmful action may injure a person whose past deeds do not warrant this type of restoration. This possibility points to the complexity of karma; it indicates that karma must be considered by looking both toward the past and toward the future.

In volume five of *Karmic Relationships*, Rudolf Steiner spoke of two general types of karma: Moon karma connected to the past, and Sun karma that points into the future (Steiner, 1997, p. 17). Moon karma entails both positive and negative sides: positive Moon karma is earned through good deeds enacted in former incarnations, and negative Moon karma results from mistakes or negative deeds from the past that must be balanced in the future. These positive and negative forces from the past influence personal destiny. The Moon rules over karmic necessity reflecting the past, while the Sun leads the human soul into the future through the impulse of freedom. Sun karma works with moral perspectives related to an individual's mission for the future. Each human being stands between these two currents of destiny.

The aspects of karma in this account relate primarily to the positive and negative forces of lunar karma, circumstances that out of necessity arise in life. Although necessity governs Moon karma, it does so only to the degree that specific people will enter a person's life or a particular event will take place. In each circumstance each individual is completely free to choose how to respond in each situation. Here destiny sets the stage and the actors write the script.

Choosing a harmful action incurs a karmic obligation to balance the deed, to make restitution in the future. Various karmic implications are possible:

1. It is possible that the person who was harmed had, in his or her past, harmed others in a similar way, in which case, the offense could be understood as the present event restoring balance to the past.
2. It is possible that the recipient of someone else's harmful actions was innocent and the event had no bearing on past circumstances. In this case fate must be borne, knowing that every harmful deed must be made good again, if not in this life, then in a later life.
3. It is also possible that a harmful event could be a chance occurrence. Steiner's description of karma allows for chance or random influence in the Universe (Steiner, 1988, p. 70).
4. It is also possible that an individual or group of people may undergo extreme suffering, not for the reason of karmic correction, but as a sacrifice to bring greater awareness of the horrors of injustice and political atrocities to the forefront of human consciousness.

Unless clairvoyant, the cause of a particular misfortune will not be known. It could be due to past karma, to free will in the present, to random chance, or to personal sacrifice.

Human freedom establishes the potential for a karmic response to modify, change, or suspend an action. It is also possible to eradicate it, but to do so requires highly developed faculties. We may not escape the consequences of our actions, but we will experience pain and suffering only if we have made the conditions ripe for this to occur. If we act in such a way that hinders reciprocity we may postpone the fruition of our karma. If we suspend it until we are in the spirit world, then we may work at this particular karma in this intermission between death and our next life. Or we may wait until another life in which we are more developed so that we can glean the educational value of reciprocity. Conversely, our life could be so unripe that blessings bestowed upon us cannot fructify until a later date or a subsequent life. These possibilities fall into the category of suspension of karma to a more propitious period or life.

When karma brings two human beings together, freedom determines the outcome. Two enemies from the past must meet again in a future life on Earth, drawn together by the unexpended forces that connected them before. Hatred activates as much a magnetic and dynamic force as love. When enemies meet, will the former recipient of hatred return hatred to the one who originally sent it forth in a former life? Or will the recipient of this hateful energy be conscious enough to transmute the negative force with the alchemy of compassion and have the ability to transform hate into love? Here we see the power of free will. We can choose to respond to hatred with love or not. Whatever the response, the energy brought into being must produce an effect. It could require many lives to restore equilibrium or harmony.

The thread of karma expresses a fundamental principle of interdependence that works in all parts of the Universe. The atom, the human body, the solar system, the galaxy, all in their structure and their workings proclaim the basic reality of harmony and interdependence as the underlying, regulating principle throughout all life. Every entity within the Universe plays a vital part in this web of connectivity.

Every action, every expenditure of energy, whether physical, mental, or moral, affects the underlying harmony and basic balance in this web of connectivity. Selfish thoughts or actions disrupt harmony and result in pain and/or suffering in the near or far future. By experiencing the effects of what we have self-created in the past, we gradually develop our own consciousness, and begin to recreate our destiny through self-directed evolution.

Karma always can lead toward the restoration of harmony, but only when consciousness matures. It is necessary that mistakes recoil back upon individuals to promote growth. Karmic adjustments result when, as conscious beings, we become servants of justice in our world of action. We ourselves decide our fate by our choice of the various alternatives that life presents, while our karma will design for the future what we have decreed.

## The Karmic Double

Each individual bears a karmic past that includes all past deeds enacted in relation to others that require a karmic correction, or restoration of harmony. The sum total of all of these misdeeds enacted in all past lives constitutes a karmic double that is formed out of an individual biography. Each human being bears a unique karmic double that consists of luciferic and ahrimanic qualities, interwoven into an inimitable configuration that reflects our personal unennobled nature.

The karmic double creates a worldly foundation for us to be able to meet the conditions of our karma. Prior to encountering the karmic relationships in which we will engage in a given incarnation, our karmic double prepares the circumstances in which these relationships may unfold. Our heredity, physical constitution, temperament, and character related to behavioral conditioning result from our karmic past. Our gender, the culture into which we are born, and the geographic location and climate of our birth arise from karmic design. All these factors set the stage for the development of our being and the conditions for encountering significant karmic relationships throughout our lives.

The karmic double then manifests through external interactions with other people and with Nature. The luciferic double can manifest as egotism, pride, self-deception, or vanity, characteristics that exist internally without necessarily requiring interaction with others. The ahrimanic double can take hold within the soul as depression, fear, greed, and amoral thinking, all of which can also live within the soul without interacting with other people. The karmic double, however, develops through human interactions, through relationships, and through deeds that affect other people's lives.

When observing human behavior one can recognize that some people tend to be more rigid, controlling, and fearful, while others live a more carefree, ambitious, glory-seeking life. Through these observations we can identify the predominance of luciferic or ahrimanic forces in any given individual. Our karmic double amalgamates these tendencies through the deeds that we enact each day in relation to others.

Our karmic double manifests as a distorted image of our true self. Through emotional confusion, our sheaths interpenetrate one another in an incongruous manner, lacking balance, and infusing the soul life with a strong force of self-interest. Astrality, or unconscious desire patterns, enters the etheric sheath and creates an etheric body full of unconscious emotion. These karmic aberrations infiltrate our thinking, feeling, and will forces, creating a false balance.

Astral forces infiltrating the etheric sheath can result in illness, an effect of the karmic double. When an imbalanced feeling life dominates our choices of food, our sleep patterns, and the rhythms in our life, our emotional energy and health suffer. This imbalance can result in a simple cold or headache, or something far more serious like lung disease, heart disease, cancer, etc.* When emotional needs drive us so that we do not care for our physical needs, our etheric body becomes depleted and unable to sustain our physical body. This is an indication that our etheric body is infused with astral forces and has become an etheric-astral oddity. When our sensibilities govern our habits so that we establish a rhythmic life of adequate sleep, healthy food, good exercise, and a harmonious emotional life, then our etheric body can support the health of our physical body. When the etheric body becomes pure, all astrality will have been purged from it. This is the condition of Life Spirit, or Buddhi, a purified etheric sheath, described in chapter 1.

As in the case with the luciferic and ahrimanic doubles, the karmic double also has a threefold nature: karmic thinking, karmic feeling, and karmic will.

---

* For further information on the relationship between karma and illness see: Steiner, R. (1947). *Manifestations of Karma*. London: Rudolf Steiner Publishing Company, chapters 3–5.

## Karmic Double Thinking

Karmic double thinking (karmic thinking) arises when emotional turmoil infiltrates one's thoughts. The pure nature of thinking gives rise to objective, clear thoughts. When astral forces permeate our thinking, thoughts become confused, emotional, subjective, and calculated for our personal advantage. The head becomes an astral organism, distorting the pure function of thought. This condition arises in relationships in response to experiences that activate karmic patterns, violate our values, or offend our ego. Karmic thinking defends, blames, justifies, and projects responsibility onto others. It polarizes individuals and groups of people, creates partisanship, and orients people in opposition to one another. When we allow our thoughts to blame and condemn others, we lose sight of the ultimate unity of all life.

Karmic thinking most commonly results in blaming others for our misfortune or discomfort. Blame protects the heart from owning the pain of the situation. We blame when we are unwilling to look within ourselves for the cause, unwilling to take responsibility for the circumstances we face, unwilling to acknowledge that we have created our lives. Many people habitually erect a barrier of blame, fortifying it with concepts of right and wrong. We blame the people who are closest to us: our family first, associates, our schools, our political systems, and our society. Rather than taking ownership for the pain, we seek comfort by placing the responsibility outside ourselves. *If only they would change, everything would be fine.*

In Leo Tolstoy's short story, "A Spark Neglected Burns the House," two neighboring families who had lived in peace and harmony for a generation, helping each other when needs arose, enact the epitome of karmic thinking. As the second-generation sons governed the households, a quarrel broke out over an egg. One of Iván's chickens flew over the fence and laid an egg in the neighbor's field, and the neighbor's wife denied that she found the egg. This dispute led to abusive arguments, physical violence, court trials, public flogging, and eventually a fire that burned half the village. The fault always lay with each other's neighbor. Karmic thinking fueled every stage of the unfolding embittered tragedy. Neither neighbor could be silent and take responsibility for the strife. Each felt driven to defend, accuse, and be right.

Iván's old father, nearing his death, counseled his son, pleading with him to look within his own soul and take responsibility for the strife between the two families.

> Ah, lad! It is you who don't see; malice blinds you. Others' sins are before your eyes, but your own are behind your back. "He has acted badly!" What a thing to say! If he were the only one to act badly, how could strife exist? Is strife among men ever bred by one alone? It is always between two. His badness is what you see, but your own you don't see (Tolstoy, 1967, p. 91).

Tolstoy exposes the relational reality of strife—it always requires two or more people to perpetuate a conflict. Not only must we realize our own culpability in situations of conflict, we must also find great courage when looking inward to scour our soul, seeking out the motives and self-deception that lead to actions of conflict. Why do I need to be right? Why am I unable to forgive? What needs drive me to continue fighting my neighbor? Is it over an egg?

Karmic thinking justifies all conflict. It underlies the false accusation of a black man raping a young white woman in Harper Lee's, *To Kill a Mockingbird* (1993). Racial injustice—driven by fear, desire for power, and projection of insecurities—overflows with karmic thinking. It fueled the British smear campaign to tarnish Mohandas Gandhi's image in the late 1930s. With Churchill's blessing they published lies and cast aspersions on his moral integrity. The millennia-long conflict in the Middle East over the rightful sovereignty of the land of Israel epitomizes the entrenched complexities bolstering the nearly impervious infrastructure of karmic thinking. It boils down to *I'm right, and you are wrong.*

## Personal Responsibility: The Antidote for Karmic Thinking

Human thoughts arise from various points of origin. Some thoughts arise from the feelings stirring within the soul. Some thoughts arise through the activity of the brain, i.e., problem solving, analysis, and critiques. Other thoughts arise as inspirations that appear mysteriously when the mind is still and receptive. For the purposes of this discussion focusing on the process of overcoming karmic thinking, it is important to delineate three types of thinking: 1) emotional thinking (astral thinking); 2) logical, rational/analytical thinking (objective thinking); 3) intuitive thinking (inspired thinking).

When contemplating astral or emotional thinking, we can imagine a cartoon caricature whose emotions have forced their way into one's thinking. Feelings of discontent dominate one's thoughts and speech. All thoughts smack of an emotional charge that defends, attacks, blames, or expresses victimhood. The force of the astral body has infiltrated the intellectual soul, disfiguring the intellect to maintain karmic patterning.

Analytical, rational thinking serves the scientific approach to knowledge. In its pure form emotion finds no place in objective thought life. The brain works with sense perception through objective processes. Repairing a broken faucet or a car requires clear objective thinking. Analyzing a proposal for city planning or critiquing a work of art may include sympathies and antipathies (personal preferences), but not emotional disharmony. Technology is a product of rational scientific thinking. Rational, objective thinking lies behind much of technological competence.

Intuitive thinking that ignites inspiration originates in the realm of the spirit. This form of thinking results from a clear mind, when the brain is still and, like a mirror, reflects cosmic thought. Inspiration pierces the silence with an ennobling, creative impulse. Rudolf Steiner's *A Philosophy of Freedom*, later published under the title *Intuitive Thinking as a Spiritual Path*, presents an in-depth explication of intuitive thinking as an experience of true human freedom.

Sense impressions received through the double are experienced as antipathy, and blame toward others for their imperfections and for ours. We can transcend this astral propelled antipathy through the cultivation of objective thoughts. This requires extricating all emotions and astral impulses from our thinking. The higher Self must override the egoistic desire to cover up one's own responsibility and project the cause onto another. The "I" surveys the situation, inquiring into our culpability in the events that have taken place. By focusing on our own culpability we expose our double, creating the potential to transform it.

Karmic thinking can be transformed through courageously honest self-examination. It is eye-opening to consider how it might be possible to take full responsibility for the ensuing circumstances, although it is in no way evident. In difficult or inexplicable circumstances, one can imagine what could possibly have happened in a past life to make the current situation a perfect learning ground. This exercise increases awareness of personal responsibility and reduces the tendency to blame and focus on the shortcomings of others.

The dissolution of egoism that permeates our thoughts leads to the development of moral imagination,* and the ability to perceive what is positive in the other person. When we replace judgment, which arises out of egotism, with empathy, compassion, and ultimately forgiveness, we dismantle karmic thinking through the strengthening forces of our true "I." When we achieve this, we become free of karmic fetters, laying the ground to think and act out of freedom. In *Foundations of Anthroposophy*, Rudolf Steiner describes that human freedom comes to expression when human actions arise out of free thinking, when a person

> reaches the point, through a moral self-training, of not allowing his actions to be influenced by instincts, passions, emotions, or by his temperament, but only by the devoted love for an action. In this devoted love for an action can develop something that proceeds from the ideal strength of pure ethical thinking. This is a really free action (Steiner, 1947, pp. 62–63).

Through moral self-training ethical thinking develops. Ethical thinking then leads to actions inspired by devoted love. These actions, free of karma, free of personal ego, free of the double, heal, transform, inspire, ennoble, and further humanity's progress in the mission of love.

---

* *Moral imagination* is the ability of imagination to translate a general moral principle into a concrete mental picture of the action to be carried out. *Moral intuition* is the capacity to experience for yourself the particular moral principle for each single situation. *Moral technique* is the ability to transform the world according to moral imaginations without violating the natural laws by which these are connected (Steiner, 1995, chapter 12).

## Karmic Double Feeling

Karmic double feelings (karmic feelings) differ from other types of feelings in that they arise as a result of interactions in personal relationships. Luciferic feelings arise out of self righteousness, assertion of self-interest, and a desire for power, while ahrimanic feelings manifest as fear, greed, hatred, despair, cowardliness, etc. These feelings can be activated independent of other people. Karmic feelings, on the other hand, arise only in relation to other people with whom we have significant relationships and can manifest as resentment, jealousy, rejection, abandonment, and betrayal.

Human emotions well up in the astral body from the subconscious realm, rising and falling in response to outer circumstances and inner imaginations, reflecting the soul's response to the situations we experience. People who believe that they have no choice in the content of their feeling response to any given situation believe that the other person caused their feelings. This belief allows one to blame the other person for one's feelings, for the misery one experiences.

It is possible that people may experience or witness the same factual situation and have a different emotional response. Many people experience emotions of hate, rage, and revenge when faced with an act of violence against a loved one. Under the same circumstances some people experience sorrow, compassion for the perpetrator, and a longing for reconciliation. This awareness leads to the realization that other people do not cause our feelings; rather, sensitivities in us stimulate reactions to particular situations according to karmic patterns.

Although emotions arise from the subconscious dimension, it is possible to consciously affect the content of emotional activity. Awareness of karmic influences active within our soul life significantly enhances this possibility. Emotional turmoil that arises in response to interactions with other people often carry layers of history that lie deep in the unconscious as powerful unseen currents of soul-memories and desires. These currents encompass the cumulative effects of ages of soul-life and many incarnations on Earth. The soul perceives life with a memory covering centuries of passion and adventure, caring and love, hatred and revenge, doubt and fear.

The circumstances that surround present relationships reflect the effects of many past-life experiences. The soul's memory of past-life activities shapes innate reactions to people, and vice-versa. When a seemingly unfounded fondness for another person arises, it is very likely due to an unconscious soul memory of the positive role he or she played in a past life or lives. On the other hand, when what seems to be an unfounded revulsion towards another person occurs, it is likely that a subconscious soul recollection occurs of that person's past actions against us, or our loved ones. As a result of these soul memories, patterns and habits form deep within our inner-consciousness, shaping behavior patterns with other people. These ingrained karmic patterns dictate our responses to situations.

Relationships in former lives that were not undertaken with positive attentiveness provide opportunities for pain and growth in present relationships. Negative feelings that arise from these circumstances can be directed inwardly or outwardly, depending on the patterned response. When turned inward with feelings of betrayal, abandonment, jealousy, rejection, or mistrust, a sense of being a victim or feeling unworthy is internalized. When directed outward, feelings of anger, accusation, vengeance, and emotional violence are often projected onto others. These negative feelings toward others resulting from emotional pain most often have the potential to reveal karmic issues and provide insights into the potential work of transformation that lies ahead.

Many challenging life experiences are karmic opportunities to neutralize patterns from the past. People are attracted to certain individuals because these relationships provide an opportunity to face karmic patterns and potentially harmonize past deeds. Karmic attraction often manifests in falling in love, for intimate relationships present the greatest possibilities to reveal, and possibly transform and harmonize, karmic patterns. Intimacy usually stimulates significant soul issues carried from the past, creating opportunities to grow. The challenges involved in transforming karmic patterns often require greater wisdom and patience than many relationships are willing to endure, evidenced by the high percentage of marriages that end in divorce.

The following examples may help build context and perspective when considering various aspects of karmic feelings. The story of Cain and Abel, the sons of Adam and Eve, portrays the archetype of the first expression of the feeling of jealousy, resulting in an act of violence. This event set the stage for the onset of a progression of karmic feelings and actions.

In the conflict between Cain and Abel, the two brothers were making offerings to God. Cain offered the fruit of the field that he tilled, and Abel offered his most beloved lamb from his flock. God received Abel's offering, as its smoke rose heavenward. In Cain's eyes God had no regard for his offering, as its dark smoke billowed out across the land. Cain grew angry, and his countenance fell. The Lord asked Cain,

> Why are you angry, and why has your countenance fallen: If you do well, will you not be accepted? And if you do not do well, sin is crouching at the door; its desire is for you, but you must master it (Gen. 4:6–7, ESV).

Here we can see that God attempted to counsel Cain to overcome his inner condition. He explained that when Cain's countenance had fallen, negative forces sought to influence him, but he must master them; he must, out of his own inner strength, overcome what lies beneath the anger and lift his countenance once again.

But Cain disregarded the words of God, and in anger and jealousy struck his brother Abel and killed him.

> Then the Lord said to Cain: "Where is Abel your brother?" He said, "I do not know; am I my brother's keeper?" And the Lord said, "What have you done? The voice of your brother's blood is crying to me from the ground. And now you are cursed from the ground, which has opened its mouth to receive your brother's blood from your hand. When you till the ground, it shall no longer yield its strength to you; you shall be a vagrant and a wanderer on the earth" (Gen. 4:9–12, ESV).

When the Lord said to Cain, "Where is Abel your brother?" He indicated that when experiencing inner turmoil, consciousness of the one who is enmeshed in our feelings is essential, carried as a brother.

"The voice of your brother's blood is crying to me from the ground." The pain resulting from all human transgressions cries out until, through the scales of karma, healing and harmony ensue. This story indicates that the suffering from human bloodshed dwells in the Earth as the collective karma of humanity (which will be discussed further later in this chapter). God lays forth the karmic law that requires each hurtful deed to be balanced. Until they are corrected, human beings shall restlessly wander the Earth.

In the story of Cain and Abel, we see the onset of a karmic thread that will weave into future incarnations. The possibility to consider further incarnations of given individualities enables a deeper understanding of the workings of karmic feelings. Rudolf Steiner indicated that Cain and Abel reincarnated in the tenth century BCE as Hiram, the master builder, and King Solomon (Steiner, 2007, pp. 379–448). Cain reentered earthly life as Hiram, representing the lineage of workers, craftsmen, and artisans whose work transforms the Earth. Abel reentered earthly life as King Solomon, carrying the impulse of the priestly line whose work unites humanity with the spiritual world. During this cycle the theme of rivalry and jealousy arose again in these two individuals.

Solomon called upon Hiram to be the master builder for the great temple in Jerusalem. During the building of the temple the Queen of Sheba came to visit Solomon. She was charmed by his wisdom and consented to be his bride. Upon meeting Hiram, she became captivated by him, arousing a mood of jealousy and rivalry between Solomon and Hiram. Subsequently, when a friend informed Solomon that three workmen were plotting to kill Hiram, King Solomon, influenced by jealousy, did nothing to stop them. Hiram was murdered, while Solomon passively allowed this to occur.

Here we observe the inversion of the fratricide of Cain. Hiram was murdered at the hands of angry, vengeful workmen. He experienced the consequence of indulged primal emotion, whereas, in his former incarnation as Cain he perpetrated the first murder as a result of his unleashed anger. On the other side of the karmic entanglement, Abel suffered death at the hand of his jealous brother, but in his subsequent incarnation as King Solomon he allowed the murder of his master builder and spiritual brother to take place, compromised by the pangs of jealous rivalry for the affection of the Queen of Sheba.

These two sets of circumstances elicit several factors. First, the length of time between these two historic events brings a perspective to the time frame of how karmic destiny unfolds. Our impatience with the circumstances of our lives, with the habits of close relationships, with the challenges and emotional trials we experience, can be tempered by understanding that the results of our actions will accompany us for centuries, or millennia, until our deeds are brought into balance. Second, we can observe how both individualities came to experience in the second scenario the challenges the other person experienced in the first scenario: Cain, having killed his brother, came to experience being murdered as Hiram. Whereas Abel, having been a victim of jealousy and anger, as Solomon experienced how jealousy can affect moral choices. Third, we can see that, although after a series of two incarnations dealing with this karmic thread, with both persons experiencing the power of subconscious emotions and the consequences thereof, there does not seem to be a resolution or completion of this karmic entanglement.

A further exploration of these two individualities is possible through the spiritual research of Uwe Lemke and Robert Powell, whose spiritual research describe these two individualities again incarnated at the time of Christ. In his book, *Das Kreuz als Lebensmotiv (The Cross as a Symbol of Life)*, Uwe Lemke describes the destinies of the women who were present at the Mystery of Golgotha. There he reveals that Mary Magdalene was formerly incarnated as the great initiate, King Solomon, at the time of the building of the Great Temple in Jerusalem (Lemke, 2000, p. 53–61). In his book, *The Mystery, Biography, and Destiny of Mary Magdalene*, Robert Powell describes Mary Magdalene's destiny in world evolution. There he indicates that Mary's brother, Lazarus,* was also incarnated as the master builder, Hiram, at the time of the building of the Great Temple in Jerusalem (Powell, 2008, p. 36).

With this third interweaving of souls, now as brother and sister, we can further consider the unfolding of karmic relationships. The themes of jealousy, rivalry, and death at the hand of another weave through the lives of Cain and Abel, and again through the lives of Hiram and Solomon. In the third cycle, Lazarus, attended by his sisters, Mary Magdalene and Martha, dies in a mysterious way. His sisters grieved bitterly at the loss of their brother. Yet it is unclear as to how the karma of the two former incarnations relate to the death of Lazarus.

A contemporary visionary, Estelle Isaacson, in her book, *Through the Eyes of Mary Magdalene*, describes in great detail how Lazarus developed an interest in the Egyptian initiation rites undergone by the pharaohs. He asked his sister, Mary, who studied the Egyptian mysteries and participated in administering the rites during her visits to Egypt, to assist him in this initiation rite. With some reservation Mary agreed to shepherd Lazarus through the death ritual that was to last three days. Isaacson describes how Lazarus lost his way and did not return to the living after the three-day initiation period. After several days of mourning, Lazarus was buried. Although Magdalene was honoring the request of her brother, she felt responsible for Lazarus's death and bitterly lamented the loss of her brother (Isaacson, 2012, pp. 173–192).

* Scholars hold various points of view as to the identity of Mary Magdalene and whether she was the same individual as Mary of Bethany, the sister of Martha and Lazarus. Mary of Bethany appears in the Canonical Gospels in Luke 7:47, 48, 10:38, 39; John 11:1, 2, 12:1–8. Mary Magdalene appears in Luke 8:2, 24:9; Matthew 27:55, 56, 27:60, 61, 28:7; John 19:25, 20:1, 2, 20:18. Based on biblical evidence it is unclear as to whether Mary Magdalene was the sister of Lazarus. There is no direct reference to this and there is also no evidence to contradict their familial ties. Susan Haskins in her scholarly volume, *Mary Magdalen: Myth and Metaphor*, addresses the issue of her identity in pp. 20–31. She details the accounts in the gospels and does not draw a conclusion to the question. Anne Catherine Emmerich, a visionary nun whose writings Rudolf Steiner validated, writes: "The parents of Lazarus had in all fifteen children, of whom six died young. Of the nine that survived, only four were living at the time of Christ's teaching. These four were: Lazarus; Martha, about two years younger; [Silent] Mary, looked upon as a simpleton, two years younger than Martha; and Mary Magdalene, five years younger than the simpleton" (Emmerich, 1954. p. 335).

If we accept this rendering as accurate, we can see a continuation of the theme of death at the hand of another, although in this case, by request. Lazarus experienced a longing for the knowledge of the spiritual world that could be attained through the Egyptian death rite. Together Mary and Lazarus prepared and supported this event, yet it failed. As a result, Mary vowed never to perform this ritual again.

When Christ finally came to Bethany, and raised Lazarus from the dead (John 11:1–44), the karmic dynamic between the individualities of Cain and Abel, Hiram and Solomon, and Lazarus and Mary resolved. The repetition of death at the hand of another interweaving between these two souls culminated with Lazarus overcoming death.*

---

* The raising of Lazarus shrouds a mystery related to death and resurrection. Various mystics and scholars present differing accounts touching on the question of whether the raising of Lazarus was actually from death or from an initiatory state. In *Jesus, Lazarus, and the Messiah,* Charles Tidball includes three perspectives on this question: the account from the Gospel of John, authored by the risen Lazarus; the writings of Anne Catherine Emmerich, a clairvoyant mystic of the nineteenth century; and Rudolf Steiner (Tidball, 2005, pp. 71–78). In the Gospel of John, chapter 11, it states: *the sisters sent word to Jesus, "Lord, the one you love is sick." When he heard this, Jesus said, "This sickness will not end in death; it is for God's glory so that God's Son may be glorified through it"* (John 11:3–4, ESV). Two days later Jesus said to the disciples: *"Our friend Lazarus has fallen asleep, but I go to awake him out of sleep." The disciples said to him, "Lord, if he has fallen asleep, he will recover." Now Jesus had spoken of his death, but they thought that he meant taking rest in sleep. Then Jesus told them plainly, "Lazarus is dead; and for your sake I am glad that I was not there, so that you may believe"* (John 11:11–15, ESV). In the Gospel of John the reference to "falling asleep" and "waking him out of sleep" refers to an initiatory sleep as performed in the ancient mystery centers of Egypt and Greece (Steiner, 1988, pp. 60–65). According to the visions of Anne Catherine Emmerich, as published in Robert Powell's *Chronicle of the Living Christ,* on Saturday, July 26, 32: *In the early hours of the morning, [Christ] Jesus went to Lazarus's grave.... He went into the vault where Lazarus's tomb was. Lazarus had been dead for several days, and his corpse had lain for some days before being entombed, for it had been hoped that Jesus would come and wake him from the dead.... There then took place the raising of Lazarus from the dead* (Powell, 1996, p. 316). In *The Gospel of St. John,* chapter 4, and in *Christianity as Mystical Fact,* chapter 8, Rudolf Steiner addresses the event as an initiation rite that Lazarus underwent. In *Christianity as Mystical Fact,* Steiner discusses the initiation process, and states: *The earthly body has really been dead for three days. New life comes forth from death. This life has outlived death. Man has gained confidence in the new life. That is what happened to Lazarus* (Steiner, 1986, pp. 138–139).

When Lazarus died

> he became submerged in the primeval original darkness of the first day of creation, and [when he came forth from the dead he] experienced the eternal transformation of darkness into light, the eternal coming into existence of consciousness as the internal transmutation of darkness into the light of understanding, of insight, of affirmation.... He experienced the universal Word such that at that moment the "Let there be light" of the world-creative Word condensed itself into the words "Lazarus, come forth" of the Son of Man ... the eternal creative Word of God—now clothed for him in a beloved human voice—commanded him to return. So it happened that Lazarus returned (Tomberg, 1992, p. 76).

In this description: "the eternal creative Word of God—now clothed for him in a beloved human voice—commanded him to return," the presence of spiritual creative power called forth life, the transmutation of death into the earthly world of time. Through the presence of his beloved friend, Christ, who could embody the eternal creative Word of God, Lazarus experienced firsthand knowledge of the transformation of primeval darkness—lifelessness, into primal light—life. The final stage of transmuting his karma required the presence of spiritual creative power. The presence of Christ activated the possibility for Lazarus to overcome death. The raising of Lazarus, the fulfillment of his karma with Mary Magdalene, required the cooperation of the purest and most genuine humanity with the most all-embracing, highest divinity.

The raising of Lazarus transformed the first karmic entanglement in the lineage of humanity—jealousy and rivalry—set in motion by the primal family, by making it known that death can be overcome. Death (or separation) does not end or resolve emotional turmoil. In the future, new circumstances will unfold to once again encounter the enduring challenges that were aborted through death, and further the process of untangling the karmic patterns from the past. The event of the raising of Lazarus demonstrates the impermanence of death, enacted for the benefit of all of humanity, and will bear fruit only to the degree to which we understand its significance.

## Objectivity: Infusing Astral Feelings with "I" Consciousness— The Antidote for Karmic Feeling

Transforming karmic feelings requires the clarity of objective thinking working in tandem with consciousness in the feeling realm. The light of higher consciousness must be engaged to raise subconscious feelings into the realm of consciousness. Chapter 1 delineates the role the human "I" plays in affecting the transformation of the double. The "I" works into the astral body and the soul sheaths to awaken consciousness, to lift the emotional swirling of the feeling life into the light of awareness and self-reflection. This allows one to objectify one's feelings, to take responsibility for one's feelings, and to shepherd one's emotions to reveal new awareness of one's self. To transform karmic thinking one must clear out all astral forces from the thinking realm. To transform karmic feeling one must infuse the astral sheath with "I" consciousness.

When, through this process, one is able to objectify or neutrally witness the events in one's life, it is possible to begin to identify karmic patterns that have been unfolding. When one has an awareness of these patterns it is possible to understand and begin to transform them. This process unfolds over time, requiring patience and continual self-inquiry. The initial step requires taking personal responsibility for your plight, followed by deep self-interrogation.

When experiencing emotional turmoil in relation to a loved one, close friend, colleague, or other immediate relationship, one must be able to step back from the surging emotions and objectively bring to consciousness that we create our own destiny through our past deeds. This is the law of karma. It must be restated here that there are events that occur that are random, that are not a result of karma. This must be kept in consciousness while further exploring avenues for transforming karmic feelings.

In difficult emotional situations, the following inquiries are submitted to bring insights and reorient thinking: *What might I have done in a past life to create this situation as a balancing correction? How might this situation be the perfect circumstance for me to learn the effects of behaviors I may have perpetrated in a previous life so as to understand how to transform my karma?*

*Can I welcome this situation as an opportunity to learn and grow? Can I see the one who stimulated the feelings as a servant of a higher purpose who has made it possible for me to heal an old pattern?* The imaginations that may arise when pondering these questions may prevent impulsive, reactive responses to many situations and promote self-responsibility. Measured words and deeds have the potential to bring healing.

If we recognize that we are considering actions that are outside our personal values, there is a high likelihood that we are being driven by karmic feelings. It was not Cain's intention to kill his brother; he expressed unrestrained emotion, not knowing what the results of his action might be. Solomon was a king of great wisdom and integrity. He brought peace to the land. He lawfully governed his people. He was beloved by the people for his wisdom and fairness. He would not, under ordinary circumstances allow the murder of another, let alone his master builder who he invited to Jerusalem to build God's Temple. Solomon blindly lost integrity with his values, driven by personal feelings of jealousy, arising out of a karmic pattern in which he was entwined. If we observe an inclination to speak or act in contradiction to our values or moral integrity, take heed, vigilant self-examination is advisable.

The transformation of karmic feelings requires patient perseverance and unmitigated self-scrutiny. The "I" of our being must penetrate the subconscious astral body and shed light on its feelings. It can be helpful to consider any predicament as a much larger complex of circumstances that go far beyond the immediate perceivable situation. The transformation of karma requires earnest dedication to personal growth.

## Karmic Double Will

Karma works in the will as a driving force. When one feels compelled to go to a particular event, travel to a specific country, or speak out about a politically charged situation that puts one at risk, one experiences the power of karmic will. The force operant in karmic will activates a conviction that compels one so strongly that it would seem impossible not to do that which one is driven to do. We are not free, but rather compelled by an unseen force.

This compelling force draws us to meet people who will prove meaningful for our development. It does not always result in harmonious relationships, but will always be fruitful for our growth. Sometimes it results in our being able to resolve or partially heal karmic entanglements that we agreed to address in this life; other times these meetings create new karma that we will have to face in the future. The actions we choose in relation to these people determine the future forces required to balance the unresolved karmic threads. Thus, we create the backdrop for the next phase of our unfolding destiny that will be propelled by our karmic will forces.

Karmic will propels our personal life into a dynamic phase, drawing us toward individuals who will engage us in our karmic patterns and significantly affect our lives. Sometimes this leads to challenges that result in significant personal growth and healing. It can also lead to tragic outcomes that result from extreme pain and resistance to societal conventions. Romeo and Juliet, passionately drawn together, defied their family loyalty for their allegiance to romantic love, culminating in their tragic deaths. Lancelot, one of the greatest knights of the Round Table, and King Arthur's most loyal and trusted knight, succumbed to his attraction to Guinevere, King Arthur's wife. Eventually Arthur's nephew exposed their love affair that led to the fall of the Round Table. Guinevere was condemned to burn to death for her infidelity. Sir Lancelot attempted to rescue her. He killed several of King Arthur's knights in the process. Lancelot ended his days as a hermit and Guinevere became a nun at Amesbury where she died.

The love affair of the French philosopher, Peter Abelard (1079–1142), one of the greatest thinkers of the Middle Ages, and Heloise d'Argenteuil (1101–1164), niece of Canon Fulbert, portrays the anguish that overshadows the lives of lovers when the unrestrained magnetism of love defies the social and moral dictates of the time. Even though twenty years her senior, Abelard pursued his love for Heloise. They bore a child and secretly married. Fulbert's ensuing violence against Heloise caused Abelard to place her in the convent of Argenteuil to protect her. Fulbert sought vengeance upon Abelard by having him attacked while asleep, and castrated. Abelard lived out the remainder of his life as a monk (*The Love Letters of Abelard and Heloise*, 1901).

In each of these examples, the magnetism of love superseded the dictates of the time. The love that burned within the hearts of these people compelled them to disregard the opposition of societal convention, loyalty to family bloodline, the king, friends, and personal safety. The pull of karma, experienced as attraction, overpowered each of these couples to disregard the forces of family, society, and in the case of Lancelot, loyalty, honor, and integrity. In all three romances a tragic ending ensued, but each one brings to light a unique element of karmic will.

On his way to the party where Romeo meets Juliet, he experiences a flash of insight into his star-given destiny. He speaks:

> my mind misgives
> Some consequence, yet hanging in the stars,
> Shall bitterly begin his fearful date
> With this night's revels; and expire the term
> Of a despised life, clos'd in my breast,
> By some vile forfeit of untimely death:
> But He, that hath the steerage of my course,
> Direct my sail (*Romeo and Juliet*, act 1, scene 4).

Romeo considers the stars as rulers of human destiny, unable to escape their decree, and consequently considers it necessary to surrender to the dictates of his destiny. In their ensuing love for one another, Romeo and Juliet challenge the ancient tribal grip of blood-guilt down through the generations. To those who follow the stream of thought that the human soul descends at birth from a spiritual existence and takes part in choosing the path of life which appears on Earth as its destiny, Romeo and Juliet appear as two human souls who have chosen their fate in order that through their sacrifice they may break the chain of the blood-feud. They embody a transition from the dominance of the bloodline to the paradigm of individual karmic relationships. The play ends with the hand of Montague clasped in the hand of Capulet with a picture of reconciliation and atonement won through love and sacrifice. The tragedy of Romeo and Juliet's unfulfilled love bore the fruit of the transformation of societal consciousness.

Lancelot and Guinevere pursued their irresistible attraction to the destruction of the Round Table and their ill-fated separation. The dramatic turns of events resulting from their romance indicate past entanglements between King Arthur, Lancelot, Guinevere, and the Round Table community. The two lovers were not able to resist the temptation of attraction to uphold the conventions of fidelity, knightly honor, and loyalty to the king. The power of their attraction demonstrates the influence of karmic will, which in this case led to the demise of the Round Table and the end of an era. The resulting tragedy presents the platform for future karmic relationships that could have the potential to balance the suffering that ensued during this incarnation, if wisdom prevails.

The love affair of Abelard and Heloise resembles that of Lancelot and Guinevere, in that the opposition that they encountered from family and the moral conventions of the time led to their separation, humiliation, and suffering. The extreme response of Heloise's uncle, Canon Fulbert, demonstrates an intensity that from a modern perspective carries a driving force that seems disproportionate to the situation. This seemingly inexplicable response indicates a veiled influence from previous incarnations. The unknown past and the powerful drama of this romance set the stage for a future constellation of relationships that will offer the possibility for compassion, love, and forgiveness to prevail.

All three of these impassioned romantic relationships ended in tragedy, but with distinctly different consequences. Romeo and Juliet sacrificed their lives with the result of societal norms transforming in response to the power of their love. Lancelot and Guinevere pursued their attraction resulting in the destruction of a culture of virtue and nobility. Abelard and Heloise met a destiny of personal violence, humiliation, and isolation, yet continued to convey their devotion through a series of love letters. Their tragic romance did not affect the larger society in the ways of the former examples, but rather demonstrated the intense dynamics of personal karmic entanglements.

We can see from these three examples that the powerful force of attraction drew all of these lovers into relationship, but the resulting outcomes varied based on the personal inner development of each individual, the complexities of their relationships with the other people involved, i.e.,

Romeo and Juliet's parents, King Arthur, and Canon Fulbert, and their destiny in the course of human evolution. To the perceptive observer the attraction of love exposes a karmic destiny that must be engaged and will play out in various possible scenarios depending on the complexities of karmic issues and the consciousness of the individuals involved.

The betrayal of a loved one raises questions of deep karmic significance. Brutus betrayed his beloved friend, Julius Caesar, valuing his allegiance to the state over his loyalty to his friend. Brutus believed that Caesar would become a dictator and, therefore, had to die in order to preserve the republic. He thrust the final knife into Caesar, sealing his death. After Caesar's ghost appeared to him on the battlefield, Brutus impaled himself on his own sword, declaring that Caesar should consider himself avenged by Brutus's death. Brutus imposed his private sense of honor on the whole Roman state. In the end, killing Caesar did not stop the Roman republic from becoming a dictatorship, for Octavius assumed power and became what Brutus feared in Caesar. Here Brutus placed himself as judge over his beloved friend, conspiring against him and participating in his murder. This deed not only created the future necessity for Brutus to balance the personal act of murder of a loved one, but also the karmic consequences of Caesar's death for the Roman republic.

In the biblical story of Samson and Delilah, Samson lost sight of his calling from God and entrusted his secret of the power of his physical strength to please the woman who captured his affections. Delilah then betrayed Sampson by divulging his secret in return for a sum of money. In the end it cost Sampson his physical sight, his freedom, his dignity, and eventually his life. Sampson broke his vow to God to win Delilah. Through the events that resulted from Delilah's betrayal of Sampson, he reaped the consequences of dishonoring his allegiance to God. The karmic consequences of her betrayal are the subject of spiritual law for future unfolding.

An archetypal example of betrayal of a loved one is Judas Iscariot's betrayal of Christ. At the Last Supper, Jesus told the disciples that one of them would betray Him. Jesus said to Judas, "What you are about to do, do quickly" (John 13:27, ESV). Judas got up and went out into the night to betray the whereabouts of his beloved teacher. When Judas realized the consequences of his actions he tried to release himself from the sequence of events that ensued. His guilt overcame him and he hanged himself before Christ's passion was fulfilled.

> When Judas, his betrayer, saw that He was condemned, he repented and brought back the thirty pieces of silver to the chief priests and the elders, saying, "I have sinned in betraying innocent blood." They said, "What is that to us? See to it yourself." And throwing down the pieces of silver in the temple, he departed; and he went and hanged himself (Matt. 27:3–5, ESV).

Judas's betrayal of Christ demonstrates the unmitigated power of karmic will. Judas had a task to fulfill and his deed bears a complex karmic condition. Rudolf Steiner points to the profundity of Judas's betrayal of Christ in a lecture cycle entitled *The Karma of Untruthfulness*, vol. 1, where he confronts the role of Judas's actions.

> Can you imagine someone who might say, You Christians owe it to Judas that your Mystery of Golgotha took place at all. You owe it to the executioner's men, who nailed Christ to the cross, that your Mystery of Golgotha ran its course! Is anyone justified in defending Judas and the executioner's men, even though it is true that the meaning of earthly history is owed to them? Is it easy to answer a question like this? Is one not immediately faced with contradictions which simply stand there and which represent a terrible destiny? Think about what I have placed before you!... What I have just said is spoken only so that you can think about the fact that it is not so easy to say: When two things contradict one another I shall accept the one and reject the other. Reality is more profound than whatever human beings may often be willing to encompass with their thinking. It is not without reason that Nietzsche, crazed almost out of his mind, formulated the words: "The world is deep, deeper than day can comprehend" (Steiner, 1989, pp. 65–66).

Here Rudolf Steiner exposes the complexities and contradictions in human destiny. Questions arise that cannot be addressed with logic or materialistic thinking. An important consideration in understanding the motivation of Judas lies in his past, in a former incarnation that helps elucidate the enigma of his destiny.

Rudolf Steiner investigated the karmic background of Judas Iscariot:

> Among the five sons of Mattathias is one who is already called Judas in the Old Testament. He was the one who at that time fought more bravely than all the others for his own people. In his whole soul he was dedicated to his people, and it was he who was successful in forming an alliance with the Romans against King Antiochus of Syria (1 Macc. 8). This Judas is the same who later had to undergo the test of the betrayal, because he who was most intimately bound up with the old specifically Hebrew element, could not at once find the transition into the Christian element, needing the severe testing of the betrayal.... It is remarkable that in this symptomatic process, the Judas of the Old Testament concluded an alliance with the Romans, prefiguring all that happened later, namely the path that Christianity took through the Roman Empire, so that it could enter into the world (Steiner, 1986, pp. 34–35).

Rudolf Steiner presents a picture of Judas Iscariot having formerly lived in Palestine during a time of great strife and religious oppression. Under the Syrian king, Antiochus, the practice of the Jewish religion was prohibited in Judea. Antiochus captured the great temple in Jerusalem, ordered the burning of all Jewish holy books, and condemned to death all the scholars who studied them. The temple was desecrated. It was Judas Maccabee, the leader of a band of Jews, having formed an alliance with the Romans against King Antiochus, who reclaimed and rededicated the temple. It is this individual who fought for seven years for religious freedom for the Jewish people, and for the reclamation of the great temple in Jerusalem, who, according to Rudolf Steiner, lived in Judea again at the time of Jesus of Nazareth as Judas Iscariot. Once again, he was threatened with the destruction of the great temple and religious oppression. The political scene was unstable, threatening the freedom and safety of the followers of Jesus and the Jewish people.

These insights into Judas's past reveal the complexity of the soul condition of Judas Iscariot. He bore a predisposition that intensified his feelings about an already explosive situation that was seething in Jerusalem. Judas had a poignant relationship with the great temple, having, in a former incarnation, reclaimed it for the Jewish people less than two hundred years before the culminating events in his life. One could easily see how he would want to preserve and protect it from destruction. He maintained a devotion to the physical temple as most sacred, the axis mundi for religious life. What then became of Judas after his betrayal, remorse, and suicide?

Rudolf Steiner investigated further into the future destiny of Judas Iscariot. The threads of his karmic past intricately weave into an artistic unfolding of human evolution.

> It was through a later reincarnation of Judas that the fusion of the Roman with the Christian element occurred. The reincarnated Judas was the first who, as we might say, had the great success of spreading Romanized Christianity in the world. The treaty concluded by the Judas of the Old Testament with the Romans was the prophetic foreshadowing of what was later accomplished by another man, who is recognized by occultists as the reincarnation of that Judas who had to go through the severe soul-testing of the betrayal. What through his later influence appears as Christianity within Romanism and Romanism within Christianity is like a renewal of the alliance concluded between the Old Testament Judas with the Romans, but transferred into the spiritual (Steiner, 1986, pp. 34–35).

Here Rudolf Steiner is referring to Saint Augustine of Hippo (354–430). This sequence of incarnations demonstrates how St. Augustine successfully spread Romanized Christianity in the world as a fulfillment on a spiritual level of the material treaty Judas Iscariot made with the Romans in an effort to align the teachings of Jesus with the Roman authorities. It is not insignificant that Pope Leo I, during whose pontificate Augustine was canonized, ordered that the feast of this saint should be observed with the same honors as that of an Apostle (Vann, 1954, p. 96).

In further consideration of the successive incarnations of Judas Iscariot and St. Augustine, in *Foundations of Esotericism*, lecture 8, Berlin, October 3, 1905, after stating that traditional Christianity has contributed to the gradual dawning of the materialistic age, partially through the suppression of the teaching of reincarnation, Rudolf Steiner brings attention to St. Augustine's doctrine of predestination as a contributing factor. Steiner indicates that already at the time of Christ it was necessary for the spiritual to be betrayed by the purely material. He states that Judas had to betray Christ. Judas was the first to attach prime importance to money—to materialism. "In Judas was incarnated the entire materialistic age. This materialistic age has obscured and darkened the spiritual" (Steiner, 1905). This picture creates a subtle backdrop for the unfolding destiny of a human soul.

In chapter 8 of *Christianity as Mystical Fact*, entitled "St. Augustine and the Church," Steiner addresses the soul quality of Saint Augustine of Hippo.

> The full force of the conflict enacted in the souls of Christian believers during the transition from paganism to the new religion is revealed in the person of St. Augustine (AD 354–430).... In Augustine's personality, out of a passionate nature, deep spiritual needs developed. He passed through pagan and semi-Christian ideas. He suffered deeply from the most appalling doubts such as attack one who has felt the impotence of thoughts in the face of spiritual problems, and who has tasted the depressing effect of the question: "Can man know anything whatever?" (Steiner, 1972, p. 183).

In his earlier life St. Augustine suffered the doubts, desires, and egotism that haunted Judas. At the beginning of his struggles, Augustine's thoughts clung to the material things of the senses. He described that he could only picture the spiritual in material images. In his *Confessions*, St. Augustine states: "When I wished to think of God, I could only imagine quantities of matter and believed that was the only kind of thing that could exist. This was the chief and almost the only cause of error which I could not avoid" (Steiner, 1972, p. 183). Here one can imagine the inner journey necessary to realign one's devotion to Christ after being the one who took on the role of the betrayer.

Judas Iscariot's betrayal of Christ bears a profound destiny that expresses not only the soul condition of his immediate life, struggling with doubt, desire, betrayal, fear, and shame, but also a greater dimension of individual human biography and history, opening a window into the unfathomable artistry of karma and human evolution. This sequence of incarnations demonstrates the governing principles of karma orchestrating the path of human destiny, if we but have eyes to see it. Without an understanding of the structure of karma and reincarnation we merely behold a succession of events that bear no architecture, no formative design fashioned in the spiritual world.

At this point in human evolution it is possible to interpret the inner progressive shaping of events, perceiving how individualities appear at defined times and bring impulses to the evolution of humanity while entangling or unraveling their karma. Learning to understand karma, individual destiny, and history in this way can bring greater insight into the workings of this present time and evoke compassion and love for individuals challenged by the trials of life.

Another important facet of karmic will drives our initiative to realize ideological convictions and serve the conscious evolution of humanity. This karmic force originates from a commitment to participate in alleviating suffering in the world and raising human consciousness for the benefit of life on Earth. Rather than balancing personal misdeeds, this expression of karma serves to balance social and cultural disharmonies. It often requires self-renunciation or personal sacrifice to achieve the ideals undertaken. Numerous examples of ideological karmic initiative infuse recorded history with purpose: Socrates, John the Baptist, Joan of Arc, Giordano Bruno, Florence Nightingale, Harriet Tubman, Susan B. Anthony, Mohandas Gandhi, Martin Luther King Jr., Caesar Chavez, Mother Teresa, Nelson Mandela, and His Holiness the Dalai Lama, to name a few. The few individuals highlighted here illustrate various dimensions at work within the driving force of karmic initiative.

Gautama Buddha, the son of a king, abandoned his wife and son in search of the meaning of suffering, old age, and death. He renounced materialism, practiced extreme asceticism, devoted himself to meditation, achieved enlightenment, and prescribed a path of practice through which people can reach enlightenment. His driving will forces fueled a life that led to the founding of a major world religion that has significantly influenced the consciousness of humanity. His family bore the weight of his unwavering devotion to his mission. His marriage and responsibilities as a parent were sacrificed to fulfill the calling within his soul.

Harriet Tubman, born a slave in Maryland's Dorchester County around 1820, risked her life leading escaped slaves to freedom in the North in the Underground Railroad. She escaped to freedom at the age of twenty-nine. She took refuge in Philadelphia, then immediately returned to Maryland to rescue her family. During a ten-year span she made nineteen trips into the South and escorted over three hundred slaves to freedom. Because she wanted freedom for all of the people who were forced into slavery, Tubman decided to help the Union Army. She was the first woman in American history to lead a military expedition. She helped Colonel James Montgomery plan and execute a raid to free slaves from plantations along the Combahee River in South Carolina in June 1863. They freed over 750 slaves (men, women, children, and babies). She worked underground, anonymously devoted to the achievement of human freedom.

Mohandas Gandhi, leader of India's independence movement, spent twenty years in South Africa opposing discriminatory legislation against Indians. As a pioneer of Satyagraha, resistance through mass nonviolent civil disobedience, he spent thirty years leading the Indian National Congress by advocating a policy of nonviolent non-cooperation to achieve independence from the British rule of India. His goal was to help poor farmers and laborers protest oppressive taxation and discrimination. He struggled to alleviate poverty, liberate women, and put an end to caste discrimination of the untouchables, with the ultimate objective being self-rule for India. Gandhi characteristically refused additional security. In the early evening of January 30, 1948, after a meeting with India's Deputy Prime Minister and his close associate in the freedom struggle, Gandhi proceeded to his prayers. As he was about to mount the steps of the podium, Gandhi folded his hands and greeted his audience with a namaskar. At that moment a young man, Nathuram Godse, came up to him, bent down in the gesture of obeisance, took a revolver out of his pocket, and shot Gandhi three times in his chest. His hands still folded in a greeting, Gandhi spoke these words: "He Ram! He Ram!" As a public figure Gandhi allowed himself to be vulnerable; he served his highest ideals with humility and openness. His unwavering commitment to Satyagraha, compounded by his tragic death, has impacted world consciousness and will continue to affect human thoughts and deeds far into the future.

Martin Luther King Jr., the primary leader in the African-American Civil Rights Movement, served the advancement of civil rights, social justice, and human dignity through nonviolent civil disobedience. His courageous resistance to bigotry positioned him at age thirty-five to be the youngest Nobel Peace Prize laureate. Threats on his life never dissuaded him from forging ahead toward his vision of equality, justice, and peace in the world. His commitment to nonviolent protest influenced the civil rights movement as a dominant force during its decade of greatest achievement, from 1957 to 1968. On April 3, 1968, the day before his assassination, Dr. King ended his final speech with the words:

> Like anybody, I would like to live a long life. Longevity has its place. But I'm not concerned about that now. I just want to do God's will. And He's allowed me to go up to the mountain. And I've looked over. And I've seen the Promised Land. I may not get there with you. But I want you to know tonight, that we, as a people, will get to the Promised Land! (Montefiore, 2006, p. 155).

Martin Luther King stated: "I just want to do God's will." This characterizes a spiritualized aspect of karmic will, seeking to serve a higher purpose than individual interest. His efforts in the civil rights movement catalyzed overt and subtle changes that laid the groundwork for the possibility for President Obama to be elected. King's courageous life dedicated to justice, equality, and peace continues to inspire people throughout the world.

The Presidential Medal of Freedom was posthumously awarded to Martin Luther King Jr. by President Jimmy Carter in 1977. The citation read:

> Martin Luther King Jr. was the conscience of his generation. He gazed upon the great wall of segregation and saw that the power of love could bring it down. From the pain and exhaustion of his fight to fulfill the promises of our founding fathers for our humblest citizens,

> he wrung his eloquent statement of his dream for America. He made our nation stronger because he made it better. His dream sustains us yet" (Carter, 1977).

These words dedicated to Martin Luther King Jr. highlight the principles of "conscience," "the power of love," and "the promises of our founding fathers"—life, liberty, and the pursuit of happiness. These principles extol qualities of the ennobled human soul, the transformed double. Here we see with individuals who work selflessly for the furtherance of human evolution, karmic forces serving the transformation of the karma of humanity rather than working to balance out individual karmic conditions.

Individuals can achieve a high level of spiritual evolution through developing their inner soul condition, so that they become a direct and self-conscious collaborator with cosmic laws. In many instances individuals who serve to transform social injustice, awaken human consciousness, who devote their lives to fulfilling social ideals, also have personal karma to balance. One karmic focus does not preempt the other.

If an individual does nothing contrary to the natural order, then there is no reaction from Nature upon him or her, and thus may be said to have "risen above karma," insofar as the term karma applies to one's own evolution, character, and activity as a human being. When one reaches the evolutionary stage of being wholly impersonal, one thereafter makes no new personal karma. One no longer weaves a web of personal destiny; the bonds of personality no longer enchain one. At this stage one becomes an impersonal servitor, living as a worker and collaborator of natural law.

Beyond the bonds of personal karma there also exists the dimension of impersonal karma, the collective karma of humanity to which all human beings are subject. We are inseparable from the family of humanity and the universal karma of cosmic history. Those who have achieved a high state of evolution devote themselves to transmuting social ills, human suffering, and the denigration of life, whether human, animal, or plant. No one is exempt from the universal karma of the world. It must be brought into balance, redeeming all the conditions contrary to natural law. I will address this topic further later in this chapter.

## Mastering the Five Currents of the Will: The Antidote for Karmic Willing

Each human being in his or her relationship to the outer world possesses five organs of action: the four limbs and the head in its function as a limb. These five organs provide means of expression for the five currents of the will. These five currents can be governed by *objective, conscious will forces*, referred to here as the light-filled currents of the will, or they can be dictated by *subjective, subconscious forces*, referred to as the five dark currents of the will.

The five dark currents of the will, as introduced in the fifth Arcanum of *Meditations on the Tarot*, manifest as follows: 1) the desire for personal greatness; 2) to take, often at the expense of others; 3) to keep, often at the expense of others; 4) to advance at the expense of others; and 5) to maintain one's position at the expense of others, each corresponding to one of the five limbs (Anonymous, 1991, p. 110). The desire to take or get hold of things is bound to the right hand; the desire to retain or keep things belongs to the left hand; the desire to advance at the expense of others corresponds to the right foot; the desire to hold onto one's position at the expense of others to the left foot. The desire for personal greatness corresponds to the head, in its function as a limb. These dark currents of the will originate as impulses that flow through our physical body and find expression in the limbs.

## The First Current of the Will: The Head as an Expression of the Heart

The desire for personal greatness—egotism, self-aggrandizement, megalomania—arises as a subconscious current inspired by luciferic forces driving thinking. However, egotism originates not in the head, but in the heart. Spiritually the head can be understood as a limb of the heart that enables the heart to act through thinking. The heart in its mature state directs its love outward to other people, to the kingdoms of Nature and to God. In an undeveloped state, the petals of the heart chakra turn inward toward the self, focusing solely on self-interest. This locus of self-centeredness in the heart then manifests as egotistical thinking in the head.

Alongside the dark current of egotism, manifesting in the thinking activity of the head, resides the potential conscious, light-filled current of humility that grows within the heart as a result of authentic experiences that increase our awareness of failings, imperfections, and how the double is motivated. Humility grows organically when shortcomings become unavoidably clear. The acknowledgement of personal imperfections, accompanied by a yearning for self-improvement, awakens humility and slowly influences thinking, transforming egocentric impulses. Humility crowns the head with the light and warmth of selfless love that flows from the heart into thinking activity.

### The Second Current of the Will: The Right Hand

The right hand expresses the subconscious current of taking property, or emotional conditions (such as reputation), at the expense of others. When a person steals, taking something out of greed, self-interest, or indifference to the consequences to others, one acts out of the subconscious or dark current of the right hand. Global economic exchanges and exploitation of resources that are solely profit-driven are prime examples.

By contrast, the conscious impulse of the right hand expresses itself in giving. Rather than taking at other people's expense, giving demonstrates the light-filled current inherent as the true nature of the right hand. When giving to another, whether it be money, volunteer work, or a kind deed, a deep human need is fulfilled. Selfless giving realizes the true nature of the untarnished current of the right hand and brings a deep sense of inner joy. Giving requires sacrifice, whether it is time, coveted privacy, material goods, or money. Thus, the transformation of the dark current of the right hand requires an interest in the well-being of others partnered with a willingness to give in order to help others flourish. Here humility makes it possible to find the right point of balance between our own well-being and that of others.

### The Third Current of the Will: The Left Hand

The subconscious force that flows through the left hand manifests as holding on, hoarding, or controlling, at the expense of others. Fear and self-interest lie behind this impulse. The belief that there will not be enough, that personal control is necessary to avoid failure, or meet desired standards, arises when one identifies one's self as isolated from others, rather than living in collaboration with others in trust and respect. A deep need for safety underlies this orientation, accompanied by a lack of trust in one's fellow human beings.

The light-filled current of the left hand activates an impulse to share, and to create trusting relationships with others. One learns to let the current of life activity flow out and flow in with confidence that there will be enough. Consideration for the well-being of others underlies this current. Trust that when in need there will be sufficient means available for all to share requires confidence in the abundance of Nature and human generosity that exist in healthy community.

### The Fourth Current of the Will: The Right Foot

The dark current flowing through the right foot advances at the expense of others. *I need to get a promotion.* An example of this arises in the story of *Othello*, when Iago strategizes to get a promotion at the expense of Cassio, as described in chapter 3. Another example rears its head in music conservatories when students steal their classmate's music so they are unable to practice for an audition or jury, so that they will win the competition. In these instances the individual operates completely out of self-interest, with no ethical concern for the other.

The counter force filled with light streaming through the right foot results in withdrawing personal desire and acting on behalf of the good of all. One might nominate someone else for a position one would like to hold, but realize that the other person would better serve the needs of the community. Life guided by the light-filled currents of the will does not seek advancement, fame, or wealth; rather it seeks to act with care and consideration for the well-being of the whole.

### The Fifth Current of the Will: The Left Foot

The force of the dark current in the left foot drives a person to maintain their position at the expense of others when it is not in the best interest of the whole. *I've been here for twenty-five years and I am going to stay until I am eligible to retire, even though my heart isn't in this job and I do not have the energy to do a good job anymore.* Whether for status, money, comfort, or fear of the unknown, acting at another's expense leads to social decay. Depletion festers in the individual soul and the soul of the organization, resulting in malady, disease, or crisis.

While the left foot unconsciously holds onto a position, bringing consciousness and light into the will releases the confines of fear and allows fluidity of actions so that the position can be released for the benefit of others. This means acting for the goodness of the whole whether the position is maintained or given up. Perhaps someone has been the head of an organization for many years and realizes that he or she no longer engages in tasks with creativity, inspiration, and heart; work has become routine. For such a person to step back may mean new life for the organization. A new leader could infuse the company or school with dynamic, forward-thinking vision. There will be times to step forward and other times to step back, as in a dance where everything needs to happen with grace and natural movement. In this way a community can move through cycles of growth with conscious, cooperative reconfiguration.

In each of the five currents of the will, engaging the light-filled current shifts the focus from one's own personal interest and what protects one's own position no matter what the consequences for others might be, to an outward orientation. The focus is on the larger community in a way in which everyone's needs are met. Each person senses his or her place in the context of the whole. Individual needs are then met through the law of mutuality in human community.

Again and again we come back to the question: where is the heart focused? We can see how many of our own actions, and the actions of organizations and governments, are based on subconscious currents of the will. Knowledge of the five currents of the will provides a context for self-awareness. If, one by one, human beings will shift their inner orientation from self-centeredness to selflessness, from self-advancement to serving the well-being of the whole through humility, we will grow closer to fulfilling our earthly mission of learning to love.

**Figure 6**

## The Five Dark Currents of the Will

HEAD

**Desire**
I am what matters.

EGOTISM
The desire for personal greatness. Megalomania, fame, self-interest, power, arrogance, and greed.

RIGHT HAND

**Doubt**
I am alone.

SEPARATION
I only take care of my own. I judge and compete with others. I take at the expense of others. Greed and self-interest. I harden my heart and am only concerned about me and mine.

LEFT HAND

**Insecurity**
It's not safe.

FEAR
I hold on at the expense of others. I do whatever keeps me safe. I fear lack, insufficiency, and vulnerability. I have a need to control.

RIGHT FOOT

**Irresponsibility**
I don't care.

POWER
I seek to advance at all costs, even at the expense of others. I take without giving back and consume without conscience. I take life for granted.

LEFT FOOT

**Apathy**
Someone else will do it.

DENIAL
I will maintain my position at all expense. I block the grief of the truth. I am convenience oriented, not conscience oriented. I don't want to know. I collude with a destructive system.

**Figure 7**

## The Five Light-Filled Currents of the Will

HEAD

Selflessness

HUMILITY

Humility before life recognition of interconnectedness. Anonymity and selfless service. I expect nothing in return.

RIGHT HAND

Redemption

INCLUSION

I choose to include and be included. I serve and give to others at my own expense. I value other's lives and needs. I promote increased global equality and unity.

LEFT HAND

Love

COURAGE

I choose to find the places inside myself that need to change. I share, having faith in plentitude. I have courage to love others in the face of any circumstances.

RIGHT FOOT

Facing the Truth

RESPONSIBILITY

I choose to protect and care for life. I concern myself with the good of all. I act and consume with conscience. I seek to understand how to live in harmony with others and Nature.

LEFT FOOT

Engagement

DISCERNMENT

I choose to consider the well-being of the planet and all life. I maintain or surrender my position for the benefit of others. My awareness leads to behavior change. I cherish all life.

## The Five Currents of the Will and the Five Wounds of Christ

The five currents of the will, as archetypes of human action, bear a correspondence with the five wounds of Christ. Christ was pierced by nails through each hand and each foot, and by a spear driven into His right side and through His heart by Longinus, a Roman soldier. From the spear wound poured a stream of water and a stream of blood, which flowed into the Earth. These five wounds of Christ symbolically prefigure the five currents of the future evolution of the human will, where each limb will be dedicated to the will of God (Anon, 1991, p. 110). The five wounds of Christ portray the immobilization of the subconscious forces of the will, allowing conscious light forces to stream into and activate the will. They represent the spiritualization of the human will as archetypes for humanity. Contemplation of the five wounds of Christ can reveal that each human being must immobilize these subconscious forces in order to purify the will.

Light-filled, divine forces worked through the limbs of Jesus of Nazareth, guiding His every action. The fact that He received the five wounds as a result of the subconscious will forces of His condemners—representatives of humanity—demonstrates the necessity for all human beings, as perpetrators of injustice and disharmony, to immobilize their subconscious forces and enable their divine nature to mature through conscious effort. We all bear the karma of the injustices in the world. The wounds of Christ symbolize the process that must eventually take place in every human being. Every human person must go through its own crucifixion of the will.

The fifth wound did not directly penetrate the head but rather pierced the heart from the thrust of the spear. Hence, the wound to the heart represents the piercing of egotism so that it will no longer influence our speech and action through the head. On His head Christ bore a crown of thorns, a crown of humility that pricks the conscience and unites it with the suffering of the world. In this way the crown of thorns augments the fifth wound in the heart.

In the fifth Arcanum of *Meditations on the Tarot*, the unknown author describes the pentagram of the Five Sacred Wounds of the stigmata as the future organs of the will (Anonymous, 1991, p. 111). These openings become available for the streaming out of divine love. The fifth wound, the piercing of Christ's side, grounded in the heart, interiorizes the alliance with God to the depths of one's being. It penetrates the blood and the holy water of our being. When human beings can dedicate their will, deeds, heart, blood, and the water of being to the divine will of the Universe, life becomes consecrated to God. This is the condition of those beings who have received the stigmata.

## Overcoming the Karmic Double

The redemption of the karmic double begins with the transformation of karmic thinking; this allows the possibility for spiritual imagination to unfold. Then it is possible to address the realm of karmic feeling. When the karmic double is robbed of its intelligence it will begin to follow the good, allowing spiritual inspiration to arise. Then the stage of spiritual intuition becomes possible as the karmic will is emptied of its own driving forces and receives, like a vessel, the grace of divine love as motivation for the will. The human will then unites with divine will.

The figure below recapitulates strategies to overcome karmic forces:

**Figure 8**

| The Transformation of the Karmic Double | |
|---|---|
| Thinking | Take personal responsibility for the circumstances of life.<br>Turn away from blame. Infuse thinking with "I" forces. |
| Feeling | Objectify the feeling life; seek the positive in all situations. |
| Willing | Self-restraint. Cultivate the five light-filled currents of the will. |

Karma unfolds through successive incarnations both as it concerns individual karma and the collective karma of humanity. Individual or personal karma has been introduced in this chapter. Collective or world karma borne by the Earth amalgamates all individual deeds perpetrated on Earth in which we all play a part as citizens of the world. When every person understands that "no man can live unto himself alone" (Rom. 14:7, ESV), that with every act and thought each of us either raises or drags down the hosts of which we are a part. Realization of the intimate ties binding us together can catalyze a sense of responsibility that will dignify life. Knowledge that human beings are one with all that exists, not merely united as members of a family, or a community, or as individuals of a nation, but like all the molecules of an organism, composing one spiritual unity, this knowledge can revolutionize the moral fiber of each soul and effect radical reform.

In studying the law of karma we can discern that rather than a law of cause and effect for the purpose of punishment or retribution, karma leads us to deeper self-knowledge, to self-responsibility, to compassion and forgiveness, and ultimately to selfless love for our fellow human beings. The law of karma ignites our will toward self-transformation.

A question that often arises for people seeking to understand the subtleties of karma concerns the appropriateness of interceding in another person's suffering. "If her suffering is a karmic condition, will I be interfering with her karma if I offer help?" Or some people think, "He deserves his suffering and must bear his karma." In response to this line of thought Rudolf Steiner stated clearly, "This is nonsense!" (Steiner, 1981, p. 76). This perspective overlooks the creative dimension of karma. The fact that we encounter a suffering person is now our own personal karma and presents us with the opportunity of bringing something positive into another's life. Helping someone creates the possibility of influencing the destiny of this person and helping him or her advance in his or her karmic journey. Having an understanding of this can activate loving deeds motivated by generosity of heart.

If we consider Christ as an archetype for demonstrating love for fellow human beings, we can see that He interceded in countless lives by healing the lame and blind, raising the dead, and forgiving the sins of repentant sinners. How did these acts of love affect the lives of those He touched? And what was the effect on their karma? What actually took place when Christ performed these deeds of healing? By examining the effects of Christ's karmic interventions it is possible to develop a template to understand personal selfless acts, if on a smaller scale.

## The Paradox Between Law and Grace

Rudolf Steiner stated that through Christ's work upon the Earth, the law of karma was replaced by the principle of grace, whereby it became possible for karmic debts (transgressions) to be forgiven. Rudolf Steiner described that at a certain point in the last two thousand years Christ became the "Lord of Karma."* According to Steiner, when a person crosses the threshold of death, upon entry to the spiritual world two beings in particular help the soul that is freed from the body review the completed life. With the help of these beings the formulation of karmic plans for the future begins. He spoke of a meeting that takes place between the soul of the deceased human being and a very special being who holds before this human soul the register of his or her past deeds. This great being who stands as a kind of record keeper of the karmic powers has appeared for many as the figure of Moses. According to Steiner this office is changing hands in the course of our age. Toward the end of the twentieth century and into the twenty-first century, human souls will ever more frequently encounter Christ as the mediator of karma instead of Moses (Steiner, 1991, p. 48). Steiner describes that when we pass through the gate of death, Christ, as Lord of Karma,

* Rudolf Steiner referred to Christ as "Lord of Karma" in three lectures in the fall of 1911: *From Jesus to Christ*, lectures 3 and 10; *Faith, Love, Hope*, lecture 1. In lecture 3 of *From Jesus to Christ*, given in Karlsruhe on October 7, Steiner spoke of the "Lord of Karma" for the first time: "A certain office in the Cosmos, connected with the evolution of humanity in the twentieth century, passes over in a heightened form to the Christ. Christ becomes the Lord of Karma for human evolution. This event is connected with the whole future evolution of humanity. And whereas Christianity and Christian evolution were hitherto a kind of preparation, we now have the significant fact that Christ becomes the Lord of Karma, so that in the future it will rest with Him to decide what our karmic account is, how our credit and debit in life are related."

is now the adjudicator who presents us with our karmic record and serves as counselor to balance the transgressions committed in the past. With the participation of the spiritual hierarchies, the necessary karmic circumstances for future incarnations are designed to create the opportunity to make restitution.

Rudolf Steiner was acutely aware of the seeming paradox between *law* and *grace*, as demonstrated in his descriptions of the different functions of Moses and Christ during the judgment of souls at the gate of death. Steiner saw the revelation of moral judgment and the process of the dispensation of grace as parallel expressions of the same moral being of the world.

According to his own statements Jesus does not oppose the laws of Moses. In the Sermon on the Mount, Jesus tells the crowds:

> Think not that I have come to abolish the law and the prophets; I have come not to abolish them but to fulfill them. For truly, I say to you, till heaven and earth pass away, not an iota, not a dot, will pass from the law until all is accomplished (Matt. 5:17–18, KJV).

Here Jesus affirms his alignment with Moses. Also at the Transfiguration on Mt. Tabor—when Jesus revealed His radiant, Sun-like nature to Peter, John, and James—Moses, the giver of the law, appeared in the light at the right-hand side of the Transfigured Christ. Moses stood beside the Christ to affirm that they work in tandem with one another.

The apparent contradictions in their approach to the law and grace can be understood when we grasp the spiritual realities that are not easily apparent to modern scholarship. Moses upholding the law of karma addresses the subjective, individual karma of humanity, which, according to Jesus will be fulfilled to the last iota. The dispensation of grace through Christ works into the objective, world karma that is borne by the Earth. Individuals can be blessed with the gift of grace through the principle of forgiveness. The following section on individual karma and world karma, and chapter 5, addressing karma and forgiveness, will shed greater light onto the complexities of the interweaving of the law of karma and the principle of grace.

## Individual Karma and World Karma

It is important at this point to understand that transgressions needing karmic adjustment exist on two planes. They not only occur on a personal level that must be compensated through our karma in the future, but also live as objective cosmic facts in the Universe, harbored in the Earth (Steiner, 1972, p. 48). On a personal level we make reparation for our misdeeds at a later time; the debt that we have personally contracted will be adjusted by our karma. But we cannot efface the misdeeds from the cosmic plane by balancing our own transgressions. We must discriminate between the consequences of our misdeeds for ourselves, and the consequences of our misdeeds for the objective course of the world.

The collective karma of humanity that exists on the cosmic plane imposes a consequence to the Earth. Steiner perceived the Earth as a living being. He stated that: "When something immoral is done anywhere on Earth it amounts to the same thing for the whole Earth organism as a little festering boil on the human body, which makes the whole organism sick" (Steiner, 1981, p. 4). The whole organism of the Earth suffers from everything immoral, and as individuals every immoral act we commit affects the whole Earth.

To grasp the significance of this cosmic reality we must realize that the Earth cannot continue to progress in its evolutionary path under accumulating weight of humanity's collective negative karma. Consider the far distant future when every human being will have completed their earthly incarnations, all karma will have been resolved to the last iota. Rudolf Steiner indicates that even though human souls will have had to balance their individual karma, the collective guilt of humanity's misdeeds will continue to live on the cosmic plane, working in the Earth. Therefore, at the end of the Earth stage of evolution, even though human beings would have balanced their karma, the Earth would not be ready to develop into a future stage of evolution because of the burden of the unredeemed collective misdeeds of human beings; humanity would be without a dwelling place.

Yet, as human beings strive to balance their individual karma, Christ works to transmute the collective karma of humanity borne within the

Earth. Were it not for Christ bearing the *sins of the world,*[*] all the transgressions that otherwise would have amassed would cast the Earth into darkness, and there would not be a planet for humanity's further evolution. Through our personal karma we can make restitution for ourselves, but not for the Earth evolution connected with the whole of humanity. Through Christ's healing work for humanity, our personal karma will not be redeemed for us, but through what occurred during the Mystery of Golgotha[**] it has become possible that our debts can be wiped out from the cosmic level of Earth evolution.

Rudolf Steiner explained that Christ may efface the karmic debts that live on the cosmic plane for human beings who inwardly have an alliance to the cosmic mission of love. Divine love must be active in the souls and deeds of those whose misdeeds are blotted out from our external world by Christ. Christ's transmutation of world karma never encroaches upon personal karma (Steiner, 1972, p. 49).

Christ united His destiny with the destiny of the Earth at the time of His sacrifice on Golgotha. Rudolf Steiner stated:

> Since then the Christ has become the Spirit of the Earth, the Planetary Spirit. The Earth is the body of the Christ; he has His dwelling place in the interior of the Earth (Steiner, 1988, p. 113).

This indicates that all the nourishment that we receive from the Earth is of Christ's body. The grain that is harvested, the sap that flows in the plants, the fruits that hang from the trees and vines, are all expressions of Christ's body.

---

* The next day John saw Jesus coming to him and said, "Behold, the Lamb of God who takes away the sin of the world! (John 1:29, ESV).

** The physical event that took place at the moment of the Crucifixion when the Christ's blood flowed onto the Earth on the hill of Golgotha is the physical expression of a spiritual event that, according to Rudolf Steiner, stands at the central point of all earthly happenings. Through this great event, the force of the Logos (The Word, as embodying the divine will, the idea of God, who is in His own nature hidden, revealing Himself in creation), which formerly radiated down upon Earth from the Sun, was taken up into the Earth's spiritual being. Since that event on Golgotha, the Logos itself has become the spirit of the Earth.

When at the Last Supper Christ gave bread to His disciples and spoke the words, "This is My body," and offered them wine, saying, "This is My blood," He revealed that the Earth and all it bears is His body. If one recognizes this as a reality, the whole of the Earth planet becomes sanctified. We begin to see that through the events of the Last Supper Christ brought to consciousness His covenant with the Earth and humanity.

Christ revealed His underlying unity with humanity when He said:

> "For I was hungry and you gave Me food; I was thirsty and you gave Me drink; I was a stranger and you took Me in; I was naked and you clothed Me; I was sick and you visited Me; I was in prison and you came to Me." Then the righteous will answer Him, saying, "Lord, when did we see You hungry and feed You, or thirsty and give You drink? When did we see You a stranger and take You in, or naked and clothe You? Or when did we see You sick, or in prison, and come to You?" And the King will answer and say to them, "Assuredly, I say to you, inasmuch as you did it to one of the least of these My brethren, you did it to Me" (Matt. 25:35–40, ESV).

The events encompassing the final week of Jesus Christ's life demonstrate the magnitude of His alliance with humanity and the cosmic unfolding of Earth evolution. In the sacred acts of the Last Supper, Christ gave His body and blood to His disciples as representatives of humanity. The following day on Golgotha, Christ gave his body and blood to Earth, sanctifying his covenant of unity with the karma of Earth, consecrating His work to transmute the cosmic level of human karma borne within Earth. The results of this covenant have given to the Earth the force to carry forward its evolution (Steiner, 1972, p. 56).

Christ came to Earth as a harbinger of love, to teach humanity about the centrality of love in human existence and demonstrate how human beings can cultivate our Christ-like nature, as in the words of St. Paul, "Not I, but the Christ in me!"* to awaken the divine nature within the human ego.

* "I am crucified with Christ: nevertheless I live; yet not I, but Christ liveth in me" (Gal. 2:20).

# CHAPTER 5

# Karma and Forgiveness: Holding the Universe Together

> Forgiveness breaks the chain of causality because he who forgives you—out of love—takes upon himself the consequences of what you have done. Forgiveness, therefore, always entails a sacrifice.
>
> —Dag Hammarskjöld*

Humanity is crowned with the mission to learn to love to its highest degree. The seed of love has been planted into the innermost depth of each human being (Steiner, 1979, p. 364). Crowning confers the power of the Divine over consciousness in sublimation of the lower self. Through individual self-development (the overcoming of our threefold double), selflessness grows, fostering the capacity to bring love to the world. The task confronting each human being at this time is to learn through selflessness, forgiveness, and compassionate wisdom, to don the crown of cosmic love.

As discussed in chapter 4, the law of karma leads to deeper self-knowledge, self-responsibility, compassion, forgiveness, and ultimately to selfless love. The five dark and light currents of the will present a picture of the

* Hammarskjöld, 1964, p. 197. Dag Hammarskjöld (1905–1961), a Swedish diplomat, economist, and author, was the second Secretary-General of the United Nations, serving from April 1953 until his mysterious death in September 1961. He was awarded the Nobel Prize posthumously.

transformative work necessary to actualize our capacity to love. The five wounds of Christ correlate to the five currents of the will creating an intuitive understanding that each individual must undergo a crucifixion of the will to become an agent of love. The dynamics of karmic thinking, feeling, and willing, and deeper complexities of karma—including the cosmic reality of individual and world karma—have laid the groundwork for the examination of the role of forgiveness in human relationships.

This chapter centralizes forgiveness as the primary virtue and guiding principle needed for our time. Forgiveness has the potential to be of immeasurable significance for human evolution. It is among the most pressing spiritual issues of our time as well as a seminal method of furthering spiritual evolution. Due to its potential to transmute karma, forgiveness plays a unique role in human relations. The metaphysics of love and forgiveness, discussed near the end of this chapter, sheds light on the process of inner transformation required to overcome the egoistic impulses that hinder our capacity for compassion, forgiveness, and love.

## Forgiveness and the Law of Karma

The question arises as to how forgiveness interfaces with the law of karma. To answer this question necessitates an inquiry as to who has the power to forgive or cancel a debt, whether moral, spiritual, or material debt. Generally only a creditor, a promisee, or a member of a social covenant has the power to do this, as they have incurred some suffering or damage from another. The objective karma (discussed in chapter 4) resulting from every human misdeed becomes a debt to all humanity that the perpetrator is unable to repay, erase, or redeem through karmic restitution. When Christ took upon Himself the karma of the Earth through His sacrifice on Golgotha, He became a surrogate for humanity to the claims resulting from human misdeeds. In Steiner's words, "Christ is the only forgiver of sins because he is the bearer of sins" (Steiner, 1972, p. 74). Therefore, Christ alone has the ability to require recompense or to forgive the objective karma borne by the Earth.

While Christ assumes all the objective karma of those who have aligned themselves with the Earth's mission of love, He has not made reparation for all the subjective consequences of those same misdeeds. The only one who can absolve these deeds are the individuals who were injured. That absolution, i.e., release of debt, can be given by the injured individuals either through their generosity in the present life or when incarnated in a later one. But Christ has transformed the unredeemable consequences of human misdeeds on the objective plane so that in the distant future a healthy balance will be restored to the Earth. For this to occur a certain consciousness is necessary—a consciousness of our individual guilt, and a consciousness that objectively Christ has the power to take these deeds upon Him and forgive them. The expression, "Thy sins are forgiven," therefore denotes a cosmic fact and not a karmic fact.

Human acts of forgiveness have the power to transform individual karma. Forgoing the inclination for revenge and renouncing the recompense that is due initiates far-reaching spiritual consequences. Sacrifice of self-interest through forgiveness liberates boundless forces of spiritual beings from the necessity of creating new future situations on Earth for the compensation of past karma, and allows others to receive needed help by means of these liberated forces. These spiritual forces are freed to work in completely new forms or structures to promote evolutionary impulses.

Forgiveness functions on the level of personal karma mirroring Christ's forgiveness of the objective karma of humanity, transmuting human transgressions. As a result of every act of true forgiveness, a liberated space, no longer filled with karmic substance, opens, into which Christ can enter and work, and to which the luciferic and ahrimanic powers have no access. A new field of grace emerges under the guidance of Christ as the Lord of Karma.

A central teaching of Hinduism advocates that one atone for one's wrongdoing (*Prayaschitta*: penance in Sanskrit), and ask for forgiveness. *Prayaschitta* expresses an aspect of the law of karma, restoring balance in the here and now, preempting the need for future karmic reconciliation. In the *Mahābhārata*, Vidura addresses Dhritarashtra saying:

> Forgiveness is a great power. Forgiveness subdues [all] in this world; what is there that forgiveness cannot achieve? What can a wicked person do unto him who carries the saber of forgiveness in his hand? (*The Mahābhārata*, 2009, Book 5: Udyoga Parva, Section 33).

Here Vidura describes the power of forgiveness as unconquerable. Similarly, in the *Bhagavad Gita* Krishna teaches that forgiveness is a characteristic of one born to realize a divine state (*Bhagavad Gita*, chapter 16, verse 3). These qualities of forgiveness create a platform for the further exploration of this human capacity.

The *Mahābhārata* teaches that one should forgive every injury regardless of the surrounding conditions. It holds that the continued survival of our species depends upon the attainment of human forgiveness. Those who conquer their wrath and show forgiveness when insulted, oppressed, and angered by those in positions of power, perform sacrifices for the furtherance of human evolution and survival. The illustrious Holy Rishi, Kashyapa,* sung the following verses in honor of those who are forgiving.

> Forgiveness is virtue; forgiveness is sacrifice, forgiveness is the Vedas, forgiveness is the Sruti.** He that knows this is capable of forgiving everything. Forgiveness is Brahma; forgiveness is truth; forgiveness is stored ascetic merit; forgiveness protects the ascetic merit of the future;

---

* Kashyapa was an ancient Indian sage. In the two lectures, *Spiritual Bells of Easter*, Rudolf Steiner speaks of two Kashyapas from the spiritual tradition of India, both of whom are relevant to the background and significance of the passage quoted here. The first Kashyapa, revered in the Hindu tradition, was one of the seven Holy Rishis who revealed the primal wisdom in the ancient Indian culture. This is the Kashyapa credited with authoring the above text. The second, honored in the Buddhist tradition, was one of Kashyapa's later incarnations in India as a disciple of Gautama Buddha in the fifth century BC, when he bore this name again. He was the disciple to whom the Buddha gave his gold brocade mantle, designating him as the Buddha's successor—the one who will become the next Buddha, the Maitreya Buddha. The text quoted here represents the wisdom of the Holy Rishis, which re-emerged in the time of Gautama Buddha, and bears great significance for our future as we prepare for the incarnation of the Maitreya Buddha.

** Sruti is the body of sacred texts comprising the central canon of Hinduism and is one of the three main sources of dharma.

> forgiveness is asceticism; forgiveness is holiness; and by forgiveness is it that the universe is held together. Forgiveness is the might of the mighty; forgiveness is quiet of mind. The man of wisdom should ever forgive, for when he is capable of forgiving everything, he attains to Brahma. Those men who ever conquer their wrath by forgiveness, obtain the higher regions.... Therefore has it been said that forgiveness is the highest virtue (*The Mahābhārata*, 2009, Book 3: Vana Parva, Section 29).

Kashyapa proclaims a multitude of attributes and empowerments of forgiveness. Among these he states that: "by forgiveness is it that the universe is held together." This and other claims that he makes indicate the imperative necessity of penetrating the depths of this virtue and the means of its attainment.

Forgiveness creates a means of experiencing divine love. True forgiveness refuses to harbor resentment, nourish a grudge, nor foster hatred. Forgiveness also cleanses one's heart of these harmful impulses. By definition, common English language understands forgiveness as the action of granting someone else, who is guilty of committing a wrong, a release from all further punishment. The aggrieved party graciously absolves the offender, releasing him or her from all obligations to provide recompense or to suffer any further punishment or karmic restitution for past misdeeds. Forgiveness, therefore, is an action, the deed of releasing another of his or her deserved punishments and obligations.

Forgiveness is not an emotion or a feeling, although many emotions are experienced in the wake of an offense and the process of coming to the choice of forgiveness or not. The common belief that forgiveness occurs when an offended person reaches a state of inner peace in relation to the wrongdoer neglects the equally important factor of the inner condition of the offender. True forgiveness addresses the healing of both the aggrieved party and the offender. It is a deed of selfless charity to grant full absolution to one who transgressed, to surrender one's rights to be compensated or be given reparations, or to seek rightful punishment.

In the biblical languages of Hebrew, Greek, and Aramaic the words translated as *forgiveness* match the contemporary understanding set forth above. In Hebrew the dominant word translated as *forgiveness* in the Old

Testament is *nasa/nasah*. It means *to lift*, as in *to lift someone's punishment from off of him* (Strong's Hebrew Lexicon). Similarly, in the New Testament the most often used Greek word translated as *forgive* is *aphiemi*. It means *to send away*, as if to say, *to send away someone's punishment* (Strong's Greek Lexicon). In Aramaic *forgive* is translated as *shbag*, which literally means *to cancel* (Ryce, 2013). This definition indicates that forgiveness constitutes an act of removing mental inclinations that generate inner realities based in hostility or fear, which compromise our ability to perceive objectively, with self-awareness and compassion.

One who is forgiven in the Bible is released from one's duly "earned" punishments or obligations of restitution. The first instance of the word *forgive* (*nasa/nasah:* to send away a person's punishment) is found in Genesis 50:17. Joseph's circumstances, as described in Genesis, illustrate a sequence of steps that identify stages of awareness in the process of forgiveness. After a transgression is committed against another person or against God, an admission of guilt (or confession) indicates self-awareness and remorse. An expression of remorse or sincere apology demonstrates contrition. A promise to never repeat the offense indicates a resolve to moral integrity that begins a process of rebuilding trust. When someone asks for forgiveness (requests release from punishment), a sense of humility rises up in the perpetrator. When the offended party grants forgiveness, a healing or reconciliation occurs. Expressing good will, care, or love to the offended party furthers the process to reestablish the relationship. It demonstrates moral integrity to make restitution for any damages that are repairable. It is the prerogative of the offended party to accept restitution or pardon the offender of any need for recompense.

Joseph's brothers begged him to forgive them and to not bear a grudge against them. They asked that he not require that they pay him back in full for all the wrong that they had done (Gen. 50:15–17). His brothers were guilty of doing him wrong, they acknowledged their guilt, and they knew they had never been fully punished (made recompense) for the hurtful actions they performed. They wanted Joseph to forgive this moral debt entirely, to take no further punitive actions, and to release them from the just penalty that they deserved. Joseph took the action of absolving them, agreeing to impose no further punishment.

The original Aramaic language of the gospels reveals deeper insights into the correlation between forgiveness and divine will. The term *koodsha* (the ancestor to the Hebrew word *kosher*, defined as *proper* in the five books of Moses) means "proper as determined by and in harmony with the Laws of Oneness for humanity, that which is divinely intended for humanity" (Ryce, 2013). *Koodsha* also represents an innate and undetectable, yet real force that can be transferred from one human being to another when the human will is aligned with the will of God.

The Hebrew word *ruach*, meaning *wind* or *breath*, is also translated as *Holy Spirit* or simply *spirit*. In the original Aramaic the word is *rookha*, generally meaning *force*, including *spirit*, *energy*, *wind*, *electricity*, etc. (Ryce, 2013). When the two terms *rookha* and *koodsha* combine, they represent one of the most sacred core concepts of archaic Hebrew psychology. *Rookha d'koodsha* literally means: "force for that which is divinely intended for humans: or Holy Spirit" (Ryce, 2013). *Rookha d'koodsha* functions as the transmitter and communicator of God's laws for humanity. At the Annunciation, the Angel Gabriel announced to Mary the "*ruksha d'koodsha* shall come upon thee, and the power of the Highest shall overshadow thee" (Luke 1:35). *Rukha d'koodsha* descended in the form of a dove following Jesus's baptism (Matt. 3:16). Following the Resurrection, Jesus told his apostles to "Receive *rukha d'koodsha*" (John 20:22). Jesus spoke of the denial of *rukha d'koodsha* as the *unforgivable sin* (Matt. 12:31–32).

> Therefore I say to you, any sin and blasphemy shall be forgiven people, but blasphemy against the Spirit shall not be forgiven. Whoever speaks a word against the Son of Man, it shall be forgiven him; but whoever speaks against the Holy Spirit, it shall not be forgiven him, either in this age or in the age to come (Matt. 12:31–32, ESV).

According to the English translation from the Greek, this passage indicates that there is a sin that is unforgiveable. Given that all karma can eventually be redeemed, this presents an apparent contradiction or questionable translation. According to Dr. Michael Ryce,* *rookha d'koodsha* is an elemental force in humans that severs the effect of errors and teaches us truth—"a force that is proper for humans, the denial of which leaves us in un-forgiveness" (Ryce, 2013).

This Aramaic interpretation specifies that to deny the Holy Spirit (*rookha d'koodsha*) keeps us in unforgiveness, where the Greek translation informs us that the denial of the Holy Spirit is the *unforgivable sin!* The Aramaic formulation indicates that we have chosen an orientation that denies the Holy Spirit and this orientation binds us in a state of inability to forgive or be forgiven. At any time we can choose to receive the Holy Spirit, at which time we are released from this state, and are able to forgive and be forgiven. The Greek formulation suggests that there is a finality that cannot be rectified, a misdeed that will never be redeemed. This contradicts the universal law of karma, which guides humanity to transform self-centered deeds to deeds inspired by selfless love.**

The following questions arise when considering the intricacies of guilt, repentance, karma, and forgiveness. In the presence of *rookha d'koodsha*, is it essential that a guilty person confesses or acknowledges guilt/culpability in order to receive forgiveness and be released from the requisite punishment? Can forgiveness atone for misdeeds in the absence of true repentance? Does the karma for that unconfessed deed remain in force against the offender or does it transfer to the forgiver? If the offender's punishment remains, then how can it be true that anyone is forgiven unless they confess?

## Seeking Forgiveness

Preparing to request to be forgiven entails a sequence of steps that are only possible if the double is in check. Seeking forgiveness requires overcoming the egotism that seeks to justify, blame, or focus on the shortcomings of the other. Acknowledgement of guilt requires a level of honesty and transparency

* Dr. Michael Ryce is a Naturopathic physician with doctorates in Naturopathic Medicine and Holistic Philosophy. His work combines body-mind principles, physics, and ancient Aramaic studies.

** This is not intended to be a comprehensive linguistic analysis.

that is foundational for the process of inner growth. When we experience the interior disposition of contrition that enables us to admit our transgressions, we actively participate in creating the transformative power of forgiveness and become not merely recipients of forgiveness, but co-participants in the unfolding process. Seeking forgiveness activates a tender and subtle negotiation between forgiver and the one forgiven. A request for forgiveness initiates a release; the forgiver is given a chance to free the offender from guilt and remorse, which in turn releases the forgiver from the bondage of not being asked to forgive. Through honesty, self-awareness, humility, and selfless love, the process of forgiveness dissolves an intricate, entangled web comprised of many ancient causal strands.

To restore wholeness after confessing one's guilt for having committed a transgression and asking for forgiveness involves freely making financial or other restitution when needed. Acknowledgment of guilt without restitution is incomplete, and implies insincerity.

## Bestowing Forgiveness

Most spiritual traditions recognize the essential need for forgiveness, precisely because it is so difficult to achieve (Bishop, n.d.). The double recoils at the prospect of forgiveness. When facing the opportunity to forgive or be forgiven, the inner process requires overcoming the stealthy deceptions of the ninefold double.

Forgiveness requires subtle discrimination, a precise understanding of one's material, and a light touch that strikes the balance between deficiency and excess. There are times when forgiveness does not seem possible, when the pain felt exceeds the capacity to let it go, and our visceral impulses are all striving towards fury. This does not always happen in proportion to the offense. Sometimes we find that a powerful blow glances easily off our backs, while some small and all but unnoticeable grievance nags at us without cease. The emotions have their reasons, which the conscious mind does not always see, and these reasons have to be respected, at least up to a point. Forgiveness often requires steering a narrow course between nursing a grudge and pretending we have pardoned someone when we have done nothing of the kind. The chief tool needed is a rigorous inner sincerity, since the grossest forms of hypocrisy are those we practice in front of ourselves.

A practical approach toward forgiveness may involve fostering a small willingness to forgive while anger and rage burn themselves for weeks or months. It may require drawing a line with someone, refusing to take further abuse while refraining from any hatred in response to it. Frequently it necessitates an inner detachment, a freedom from emotional dependence on others. Sometimes it entails looking at the situation from the other people's perspective (*tout comprendre, c'est tout pardonner:* to understand all is to forgive all). Forgiveness takes forms as diverse and unpredictable as human beings themselves. For some, generous and munificent, it comes naturally and spontaneously, while others may find that it has to be cultivated with effort in the hard soil of their natures. It is wise to be honest with ourselves about such things, and also wise to remember that forgiveness is to be bestowed inwardly as well as outwardly; the ability to grant mercy to ourselves often makes it easier to extend this kindness to others.

## Forgiveness as a Gift of Grace

There are times when transgressions can be forgiven without any acknowledgment of culpability from the offender or without being asked for forgiveness. Release from corrective measures without acknowledgement of guilt or requesting forgiveness is a gift of grace to the perpetrator of a transgression. In such matters, especially when the relationship is otherwise unharmed, one may choose to inwardly discharge the incident, forgive the person in one's heart and never seek punishment or restitution. True forgiveness in this kind of situation necessitates never again mentioning the matter and going into the future with compassion and restoration of the former relationship.

There are times when an offender does not acknowledge guilt or awareness of any transgression and the injured party does not feel safe in relation to the offender. In cases like this a sense of distrust often lives in the soul of the injured party. Lack of self-awareness, dishonesty, or differing values on the part of the offender undermines trust. In situations like this the injured party is free (to the degree the emotions allow) to choose how to go forward.

In some cases the act of releasing an assailant of all responsibility for a transgression places others in danger of repeated offenses. In such cases the most far-sighted loving approach calls for judicial intervention for the protection of the larger community. In the Buddhist short story, "The Compassionate Ape" (McGinnis, 2004), the main character demonstrates a benevolent, yet self-protective response to a violent assault (attempted murder) by a man who the ape had just rescued from sure death. The ape continued to show kindness to the man and guided him to the path to his home. The ape said:

> "Come, I will take you to the edge of the mountain and show you the path to your village, but you walk in front of me, as you are not to be trusted in the least." His parting words were, "I have more compassion for you now than I did when you were at the bottom of that pit. Your evil deed will return on you multifold, for goodness returns goodness and wickedness returns wickedness" (McGinnis, 2004, p. 107).

The compassionate ape did not let the man's attempt to kill him affect his value of kindness, nor alter his proclivity to help the man find his way home. He did, however, establish a boundary of safety, honoring his own self-worth and dignity. A measure of forgiveness is implicit here, in that the ape directed his concern for the man's future consequences and did not bear animosity. The ape upheld his integrity while engaging the wisdom to protect himself.

Archbishop Desmond Tutu faced the challenge of healing a nation when President Nelson Mandela named him Chairman of the Truth and Reconciliation Commission at the dissolution of apartheid. The establishment of South Africa's Truth and Reconciliation Commission pioneered an unprecedented transformation from despotism to democracy by exposing the atrocities committed in the past and achieving reconciliation with its former oppressors. In his book, *No Future Without Forgiveness,* Tutu brings the essential act of forgiveness to the fore, offering his reflections on the profound wisdom he gained through this painful experience.

One aspect of restorative justice developed in his manuscript addresses a central theme of the African weltanschauung known in the Nguni group of languages as *ubuntu. Ubuntu* literally means "human-ness," and is often translated as *humanity towards others*. When used in a more philosophical sense it indicates the belief in a universal bond of sharing that connects all humanity. "A person is a person through other people. We are bound up in a delicate network of interdependence" (Tutu, 1999, p. 31). This ideal suggests that humanity is not embedded in my person solely as an individual; my humanity is co-substantively bestowed upon the other and me. "To forgive is not just to be altruistic. It is the best form of self-interest. What dehumanizes you inexorably dehumanizes me" (Tutu, 1999, p. 31). Failure to forgive corrodes the "summum bonum, that greatest good, communal harmony that enhances the humanity and personhood of all in the community" (p. 35). Tutu ultimately concludes that failure to forgive constitutes metaphysical suicide.

To forgive in the face of long-standing social injustice and horrific personal tragedy requires spiritual presence. For genuine forgiveness occurs when the injured person can look the offender in the eyes and with honesty state, "I hereby extend God's mercy to you and waive any further punishment you rightly deserve and eliminate any further restitution or reparations you may owe to me. Your debt is entirely and fully gone. You are free of any further liability in this matter." The offender is pardoned.

On the cross Jesus Christ uttered an immortal plea on behalf of humanity: "Father, forgive them, for they know not what they do." This example of supreme forgiveness demonstrated Jesus Christ's sense of oneness with humanity that enabled Him to make such a universal entreaty. He empathized with the limited human perspective and at the same time did not want those living in ignorance (the Roman soldiers and the whole of humanity) to remain bound. Not only did He plea for God's mercy for humanity, but an equally important subtext implies that He aspired for humanity to transcend ignorance and comprehend world existence with knowledge of the law of karma and the wisdom to live by the commandment of love.

As humanity struggles to develop the capacity to forgive inner and outer misdeeds, the spiritual world longs for human consciousness to increase and receptivity and oneness with the Divine to grow. True forgiveness not only pardons adverse actions, it sparks an awakening of consciousness within both the forgiven and the forgiver. Ignorance becomes not just temporarily absolved but transformed. Forgiveness engenders illumination and initiates a process of purification that transpires in relation to one another. Forgiveness also leads to transcendence and responsibility. Transcendence denotes moving beyond the moment of hurt, fear, trauma, anger, judgment, and criticism to a condition of inner harmony and love. It requires personal strength and the ability to initiate action from love.

Furthermore, the ability to forgive others for their misdeeds influences our worthiness to receive forgiveness for misdeeds. In the parable of the unforgiving servant, Jesus spoke of a slave who owed his master ten thousand talents (an exorbitant sum of money). The servant could not pay and begged for patience and promised he would pay. The master had compassion and forgave him the debt. The slave then turned to a fellow slave who owed him a hundred denarii (a small amount), demanded payment, and when payment was not forthcoming, cast him into debtors' prison. The master heard of this and thus had the first slave cast into debtors' prison as well, saying,

> I forgave you your debt because you pleaded with me. Should you not also have had mercy on your fellow slave, in the same way that I had mercy on you? My heavenly Father will also do the same to you, if each of you does not forgive his brother from your heart (Matt. 18:23–35, ESV).

The law of karma is inexorably linked with that of forgiveness. Jesus clearly indicated this when He said: "For if you forgive others their trespasses, your heavenly Father will also forgive you. But if you do not forgive others their trespasses, neither will your Father forgive your trespasses" (Matt. 6:14–15, ESV). The forgiven life is the forgiving life. Human forgiveness reflects our experience and understanding of divine forgiveness.

This parable comes in response to Peter's inquiry about repeated offenses and repeated requests for forgiveness.

> Then Peter came and said to Him, "Lord, how often shall my brother sin against me and I forgive him? Up to seven times?" Jesus said to him, "I do not say to you, up to seven times, but up to seventy times seven" (Matt. 18:21–22, ESV).

Peter, in his guess of "up to seven times," was still thinking in the limited terms of the law, rather than in the unlimited terms of grace. By saying we are to forgive those who sin against us seventy times seven, Jesus was not limiting forgiveness to 490 times—a number that is, for all practical purposes, beyond counting—but rather asserting that there is no quantifiable limit to forgiveness. It is not to be meted out in a measured fashion, but is to be measureless.

## Receiving the Gift of Forgiveness

Most discussions on the topic of forgiveness focus on the positive effects for the offended party who, after releasing the negativity harbored in the soul, finds inner peace. This excludes the effect of forgiveness in the soul life of those who have transgressed and been forgiven. Yet this is half the equation, and equally important.

Relevant to this discussion is a personal experience of being forgiven that has profoundly affected my life. It does not involve a personal offense against another person, and therefore the resulting effects are no doubt less dramatic, but nevertheless the transformative experience of being forgiven has given me great pause to reflect on the fundamental (primary) necessity for and magnitude of power contained within the act of forgiveness. Here is the account in brief.

At the outset of an hour-long drive to teach a class, a police officer pulled me over for speeding. I was so shocked when he came to speak to me that I could hardly respond to his questions. He thought I was being rude and said sternly, "Did you hear me?" I felt such a deep sense of fear, guilt, and contrition, for I knew I had been speeding.

While performing his law enforcement checks, he noticed my bumper sticker—*Blessed are the Peacemakers.* Upon his return he asked me if I knew the source of the words on my bumper sticker. I said, "Yes, they are the seventh beatitude from the Sermon on the Mount." He responded, "Yes, Matthew 5:1–12." I paused and then told him that I teach a course on the Beatitudes of Christ.

I eventually managed to eek out the question, "Is it possible to receive a warning?" He said he would have to see if it would be possible. After some time checking police files in his computer he came back and said to me, "It is possible to receive a warning. Drive safely and within the speed limit. God bless you." I said, "Thank you," as tears welled up in my eyes. There was a numinous presence that touched me to the core of my being. I drove off to my class as an unidentified spiritual reality was being seeded in me.

I had no idea at the time how deeply I was affected by this experience. The officer's forgiveness of my offense against the law began to work on me. Firstly, out of respect and gratitude to the officer for his pardon, I wanted to honor his injunction: "Drive safely and within the speed limit." In reflection, his words resembled the situation when the adulteress was brought before Christ, when at the conclusion He said to her, "Neither do I condemn you; go, and from now on sin no more"* (John 8:11, ESV). Like the adulteress, I was left with my inner reflections. Rather than focusing on punishment, my thoughts were free to focus on changing my life.

---

* A woman caught in the act of adultery was brought to Jesus by scribes and Pharisees who said to Him: "Master, this woman was caught in adultery in the very act. Now Moses in the law commanded us that such women should be stoned; what do you say?" They said this to test Him, so that they might have grounds for accusing Him. But Jesus stooped down and with His finger wrote on the ground. So when they continued asking Him, He lifted Himself up and said to them, "Let him who is without sin among you be the first to cast a stone at her." And again He stooped down and wrote on the ground. But when they heard this, being convicted by their own conscience, they went out one by one, beginning at the eldest even unto the last: and Jesus was left alone with the woman standing before him. Jesus stood up and said to her, "Woman, where are your accusers? Has no one condemned you?" She said, "No one, Lord." And Jesus said, "Neither do I condemn you; go, and from now on sin no more" (John 8:4–11, ESV). Jesus did not respond to the accusations of the scribes and Pharisees, but silently drew a symbol upon the Earth that conveyed to the accusers that the events that have taken place are inscribed within the Earth as part of the record of the cosmic karma of humanity. When He then responded with the injunction "let he who is without sin cast the first stone," He activated the consciences of the accusers, indicating that all of their misdeeds are also inscribed in the Earth. When they withdrew in shame, He turned the woman's thoughts away from all ideas of outer judgment and pointed her to reflect inwardly upon her deeds. Rather than focusing on punishment, Jesus turned her thoughts to changing her life.

Secondly, the tension in me that drove me to speed, for fear I would be late, began to dissolve. Something changed in my physiology, in my nervous system, that released a lifelong habit of tension. A peace has come over me when I am driving. My whole driving style has changed; I no longer feel the pressure and need to speed when driving. If I am concerned about being late, I think of the officer and remember his kindness to me. He did not have to pardon me. He chose to do it as a free deed. I felt Christ's weaving in that instance and His presence and the powerful mechanism of forgiveness continues to work in me.

Thirdly, this simple event catalyzed a deep inquiry into the ramifications of the act of forgiveness, the results of which are contained here. I know now from personal experience that forgiveness has the power to catalyze transformation. It redirects the experience of guilt from the jaws of punishment (a form of retribution) to the creative forces of transformation. A spiritual stimulus unleashes a new frequency of awareness that begins to work within the human soul. When touched by this power of divine love, the transformative effect penetrates to the depths of one's being. I am not suggesting that the illness or offense will not recur (it may or may not depending on multiple factors), but rather that the impact of the healing power of love will remain as a strengthening force, and allegiance to Christ's teaching that *we must forgive seventy times seven times* will carry over from incarnation to incarnation.

I have often thought about what might have happened if the officer had given me a ticket—punished me—for speeding. I believe I would have felt anger, concern about money, resentment, projected all kinds of thoughts about the situation, and continued to feel the tension in my body about being late. He would have given a mechanical response that would likely have engendered fear when driving, and probably a feeling of bitterness about law enforcement. Whereas, the officer touched me with an act of grace that powerfully changed my life. I have gleaned from this experience that we have the power to be each other's redeemers.

An interesting point to consider is that the officer has no idea that any of this has happened to me. He left me in Christ's hands. And I do not know what affect his deed had on him. This is part of the great mystery of how we touch one another's lives and leave the fruits to God.

The experience of being forgiven lifts us to a new dimension of life, to a higher, more subtle frequency of consciousness where we experience a veiled encounter with the Lord of Karma. His potent love assists us beyond measure in our climb up the steep side of life's mountain where karma can be balanced with much greater awareness and alacrity. The experience of being forgiven leads to cognition of the reality that in bestowing forgiveness upon another an agency of divine magic occurs, the science of love.

## The Metaphysics of Love and Forgiveness

Comprehension of the metaphysics of love and forgiveness requires an awareness of a collaborative effort between human beings and the activity of spiritual beings that actively engage in the evolution of life on the Earth. George Ritchie's* book, *Return from Tomorrow*, offers an extraordinary example of this elusive reality. In May 1945 a holocaust survivor, referred to by the pseudonym Bill Cody, related to Ritchie a seminal event in his life that demonstrates the potential power of forgiveness. Bill recounted the moment in 1939 when the Germans entered his neighborhood in the Jewish section of Warsaw where he lived with his wife and five children. When they reached his street they lined everyone against a wall except Bill and opened fire with machine guns. Bill begged to be allowed to die with his family, but because he spoke German they put him in a work group. He recounts thinking he had to decide right then whether to let himself hate the soldiers who had done this. He said it was an easy decision. He was a

* Dr. George G. Ritchie, MD, held positions as president of the Richmond Academy of General Practice; chairman of the Department of Psychiatry of Towers Hospital; and founder and president of the Universal Youth Corps, Inc. for almost twenty years. At the age of twenty, George Ritchie apparently died in an army hospital and was pronounced dead twice by the doctor on duty. Nine minutes later he returned to life. Dr. Ritchie wrote of his near-death experience in *Return from Tomorrow*, published in 1978. Ritchie's story was the first contact Dr. Raymond Moody, PhD, had with near death experiences, during his post-graduate studies and residency in Psychiatry at the University of Virginia. This led Moody to investigate over 150 cases of near death experiences in his book *Life After Life* and two other books that followed.

lawyer. In his practice he had seen too often what hate could do to people's minds and bodies. Hate had just killed the six people who mattered most to him in the world. At that moment he decided that he would spend the rest of his life, whether it was a few days or many years, loving every person he came in contact with (Ritchie, 2007, pp. 119–120).

Ritchie met Bill Cody just after Cody had survived six years in Wuppertal concentration camp. Although he had been exposed to the same abusive eating and sleeping conditions as the other inmates, reports indicated that he showed no physical or mental deterioration. When compared with all the other survivors, most of whom could hardly walk, Bill's posture was erect, his eyes bright, his energy indefatigable. His whole physical and emotional demeanor was incomprehensible to Ritchie. After intensive interviewing, the only distinguishing characteristic Ritchie could find that separated Bill from his fellow prisoners was his deep commitment to love. It appears that as an agent of love, his physical and soul forces had been nourished by the presence of spiritual forces working in his etheric body.

Exploration of the metaphysics of love and forgiveness leads us back to the nine sheaths of the human being described in chapter 1. To begin to understand what takes place within these sheaths during the process of forgiveness we must first recognize a fundamental principle expressed by Rudolf Steiner in the second lecture of the curative education course (Steiner, 1924). Here he described that the positive influence of one sheath of the human being upon another can only be brought to bear by a higher sheath (higher indicating more spiritual capacity) upon a lower sheath. He gave the examples that an etheric sheath can positively influence the physical sheath. In like manner, an astral sheath can positively influence an etheric sheath. A soul sheath can positively influence an astral sheath, etc. Rudolf Steiner addressed the stage pertinent to the process of forgiveness: "an ego can be influenced only by what is living in a Spirit Self" (Steiner, 1924). The Spirit Self alone has the capacity to positively influence the ordinary human ego (or lower self) and further its growth and evolution.

**Figure 9**

## The Nine Sheaths of the Human Being

Spirit Human
Life Spirit
Spirit Self

---

Higher Ego—"I"

---

Lower Ego
Consciousness Soul
Intellectual Soul
Sentient Soul

---

Astral Body
Etheric Body
Physical Body

For clarity, the lower ego, also known as the lower self, consists of the three soul sheaths: the sentient soul, the intellectual soul, and the consciousness soul. Consciousness soul integrates the will forces into the thinking and feeling soul realms, infusing consciousness into human deeds. When the soul instills truth and goodness into itself through selflessness, it becomes an instrument of higher consciousness such that spiritual forces can work through it. Consciousness soul becomes the prepared soil of the soul life in which the spirit can take root. The development of this sheath establishes a bridge to the higher spiritual sheaths of the human being.

The "I," also known as the higher Ego or higher Self, interfaces between the three soul sheaths and the three spirit sheaths—Spirit Self, Life Spirit, and Spirit Human. It gradually establishes greater influence over the body and soul and subsequently creates a vessel for the spirit to enter into human consciousness.

## Metaphysics of Love and Forgiveness: Step 1

### The Higher Ego Permeating the Consciousness Soul, Intellectual Soul, and Sentient Soul

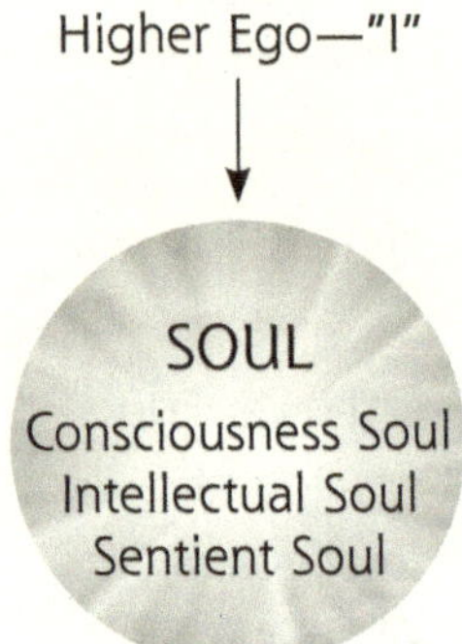


**Figure 10:** The above diagram illustrates the higher Ego, also known as the "I," influencing the three soul sheaths, or lower ego. The substance of the higher Ego spiritualizes the lower ego, establishing greater consciousness in preparation for the next stage of development.

The Spirit Self emerges as the astral body becomes transformed or purified through the influence of the "I." For the Spirit Self to be birthed, the "I" must prepare the three soul sheaths and the astral body. This preparation or transmutation of the soul brings consciousness to the inner life of the astral body. At this stage, through moral thinking the human ego is able to influence the senses and educate them towards perceiving objectively all that one experiences with a consideration for truth, moral goodness, and beauty.

When the "I" has become strong enough to generate the purification of the astral sheath, it becomes the birthplace of the Spirit Self. This spiritual dimension of the human being bears the capacity for spiritual seeing through transformed thinking, what Rudolf Steiner called *intellectual clairvoyance* (Steiner, 1984, p. 111).

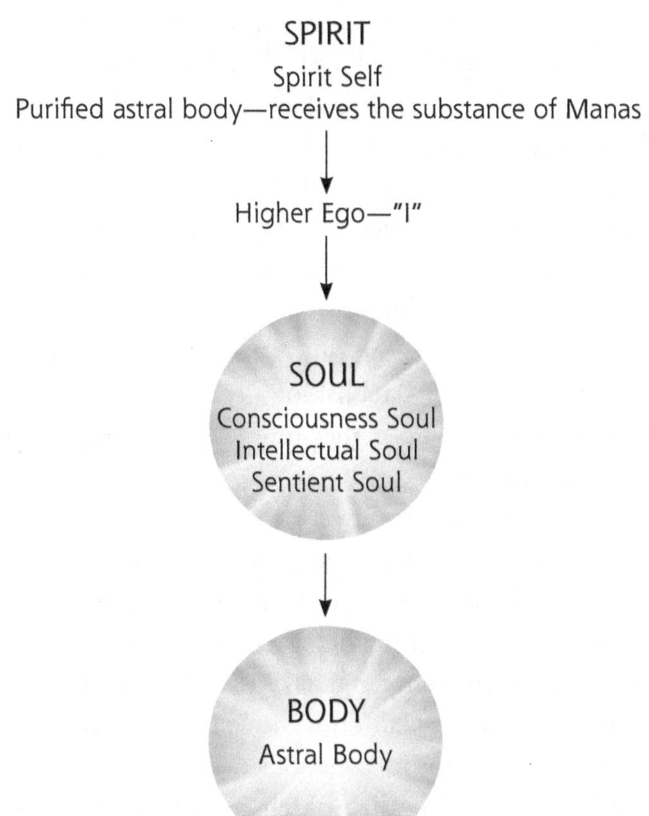


**Figure 11:** The above diagram illustrates the Spirit Self emerging as the astral body becomes transformed or purified through the influence of the "I." In order for the Spirit Self to emerge, the "I" must prepare the three soul sheaths and the astral body. The purified astral body then becomes the Spirit Self.

The fundamental relationship between the Spirit Self, the "I," and the lower ego establishes a primary aspect of the inner process of forgiveness. The capacity to forgive is directly determined by the degree to which the Spirit Self influences the lower ego through the intercession of the "I," and concomitantly, what our Spirit Self accomplishes by way of influencing the lower ego will be expressed through our deeds of forgiveness throughout life. This includes forgiveness for all the countless mistakes and errors perpetrated by our lower ego and the lower egos of others that in the vast majority of cases are due to complete or partial ignorance, and not influenced by the guidance of the Spirit Self.

The act of forgiveness requires an effort of moral will to override the memory of an offense or injustice residing in the lower ego. This creates an interval devoid of memory into which the substance of the higher Ego, the substance of spiritual love, can flow. This substance of the higher Self spiritualizes the human ego, establishing greater consciousness. The permeation of the human ego by higher moral forces brings it closer to an experience of its archetype.

As the Spirit Self then permeates the human ego, it strengthens and inspires the ego to such an extent that it may in time become possible for it to perceive the world not only with the physical senses but also with the spiritual organs of perception of the etheric body. In the same way that one's earthly ego needs the sense organs of the physical body to experience a conscious state of existence, so does the Spirit Self need the perceptive organs of the etheric body for its conscious existence.

In the same way that moral thinking influences the senses, the permeation of the Spirit Self upon the lower ego can shape the etheric body through the act of forgiveness. The Spirit Self gradually dissolves the scars and murkiness of inner duress that arise as a consequence of our errors, the moral inadequacies of our character, and the dynamics of our double. At the moment of forgiveness, when under the influence of our higher Ego, one consciously liberates the etheric body from all of its harmful and negative elements. As one dissolves them in an act of forgiveness, the etheric body is revitalized and becomes more radiant and transparent.

# Metaphysics of Love and Forgiveness: Step 3

## Manas and Buddhi Permeating the Astral and Etheric Bodies

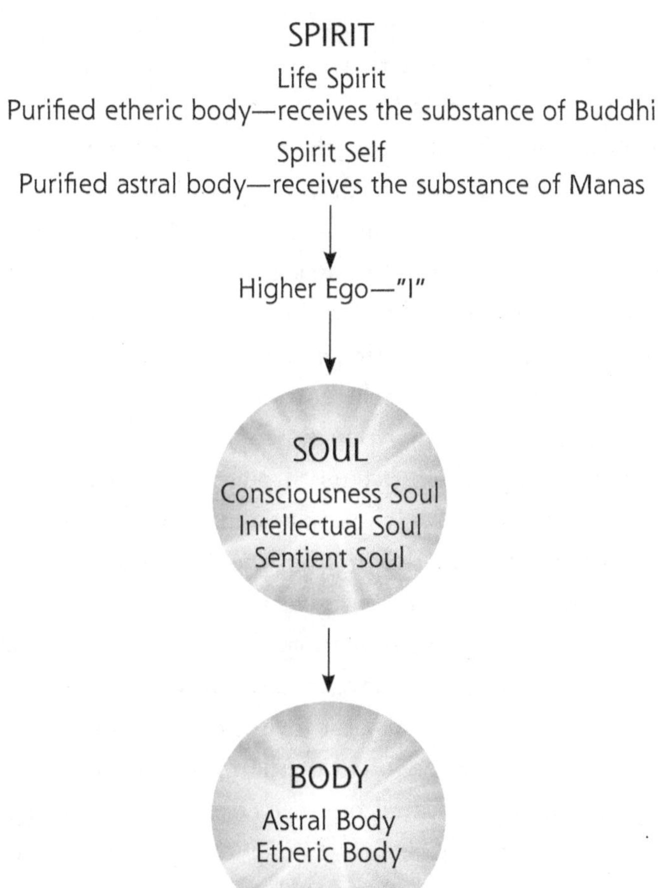


**Figure 12:** The above diagram illustrates Life Spirit emerging as the etheric body is purified through the influence of the "I" and the Spirit Self. The Spirit Self permeates the higher Ego, or "I," which then works into the etheric forces, revitalizing the etheric body so that it becomes radiant and transparent. The purified etheric body becomes Life Spirit or Buddhi.

Depending upon the degree to which the Spirit Self is able to strengthen the higher Ego to affect the etheric body, it may lead to the forming of supersensible organs of a higher nature, that of *Spiritual Inspiration*, also known as *clairaudience*. An alternate possibility may lead to receptivity to perceive the macrocosmic forces of the universal etheric life (Prokofiev, 1995, p. 54). Through the act of forgiveness, an individual can achieve a degree of purification of his or her etheric body that allows the individual to access it as an inexhaustible source of cosmic life. This interpenetration creates the possibility for spiritual forces to permeate the human being, giving strength and vitality to work in alliance with the driving force of the Universe—love. The sustained vitality of Bill Cody demonstrates this phenomenon.

At the level of Life Spirit, the capacity for forgiveness encompasses a heightened sense of responsibility for the actions of fellow human beings, communities, or possibly an entire nation, race, ethnic group, language group, or religion. This often includes consciously taking upon one's self the karma of another person or group of people, through purely selfless and fully spiritualized love, which occurs through the process of forgiveness. Christ exemplified this when He took upon Himself the karma of humankind at the Mystery of Golgotha through the deed of forgiveness and love.

The highest stage of love and forgiveness entails participating in bearing the karma of the whole of humanity. Continually and steadfastly forgiving humanity for acts that have caused suffering (past, present, and future) exemplifies a vast capacity for love and forgiveness. This results in the development of the inner forces of the individual Ego that then can form organs of higher perception out of its own essence, permeating itself with the substance of the Spirit Self, Life Spirit, and Spirit Human.

Spirit Human consciousness awakens the capacity to experience Christ on the Higher Devachan.* Here Christ appears directly in His innermost essence without any of the veils that were necessary to adopt at lower planes of existence (on the astral plane in an etheric garment and on the Lower Devachan** in an astral garment) to accommodate the lack of human

* The Higher Devachan is the spiritual plane of life ether, the domain of the Archai.

** The Lower Devachan is the spiritual plane of sound or chemical ether, the domain of the Archangels.

# Metaphysics of Love and Forgiveness: Step 4

## Manas, Buddhi, and Atma Permeating the Astral, Etheric, and Physical Bodies

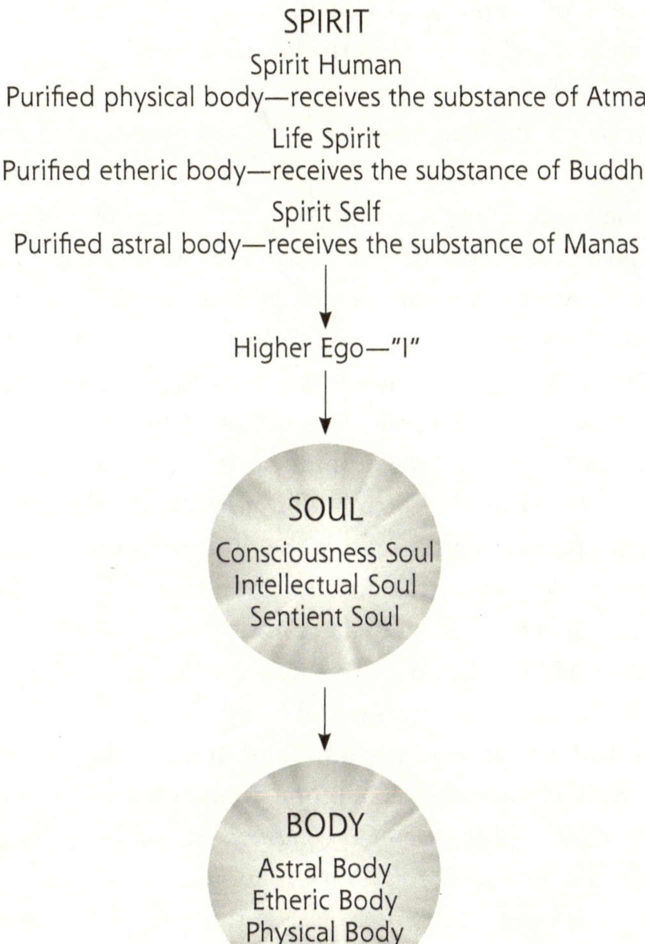


**Figure 13:** The above diagram illustrates Life Spirit emerging as the etheric body is purified through the influence of the "I" and the Spirit Self. The Spirit Self permeates the higher Ego, or "I," which then works into the etheric forces, revitalizing the etheric body so that it becomes radiant and transparent. The purified etheric body becomes Life Spirit or Buddhi.

capacity for spiritual perception. At this stage of consciousness all the intermediary forms fall away and the individual Ego perceives Christ as the cosmic, universal Ego.

This stage of Spirit Human presents a picture of the far distant future for humanity, at this time attainable only by the highest initiates. It is included here to offer an overarching perspective for the potential cultivation of forgiveness and love within the human heart.

In the act of forgiveness the forces and substance of the higher Ego permeate the lower ego. This transforms the lower tendencies of the human double. True forgiveness always has a sacrificial character, namely, the overcoming of the lower ego by the higher Ego. Through the force of egoism, the lower ego resists forgiveness in every possible way and grasps at any opportunity to avoid this step. The difficulty or ease in forgiving is determined above all by the extent of the activity of the higher Ego exerting mastery over the lower ego. Each individual's capacity to forgive acts as an inner barometer that indicates the extent of the presence and maturity of the higher Ego. The present mind-set of contemporary western culture alternates between the thoughts of *guilt* and *forgiveness*. The battle between guilt and forgiveness reflects the dilemma in modern consciousness between an old moralistic thinking that blames and punishes, and the advent of a new moral thinking that embraces a greater context of freedom, responsibility, and love. To attain to a new moral thinking requires a shift into a spiritualized consciousness out of free volition, in which responsibility becomes the foundation of a new understanding of forgiveness, a necessary step to realizing a new level of moral awareness and evolution.

In *The Occult Significance of Forgiveness*, Sergei O. Prokofiev* places the fifth petition of the Lord's Prayer, "forgive us our trespasses as we forgive those who trespass against us," as the task of the current age of Consciousness Soul. He sees this petition as the guiding principle of our entire spiritual evolution. It is an indication of the path of spiritual ascent that all humanity will tread in the course of the remaining stages of earthly

* Sergei O. Prokofiev, Russian anthroposophist and co-founder of the Anthroposophical Society in Russia, was a member of the Executive Council of the Anthroposophical Society in Dornach, Switzerland.

evolution. Prokofiev refers to forgiveness as an occult path of cognition that leads both to a direct experience of the Christ Being and to a deeper knowledge of Him (Prokofiev, 1995, pp 7–9). Developing the capacity to forgive will enable modern human beings gradually to become fully conscious coworkers of Christ in the process of accomplishing the attainment of cosmic love on Earth.

## The Deeper Responsibility of Guilt

Discovering the responsibility underlying guilt advances the shift in consciousness to a new moral thinking. An honest, fearless, moral inventory brings a recognition that the wrongs committed by self or others, social ills, and human atrocities derive from complex personal, cultural, and historical factors. When the inquiry of self-responsibility reaches deep enough, not only does an immediate and actual cause become evident, but it also becomes apparent that the underlying origin of transgression is the essence of separateness, the core of selfness, unwillingness, not giving, not yielding, not forgiving. This level of self-awareness awakens a reality of mutual guilt.

The following true account demonstrates the power of forgiveness to transmute karma through shared guilt. Dr. Ihaleakala Hew Len, a consulting clinical psychologist, spent four years at the Hawaii State Hospital in the 1980s, overseeing a ward of the most dangerous, violent, "mentally ill" criminals in Hawaii (Vitale, 2007, pp. 11–18). It was an untenable work environment with continual staff turnover, and when on duty, staff members would walk through the ward with their backs against the wall, afraid of being attacked by patients.

Dr. Len accepted the position on the condition that he did not have to have direct contact with the patients. After a few months of Dr. Len's presence at the hospital, patients that previously had to be shackled were being allowed to walk freely. Others who had been heavily medicated were being taken off their medications. Staff absenteeism and turnover disappeared. Patients who had had no chance of ever being released were being set free. After four years the ward was closed.

When asked, "How did you cure a complete ward of mentally ill criminals without ever seeing any of them?" Dr. Len replied, "I simply worked on healing the part of myself that created them." When asked how he went about healing himself, Dr. Len answered, "I just kept saying, *I am sorry* and *I love you* over and over again."

He would read the patients' charts, write down their names, and then work to transform himself. He cleansed his judgments, beliefs, and attitudes, and he asked the Divinity what he could do for the patients. As he worked on himself, patients began to heal.

Dr. Len used a Hawaiian healing process called ho'oponopono, a process of repentance, forgiveness, and transmutation developed by Kahuna Lapa'au Morrnah Nalamaku Simeona,* in which erroneous thoughts within one's self and within another person are transmuted into perfect thoughts of love.

He claims that the process of repentance and forgiveness is achieved through the inner dialogue, *I am sorry for the erroneous thoughts within me that have caused the problem for me and for the client; please forgive me.* In response to the repentance and forgiveness appeal of the therapist, love begins the mystical process of transmuting the erroneous thoughts. In this spiritual correction process, love first neutralizes the emotions that have caused the problem, be they resentment, fear, anger, blame, or confusion. In the next step, love then releases the neutralized energies from the thoughts, leaving them in a state of void, of emptiness, of true freedom, so that love can stream in, and healing is possible.

Dr. Len explained that because he is fully responsibility for everything in his life, it is possible to transform everything in his life. He uses the healing words: *I love you, I am sorry, please forgive me, thank you.*

This transmuting power of love and forgiveness, practiced by a Hawaiian Kahuna, aligns with Christ's deed of taking the sins of the world upon Him,

---

* Morrnah Nalamaku Simeona (1913–1992), a native Hawaiian Kahuna and gifted healer, developed a new system of healing based on the ancient spiritual tradition, ho'oponopono. In addition she attended Catholic school where the way of Christ deeply influenced her spiritually. Eventually she went on to study the metaphysical traditions of India and China, and later the works of Edgar Cayce.

and accepting the guilt of humanity as His own. The choice of taking this step becomes a radical shift to form the capability, through our alignment with the Lord of Karma, to heal the Earth. This is the work of future humanity—to share the guilt of the world, and transmute it through forgiveness.

## The Capacity to Forgive

The capacity to forgive develops with a deepening of our moral life in which the higher Ego permeates through and supersedes the lower ego. This can only come about through training in *unselfishness.* Christ's appearance upon Earth offered a supreme example of selflessness. Understanding Christ's life can become a school of unselfishness for the conscious development of the human soul.

In a lecture entitled "The Four Sacrifices of Christ," Rudolf Steiner described how our eyes, as well as all the senses, are selfless. We see through our eyes, but we do not feel them. The eyes are separate from the process of perceiving. They allow light to pass through them to the optic nerve without interference. If our eyes were self-seeking they would use up the color immediately within themselves instead of letting it pass through. Steiner asserts that if our eyes wanted to experience the color blue we would feel a sort of suction in our eyes. If our eyes were as selfish as we are in our moral, intellectual, and emotional life, and they wished to experience the effect of red, we would feel a sharp stab. If our eyes were self-seeking, all our color impressions would result in sucking or stabbing pains. We would be painfully conscious that we have eyes. However, humanity experiences color and light without having to think of the seeing process. The eye is selflessly extinguished during perception. It is a pure organ through which light passes so that we may see (Steiner, 1981, pp. 3–4). This selfless capacity within the eyes, and all the senses, which according to Rudolf Steiner came about through an earlier sacrifice of the Christ Being in preparation for the Mystery of Golgotha, can be seen as a prefiguring of the work required by the human "I" at our current time in the evolution of human consciousness.

It is through individual self-development that we are able to begin to develop the capacity of selflessness and foster love in the world. As each individual yearns for self-knowledge and earnestly strives to mature, the world moves one step forward from selfishness to selflessness, from individual self-interest to loving community. The task confronting each of us at this time is to learn through selflessness, forgiveness, and compassionate wisdom, to bear within us the power of cosmic love.

All that the "I" of each human being consciously brings to development will grow into cosmic love. The seed of love has been planted into the innermost depth of each human being (Steiner, 1979, p. 364). The knowledge humans acquire, and every deed humans do with true understanding and selflessness, sow seeds that will eventually ripen into divine love. For it is love that will grow into the potent forces that will lead humanity to fulfill the creative work necessary for the future unfolding of human consciousness, the completion of our karma, and the fulfillment of the mission of Earth, to become beings of cosmic love.

# Conclusion: Charting the Course

> The work on the shadow is only a preparation for a life of service. The shadow teaches us the lesson of humility. Having experienced the depths of our own darkness we can never judge another person, nor can we be frightened by the darkness.
>
> —Llewellyn Vaughan-Lee*

> We are living in what the Greeks called the *kairos*—the right moment—for a "metamorphosis of the gods," of the fundamental principles and symbols....
>
> So much is at stake and so much depends on the psychological constitution of modern man.... Does the individual know that *he* (and she) is the makeweight that tips the scales?
>
> —Carl Gustav Jung**

Thus far, this book has attempted to express the imperative need to consciously develop heart thinking. Now the focus turns toward the essential need to cultivate will forces. Advancement on the path of the evolution of consciousness requires effort, whether for individuals, communities, nations, or humanity as a whole. Spiritual progress necessitates individual, focused practice.

---

* Vaughan-Lee, 1994, p. 57.

** Jung, 1970, p. 304.

The Buddha called his teaching a raft. To cross a turbulent river one may need to build a raft. When built, we single-mindedly and with great energy make our way across. Once across we do not need to cart the raft around with us. We need not cling to anything including the teachings. However, we must use them before letting them go. It is no use knowing everything about the raft and not getting onto it.

The following appendices offer core teachings from Judaism, Buddhism, and Christianity to transform the double and awaken spirit consciousness. Appendix E presents a meditation course for inner development. The path lies ahead for humanity. How it will be tread will be determined by individual choice. The choice is yours.

# APPENDIX A

## The Universality of the Golden Rule and the Law of Reciprocity

The Golden Rule or the ethic of reciprocity is found in the scriptures of nearly every religion. It is often regarded as the most concise and general principle of ethics.

> You shall love your neighbor as yourself.
>
> *Judaism and Christianity. Bible, Leviticus 19:18*

> Whatever you wish that men would do to you, do so to them.
>
> *Christianity. Bible, Matthew 7:12*

> Not one of you is a believer until he loves for his brother what he loves for himself.
>
> *Islam. Forty Hadith of an-Nawawi 13*

> A man should wander about treating all creatures as he himself would be treated.
>
> *Jainism. Sutrakritanga 1:11:33*

> Try your best to treat others as you would wish to be treated yourself, and you will find that this is the shortest way to benevolence.
>
> *Confucianism. Mencius VII.A.4*

One should not behave towards others in a way which is disagreeable to oneself. This is the essence of morality. All other activities are due to selfish desire.

*Hinduism. Mahābhārata, Anusasana Parva 113:8*

Tsekung asked, "Is there one word that can serve as a principle of conduct for life?" Confucius replied, "It is the word shu—reciprocity: Do not do to others what you do not want them to do to you."

*Confucianism. Analects 15:23*

Comparing oneself to others in such terms as "Just as I am so are they, just as they are so am I," he should neither kill nor cause others to kill.

*Buddhism. Sutta Nipata 705*

One going to take a pointed stick to pinch a baby bird should first try it on himself to feel how it hurts.

*African Traditional Religions. Yoruba Proverb (Nigeria)*

One who you think should be hit is none else but you. One who you think should be governed is none else but you. One who you think should be tortured is none else but you. One who you think should be enslaved is none else but you. One who you think should be killed is none else but you. A sage is ingenuous and leads his life after comprehending the parity of the killed and the killer. Therefore, neither does he cause violence to others nor does he make others do so.

*Jainism. Acarangasutra 5:101–102*

The Ariyan disciple thus reflects, Here am I, fond of my life, not wanting to die, fond of pleasure and averse from pain. Suppose someone should rob me of my life ... it would not be a thing pleasing and delightful to me. If I, in my turn, should rob of his life one fond of his life, not wanting to die, one fond of pleasure and averse from pain, it would not be a thing pleasing or delightful to him. For a state that is not pleasant or delightful to me must also be to him also; and a state that is not pleasing or delightful to me, how could I inflict that upon another?

As a result of such reflection he himself abstains from taking the life of creatures and he encourages others so to abstain, and speaks in praise of so abstaining.

*Buddhism. Samyutta Nikaya v.353*

A certain heathen came to Shammai and said to him, "Make me a proselyte, on condition that you teach me the whole Torah while I stand on one foot." Thereupon he repulsed him with the rod which was in his hand. When he went to Hillel, he said to him, "What is hateful to you, do not do to your neighbor: that is the whole Torah; all the rest of it is commentary; go and learn."

*Judaism. Talmud, Shabbat 31a*

"Teacher, which is the great commandment in the law?" Jesus said to him, "You shall love the Lord your God with all your heart, and with all your soul, and with all your mind. This is the great and first commandment. And a second is like it, You shall love your neighbor as yourself. On these two commandments depend all the law and the prophets."

*Christianity. Bible, Matthew 22:36–40*

# APPENDIX B

## The Ten Commandments of Moses

The Ten Commandments given by Moses constitute guidelines for human life, and guidance for individuals engaged on a path of spiritual practice. They were given by Moses to help the people of Israel (and in a deeper sense the whole world) in the struggle against the forces of the double.

> The Ten Commandments signify much more than simply a moral code of daily life. They signify, further, the hygiene, the method, and the conditions of fructification of the spiritual life, including all forms and degrees of practical esotericism (Anonymous, 1991, p. 296).

The path of practical esotericism includes *mysticism*, *gnosis*, *sacred magic*, and *hermeticism*, which are addressed in the first four commandments. Mysticism is the experience of mystical union or direct communion with ultimate reality. It is the seed of gnosis, the knowledge of spiritual truth that grows out of mystical revelation and can be brought to communicable expression. Sacred magic is the child of mysticism and gnosis; it is the putting into practice of that which mystical revelation has made known, through the union of divine will and human will working toward the restoration of true freedom. Hermeticism is the manifestation of the unity, mysticism-gnosis-magic. The ideal of hermeticism is to awaken from sleep ever-deeper layers of consciousness. Essentially, the more one becomes truly human, the more one manifests the divine element underlying human nature, which is the "image and likeness of God." The Ten Commandments give the spiritual laws for these dimensions of inner development.

## The First Commandment

**"Thou shalt have no other gods before me."** Mysticism is the awakening of the soul to the presence of God. The first commandment calls upon us to acknowledge the God who transcends the self, the living God of Creation, and that no other gods be acknowledged as equal. This is the living God whose breath is the "vertical line" that supports increasing interiorization. This is the living God who guides our development from subjective conscience to the conscience of the world, from expansion of the individual self to its very own source from which all selves radiate out. "He who is" has a claim to undivided devotion from the center and essence of the whole consciousness of human beings. This is the God who "is more I than I myself am." "Other gods"—beings of the spiritual hierarchies who serve the living God—are of a lesser order than the living God. And beings of the sub-earthly spheres, who can enslave the self and block its path to true freedom, are not to be worshipped or considered as gods. *Love the Lord thy God with all thy heart, with all thy soul and with all thy might. Surrender to the living God.*

## The Second Commandment

**"Thou shalt not make for thyself a graven image, or any likeness."** The fundamental law of gnosis is not to substitute imagery drawn from the human mind, or from Nature, for the reality of the living God. The encounter of the being of the soul with the being of God, the reality of God, the truth of God, is not possible through ordinary seeing or knowing. It happens in the reciprocal permeation of the love of God and of the love of the soul. This takes place beyond the level of ordinary images and ideas. It is the radiance of the reality of God—the truth of God—that permeates and envelops the soul of the human being.

## The Third Commandment

**"Thou shalt not take the name of the Lord thy God in vain."** The fundamental law of sacred magic is to act in and through the name of the Divine, whilst guarding against making the name of the Divine an instrument of one's own will. This includes activity in the name of God without making use of His name in order to adorn one's self with it. The spoken name of God releases the summoning power contained in it, signifying a magical invocation. Herein lies the possible serious misuse of the holy name of God. If God becomes viewed as a kind of "religious superstructure" rather than the original divine ideal, the name of the Lord is misused.

## The Fourth Commandment

**"Remember the Sabbath day, to keep it holy."** Meditation is "sanctified rest," where thought is turned towards that which is above. Meditation is the turning within of the soul that is devoted to the search for truth. Meditation is also a turning away from the outside world and its concerns, influences, after-effects, and memories thereof. Ideally, one seventh of the time ought to be consecrated to turning within, to rising up out of the stream of daily life. Meditation is the "hallowing of the Sabbath." It signifies the fulfillment of the command to turn within for inner reflection. Meditation, contemplation, and prayer all belong to inner reflection or "hallowing the Sabbath." Spiritualization is the goal and meaning of turning within. Turning within mirrors the divine work of creation and rest. The resting which follows the work of God's creation is a spiritualization of the preceding work of creation. Meditation first purifies its own source, the soul, from which it arises. The fundamental law of hermeticism is "as above, so below." And just as God rested on the seventh day, in contemplation and meditation, so—by way of analogy—are human beings also called to devote a certain amount of time to the "sanctified rest" of meditation.

## The Fifth Commandment

**"Honor thy father and thy mother."** All progress presupposes continuity—coherence between the past, present, and future. One must abstain from all action that breaks continuity, cutting the current of life. It is the fundamental law of a constructive attitude, which is essential in spiritual life, and is the foundation of all tradition, all continuity in progress, growth, development, and evolution. To honor "father" and "mother" is the spirit and soul of tradition, of constructive continuation from the past to the present, of true progress across the ages, of the path of the life of humankind towards truth. It is the very essence of the life of the spirit and the soul. Interiorization in peace and quiet makes possible the becoming aware of father-love and mother-love as mirrors of divine love. It is the experience of honored paternal love that renders us capable of opening our hearts to the Divine, and honoring the Divine Father of Creation. It is the experience of honored maternal love that underlies our ability to recognize and hallow the Divine Mother of Creation. *Honor thy father and thy mother, as in heaven, so also upon the earth.*

## The Sixth Commandment

**"Thou shalt not kill."** The fundamental law of a constructive attitude is essential in spiritual life. "Thou shalt not kill" encompasses all physical acts of destroying life, all negative or destructive thoughts, all negative or hurtful feelings, and all harmful or negatively motivated words and deeds. Thou shalt not kill also applies to the realm of knowledge. One who denies the life of symbols, kills them in his thought. To deny that which reveals means to kill that which lives in the domain of thought. To deny is to kill; to forget is to bury. To honor and appreciate is to preserve the living; to restore to memory is to recall to life. Evil or error cannot be overcome by killing or destruction. The only way to overcome error is by way of transformation—ennoblement through purification. Contemplation leads to an inner deepening—along the paths of tolerance, peaceful coexistence, and the open confrontation between error and truth, between what is useful and what is good, between what is impressive and what is nobly beautiful. In the realm of the spirit it is impossible to kill something living. What takes place is simply an inner transformation, an alchemical process of purification and interiorization or spiritualization, but no extinction.

## The Seventh Commandment

**"Thou shalt not commit adultery."** Continuity—or tradition and life—implies faithfulness to the cause that is espoused, to the direction taken, to the ideal that one has as a guide, and to all alliances with entities above and with human beings below, for the sake of the continuity of life. There is carnal adultery, psychic adultery, and spiritual adultery. Unfaithfulness on the physical level is autonomy of carnal desire, which destroys the unity of body, soul, and spirit, shredding the etheric fabric of a marriage union. Psychic adultery constitutes an unfaithful soul life, where one allows one's feelings to become involved with another beyond the appropriate bounds prescribed by psychic loyalty to one's partner. Spiritual adultery is the exchange of a higher moral and spiritual value for a lower moral and spiritual value. Every living spiritual tradition ought to be faithful to its original impulse. Adultery is essentially a form of killing—of separating soul and body, whose union is the archetype of marriage. Our eternal covenant with God requires eternal loyalty. In the bond of marriage between man and woman is mirrored the marriage covenant of God with each human soul.

## The Eighth Commandment

**"Thou shalt not steal."** Theft is the desire to obtain without effort or sacrifice that whose worth implies effort and sacrifice. Stealing of material goods, of another's feelings or ideas, stealing social, occupational, or spiritual gain: all constitute theft. All "tricks" of a technical nature, having as their aim the dispensing with the effort and sacrifice required for normal spiritual growth and development, fall under the heading of theft. You will harvest only after having tilled the earth, only after having sown, and only after having waited for the time when the fruit will be ripe for harvesting. All other gain is false.

## The Ninth Commandment

**"Thou shalt not bear false witness against thy neighbor."** This commandment warns against the spirit of rivalry manifested as negative criticism. All action should be motivated by love for the cause and ideal rather than by a spirit of rivalry. Anyone who takes on himself the mission of judge can act only in the sense of destruction. Anyone who begins to criticize soon passes to censure and ends up condemning, which leads inevitably to division into hostile camps and to other forms of destruction. Criticism and polemicism are mortal enemies of the spiritual life. They signify the substitution of destructive electrical energy for constructive vital force. Slander—"false witness against your neighbor"—is a killing of the good reputation, respect, and trust of another human being; the extended soul life of another is distorted and destroyed. Slander is moral murder and robbery.

## The Tenth Commandment

**"Thou shalt not covet thy neighbor's house."** This commandment expresses the spirit of rivalry manifesting as envy. The life, marriage, possessions, and honor of another human being are just as inviolable as they are for one's self. The physical body is a possession or extension of the human soul that allows the soul to live in the world as the place of the development of his or her consciousness. The portion of the outer world perceived as "possession," or property, is a kind of extended body, an extension of the field of action of the human soul. This is also the realm of the development of consciousness for each human soul. The house, yard, garden, and field of my neighbor is his or her "extended body," an extension of the field of action of the human soul. To desire thy neighbor's possessions is to violate his or her development. Coveting is a form of psychic murder and robbery.

The Ten Commandments could be seen in two groups, guiding the human soul into right relationship with spiritual and earthly aspects of our being. The first four commandments establish a rightful relationship to the spiritual world. This could be seen as a vertical axis between humanity and the world of spirit. The remaining six commandments state the fundamental laws of spiritual culture or discipline pertaining to human relationships. These could be imagined as forming a horizontal axis representing human relations with one another. Together we have the formulation for an inner cross of moral guidance, which is illustrated on the following pages. (See also, *Meditations on the Tarot*, Arcanum 11.)

**Figure 14**

The Ten Commandments
as an Inner Cross of Moral Guidance

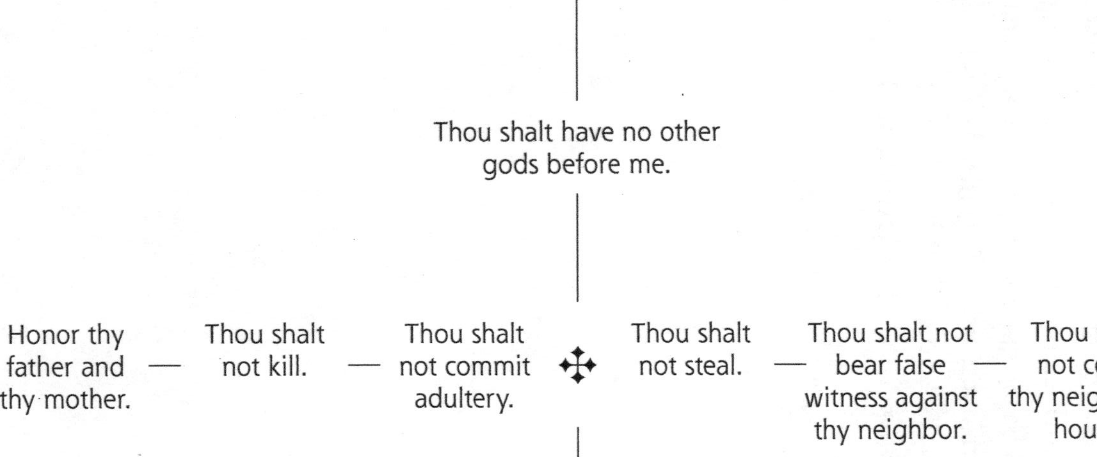

Thou shalt not make for thyself
a graven image, or any likeness.

Thou shalt not take the name
of the Lord thy God in vain.

Remember the Sabbath day,
to keep it holy.

# APPENDIX C

# The Eightfold Path of Gautama Buddha

The essence of the Buddha's teaching can be summed up in two principles: the Four Noble Truths and the Noble Eightfold Path. The Four Noble Truths present doctrine, and elicit understanding; the Noble Eightfold Path requires discipline, and calls for practice. These two principles work together as an indivisible unity.

The Noble Eightfold Path is the fourth of the Four Noble Truths.

## The First Noble Truth

**The reality of Dukkha (suffering) as part of conditioned existence.** Dukkha is a multi-faceted word, literally meaning "that which is difficult to bear." It can mean suffering, stress, pain, anguish, affliction, or lack of satisfaction. It can be gross or very subtle, from extreme physical and mental pain and torment to subtle inner conflicts and existential malaise.

## The Second Noble Truth

**Dukkha has a causal arising.** This cause is defined as grasping and clinging or aversion. Because all conditioned existence is impermanent it gives rise to Dukkha.

### The Third Noble Truth

**There is an end of Dukkha.** Nirvana lies beyond grasping and control and conditional existence. It is waking up to the true nature of reality, and to true nature of one's self, Buddha Nature. Nirvana literally means *unbound*, as in "Mind like fire unbound." This image is of a flame burning and giving off light and warmth without external fuel. The flame is self-fueling.

### The Fourth Noble Truth

**The path that leads to awakening is the Noble Eightfold Path.** The eightfold path is a process to help remove or move beyond the conditioned responses that obscure one's true nature. Ultimately, the eightfold path requires unlearning rather than learning. The teachings are skillful means or expedient method.

The tenets of the eightfold path presented below are adapted from Rudolf Steiner's inclusion of these tenets in *Guidance in Esoteric Training* (Steiner, 1994, pp. 24–27.) They are included in the meditation course in Appendix E with guidelines as to how one may practice them.

### Saturday: Right Thought

Strive to be attentive to every thought, separating the essential from the nonessential, the eternal from the transitory, the truth from opinion or falsehood. In listening to the words of others, become still inwardly, foregoing all judgments, favorable or unfavorable. In the face of all circumstances, bring one's thoughts away from criticism, rejection, and negativity; direct one's thoughts to what is objectively true, helpful, loving, and potentially healing.

### Sunday: Right Resolve

Strive to practice discernment and discretion in all matters, no matter how insignificant. All thoughtless behavior and meaningless action should be eliminated from the life of the soul. Deliberated reasoning should accompany all decisions, abstaining from doing things for which there is no significant reason. When one is clear about the rightness of a decision, made independently of sympathies and antipathies, one formulates a resolve, holding to it with inner steadfastness.

### Monday: Right Word

Strive to only speak words that are true, helpful, and purposeful. Avoid any speech which is harmful, divisive or condemning, deceptive, slanderous, or that trivializes. Talking for the sake of talking is harmful. Never speak without purpose; enjoy silence. Listen with inner stillness, reflect on what is said to you, then respond with objectivity and with thoughtful words that have the potential to bring insight, healing, and the presence of the Divine.

### Tuesday: Right Action

Strive to do deeds that bring harm to no one. Take up the work that is before you with gladness. Do not put off until tomorrow what can be done today. Find joy in doing acts of kindness for others. When one is called to act out of one's inner being, consider carefully the effects of one's actions. Before acting out of one's own initiative, contemplate discerningly the motives and effects of your actions. Act for the good of the whole, with consciousness of the other and of the eternal.

### Wednesday: Right Livelihood

Strive to create balance between the inner life and one's activities in the outer world, living in harmony with Nature and spirit. Avoid all that brings stress and haste into one's life. Do not become overwhelmed by the trivialities of life. Hurry over nothing, nor be slothful or lazy. Create rhythm to allow one's life to be lived as a means for working toward the development of higher consciousness. Find the standpoint from which you can work inwardly and in the world.

## Thursday: Right Endeavor

Strive for wisdom in formulating one's ideals, one's commitments to life endeavors such as family, marriage, friends, careers, education, nutrition, spiritual practice, the times in which we live, etc. Looking beyond the momentary, everyday situations, set one's vision on the aims and ideals of the highest potential of being human. Be mindful to do nothing that is beyond one's abilities and to leave nothing undone that is within one's abilities.

## Friday: Right Memory

Strive to learn as much as possible from life experiences. Focus one's memory on events from which one can learn, in order that one can improve in a future situation. In recollecting events that stir discomfort or antipathy, seek to discover the intolerance or self-delusion that may be unconsciously active. In remembering events that have no particular interest to you, it is possible to learn about areas of life to which you have hitherto not brought value or appreciation. Right memory fosters growth. Seeking to find a sense for the meaning within each experience brings us to a consciousness of our destiny.

## Every Day: Right Contemplation

Turn to the depths of one's being and strive to identify the essential, the enduring; earnestly and steadfastly work toward goals in accord with it. Seek to perceive the virtues that are yet to be acquired and set the course to attain them. Seek to observe the vices that arise in one's life and identify a means of dissolving them.

# APPENDIX D

## The Nine Beatitudes of Christ

The nine Beatitudes of the Sermon on the Mount are the description of the conditions of the ninefold reality which the *makarioi* (blessed) have to pass through in the nine members of their human nature in order to bring about that which lies in the positive karma of humanity. Blessed, from the Greek *makarioi*, means that the positive karma of humanity will consist, not in an escape from suffering and pain, but in the experiencing of a new type of suffering and pain. The *makarioi* (blessed) are those who in the joy of their good fortune will not forget the ill-fortune of others, whereas in ill-fortune they will have present with them the felicity of the Holy Spirit.

| **Matthew 5:3–12**<br>*(revised standard version)* | **The Gospel of St. Matthew**<br>*lecture 9, by Rudolf Steiner* |
|---|---|
| Blessed are the poor in spirit, for theirs is the kingdom of heaven.<br>(Physical body) | Blessed are they who are begging for the spirit; for when the way is opened for them by Christ, there flows into their Ego what we may call the "Kingdoms of Heaven." |
| Blessed are they that mourn, for they shall be comforted.<br>(Etheric body) | Blessed are they that mourn, if living for Christ, they realize the new truth, and experience in themselves comfort for all suffering. |

| | |
|---|---|
| Blessed are the meek, for they shall inherit the earth. (Astral body) | Blessed are the meek (conquerors of Lucifer) through their own initiative, through the power of the Ego, for it is they who will inherit the Earth (the terrestrial kingdom). |
| Blessed are those who hunger and thirst for righteousness, for they shall be satisfied. (Sentient soul) | Blessed are those who fill the Sentient Soul with the Christ-power, for they can find within Him the possibility of satisfying their thirst after righteousness. |
| Blessed are the merciful, for they shall obtain mercy. (Intellectual soul) | Blessed are those who take the Christ-power into themselves, and whose qualities pass from like to like. What streams forth, streams back again. |
| Blessed are the pure in heart, for they shall see God. (Consciousness soul) | Blessed are those who experience Christ in their Ego, for they will find God in their heart, the expression of the Ego in the blood. |
| Blessed are the peacemakers, for they shall be called the children of God. (Spirit Self) | Blessed are they who draw to themselves the Spirit Self as the first purely spiritual member of their being, for they will be called the children of God. The first member of the higher triad has entered into them and they have become an outward expression of the God-head. |

Blessed are those who are persecuted for righteousness sake, for theirs is the kingdom of heaven.

(Life Spirit)

Blessed are those chosen individuals in whom the Christ-impulse has permeated from the Ego down to the vital body, for theirs is the consciousness of the Third Kingdom, not of this world.

Blessed are you when men revile you and persecute you and utter all manner of evil against you falsely on my account. Rejoice and be glad, for your reward is great in heaven.

(Spirit Human)

Blessed are those most intimate disciples whose karma has become one with the cosmic karma of the Christ-impulse.

# APPENDIX E

# Meditation Course for Inner Development: Encountering the Double

The meditation materials offered here address the inner challenges that all spiritual aspirants encounter as they strive for spiritual consciousness. The journey upon a spiritual path entails experiences of ever-greater and more subtle challenges, temptations, and trials. This course is intended to enable spiritual consciousness to permeate and influence subconscious soul forces, facilitating an interweaving between the soul and spirit, a respiration between consciousness soul and Spirit Self.

Inner development or the path of inner purification is the process of the transfiguration of the chakras. The meditations offered here address the pitfalls and challenges that humanity encounters in relation to each of the chakras in correspondence with the complex nature of the subconscious realm. The human subconscious is penetrated with the activity of impulses that obstruct one's path of spiritual development; the source of this obstruction is often referred to as the human shadow or double. Rudolf Steiner spoke of this aspect of the soul as the "doppelgänger." C.G. Jung called this aspect of the subconscious realm the "shadow." Valentin Tomberg addressed this dimension of the soul as the "double" in his lectures on inner development and also in his *Our Mother Course.*

In *Blessed Among Women* by Arnold Michael, Jesus described to his disciples that the enemy is within, our greatest foe being ourselves.

> "How can we know when the enemy within ourselves has been overcome?" Jesus's reply came straight away. "When no longer do you judge your fellow man! A heart that is free from accusation and condemnation is a heart that has overcome anger, greed, and desire, and therefore it is a pure heart."

The transformation of the impure aspects of the human condition allows an inner receptivity wherein divine forces may work. This process of transformation continues throughout the stages of the purification of the astral body, the etheric body, and the physical body. Thus, it is ever possible to deepen and broaden one's capacity to strip away the impure aspects of the individual and become resonant to the divine outpouring of light and warmth, of wisdom and love.

## The Structure of the Meditations

The meditations are ordered on a seven-day cycle, applying the correspondence that Rudolf Steiner gave relating the days of the week to the tenets of the Buddhist eightfold path.

Saturday (Saturn Day)—Right Thought
Sunday (Sun Day)—Right Resolve
Monday (Moon Day)—Right Word
Tuesday (Mars Day)—Right Action
Wednesday (Mercury Day)—Right Livelihood
Thursday (Jupiter Day)—Right Endeavor
Friday (Venus Day)—Right Memory
Every Day—Right Contemplation

Each week a different meditation designed to address a specific aspect of the subconscious realm will be undertaken through the portals of these eight precepts. Following are descriptions of the tenets of the eightfold path in relation to the days of the week. They have been formulated specifically for this course from the inspiration of Rudolf Steiner.

## Saturday: Right Thought

Strive to be attentive to every thought, separating the essential from the non-essential, the eternal from the transitory, the truth from opinion or falsehood. In listening to the words of others, become still inwardly, foregoing all judgments, favorable or unfavorable. In the face of all circumstances, bring one's thoughts away from criticism, rejection, negativity; directing one's thoughts to what is objectively true, helpful, loving, and potentially healing.

## Sunday: Right Resolve

Strive to practice discernment and discretion in all matters, no matter how insignificant. All thoughtless behavior and meaningless action should be eliminated from the life of the soul. Deliberated reasoning should accompany all decisions, abstaining from doing things for which there is no significant reason. When one is clear about the rightness of a decision, made independently of sympathies and antipathies, one formulates a resolve, holding to it with inner steadfastness.

## Monday: Right Word

Strive to only speak words that are true, helpful, and purposeful. Avoid any speech which is harmful, divisive or condemning, deceptive, slanderous, or that trivializes. Talking for the sake of talking is harmful. Never speak without purpose; enjoy silence. Listen with inner stillness, reflect on what is said to you, then respond with objectivity and with thoughtful words that have the potential to bring insight, healing, and the presence of the Divine.

## Tuesday: Right Action

Strive to do deeds that bring harm to no one. Take up the work that is before you with gladness. Do not put off until tomorrow what can be done today. Find joy in doing acts of kindness for others. When one is called to act out of one's inner being, consider carefully the effects of one's actions.

Before acting out of one's own initiative, contemplate discerningly the motives and effects of your actions. Act for the good of the whole, with consciousness of the other and of the eternal.

### Wednesday: Right Livelihood

Strive to create balance between the inner life and one's activities in the outer world, living in harmony with Nature and spirit. Avoid all that brings stress and haste into one's life. Do not become overwhelmed by the trivialities of life. Hurry over nothing, nor be slothful or lazy. Create rhythm to allow one's life to be lived as a means for working toward the development of higher consciousness. Find the standpoint from which you can work inwardly and in the world.

### Thursday: Right Endeavor

Strive for wisdom in formulating one's ideals, one's commitments to life endeavors such as family, marriage, friends, careers, education, nutrition, spiritual practice, the times in which we live, etc. Looking beyond the momentary, everyday situations, set one's vision on the aims and ideals of the highest potential of being human. Be mindful to do nothing that is beyond one's abilities and to leave nothing undone that is within one's abilities.

### Friday: Right Memory

Strive to learn as much as possible from life experiences. Focus one's memory on events from which one can learn, in order that one can improve in a future situation. In recollecting events that stir discomfort or antipathy, seek to discover the intolerance or self-delusion that may be unconsciously active. In remembering events that have no particular interest to you, it is possible to learn about areas of life to which you have hitherto not brought value or appreciation. Right memory fosters growth. Seeking to find a sense for the meaning within each experience brings us to a consciousness of our destiny.

### Every Day: Right Contemplation

Turn to the depths of one's being and strive to identify the essential, the enduring; earnestly and steadfastly work toward goals in accord with it. Seek to perceive the virtues that are yet to be acquired and set the course to attain them. Seek to observe the vices that arise in one's life and identify a means of dissolving them.

## PART 1
## The Eightfold Path

During the first four weeks of the course, work solely with the above descriptions for the days of the week. Beginning on the first Saturday of the month, during your meditation time, read the ideal for "Right Thought," close your eyes, and hold this ideal for a few moments. When you are ready to open your eyes, speak the words: "Within my heart let dwell the Cosmic Word." Then turn to the tenet of "Right Contemplation," and hold this ideal for a few moments. Again speak the words: "Within my heart let dwell the Cosmic Word."

On the following day, Sunday, during your meditation, read the ideal for "Right Resolve," ending with the speaking of the words: "Within my heart let dwell the Cosmic Word." Then turn to the tenet of "Right Contemplation," and hold this ideal for a few moments. Again speak the words: "Within my heart let dwell the Cosmic Word."

Continue to work in this way with the tenets of the eightfold path for each of the seven days of the week. This cycle is repeated for four weeks, allowing the content to permeate in a fourfold manner, penetrating the higher Self or spirit consciousness in the first week, the astral level in the second week, the etheric level in the third week, and the physical level in the fourth week. This fourfold repetition allows the content of the meditations to integrate more deeply into each of the sheaths of our being, until it begins to work in the will.

### Meditation Exercise: Weeks 1–4

When sitting comfortably:

Inhale the breath of divine light outpouring from the Cosmos; exhale the breath of human love, streaming toward all of creation.

Find inner equilibrium. Become empty.

Read the tenet of the eightfold path for the given day of the week: e.g., Saturday—Right Thought, Sunday—Right Resolve, etc.

Hold in meditation the tenet of the eightfold path. At the close of the meditation, speak the words: "Within my heart let dwell the Cosmic Word."

Turn to the reading on Right Contemplation.

Hold in meditation the tenet of Right Contemplation. At the end of the meditation, again speak the words: "Within my heart let dwell the Cosmic Word."

Repeat each day of the week with the corresponding tenet of the eightfold path.

## PART 2
## The Ten Commandments

The Ten Commandments given by Moses constitute guidelines for human life, and guidance for individuals engaged on a path of spiritual practice. They were given by Moses to help the people of Israel (and in a deeper sense the whole world) in the struggle against the forces of the double. When understood and practiced, the Ten Commandments can bring one into harmony with the purified astral body, with the Virgin, Sophia.

> The Ten Commandments "whisper" their message of the integral being of the Virgin, who was the instrument of realization of the aim of the Sinai alliance—the Incarnation of the Word....
>
> The Ten Commandments signify much more than simply a moral code of daily life. They signify, further, the hygiene, the method, and the conditions of fructification of the spiritual life, including all forms and degrees of practical esotericism (Anonymous, 1991, pp. 295–296).

The path of practical esotericism includes that of *mysticism*, *gnosis*, *sacred magic*, and *hermeticism*, which are addressed in the first four commandments. Mysticism is the experience of mystical union or direct communion with ultimate reality. It is the seed of gnosis, the knowledge of spiritual truth that grows out of mystical revelation and can be brought to communicable expression. Sacred magic is the child of mysticism and gnosis; it is the putting into practice of that which mystical revelation has made known, through the union of divine will and human will working toward the restoration of true freedom. Hermeticism is the manifestation of the unity, mysticism-gnosis-magic. The ideal of hermeticism is to awaken from sleep ever-deeper layers of consciousness. Essentially, the more one becomes truly human, the more one manifests the divine element underlying human nature, which is the "image and likeness of God." The Ten Commandments give the spiritual laws for these dimensions of inner development.

The Ten Commandments could be seen in two groups, guiding the human soul into right relationship with spiritual and earthly aspects of our being. The first four commandments establish a rightful relationship to the spiritual world. This could be seen as a vertical axis between humanity and the world of spirit. The remaining six commandments state the fundamental laws of spiritual culture or discipline pertaining to human relationships. These could be imagined as forming a horizontal axis representing human relations with one another. Together we have the formulation for an inner cross of moral guidance, which is illustrated on pages 212 and 213. (See also, *Meditations on the Tarot*, Arcanum 11.)

The meditations during the next ten weeks include concentration on one of the Ten Commandments in conjunction with the weekly cycle of the eightfold path. During the first week the focus of concentration will be on the first commandment: "Thou shalt have no other gods before me." On Saturday this concentration on the first commandment will be held in the light of "Right Thought"; on Sunday the first commandment will be held in the light of "Right Resolve"; and so forth. Following are short passages to help enter into the essence of each commandment. For a more in-depth commentary on each of the Ten Commandments, see Valentin Tomberg's *Covenant of the Heart*, part two.

## Meditation Exercise: Weeks 5–14

When sitting comfortably:

Inhale the breath of divine light outpouring from the Cosmos; exhale the breath of human love, streaming toward all of creation.

Find inner equilibrium. Become empty.

Read the commandment for the given week and the following passage for that commandment.

Turn to the concentration for the day of the week: e.g., Saturday—Right Thought, Sunday—Right Resolve, etc.

Hold in meditation the commandment in the light of the tenet of the eightfold path. At the close of the meditation, speak the words: "Within my heart let dwell the Cosmic Word. Within my will let work the Will of God."

Turn to the concentration on Right Contemplation. At the end of the meditation, speak the words: "Within my heart let dwell the Cosmic Word. Within my will let work the Will of God."

Repeat each day of the week with the corresponding tenet of the eightfold path.

## Week 5: The First Commandment

**"Thou shalt have no other gods before me."** Mysticism is the awakening of the soul to the presence of God. The first commandment calls upon us to acknowledge the God who transcends the self, the living God of Creation, and that no other gods be acknowledged as equal. This is the living God whose breath is the "vertical line" that supports increasing interiorization. This is the living God who guides our development from subjective conscience to the conscience of the world, from expansion of the individual self to its very own source from which all selves radiate out. "He who is" has a claim to undivided devotion from the center and essence of the whole consciousness of human beings. This is the God who "is more I than I myself am." "Other gods"—beings of the spiritual hierarchies who serve the living God—are of a lesser order than the living God. And beings of the sub-earthly spheres, who can enslave the self and block its path to true freedom, are not to be worshipped or considered as gods. *Love the Lord thy God with all thy heart, with all thy soul and with all thy might. Surrender to the living God.*

## Week 6: The Second Commandment

**"Thou shalt not make for thyself a graven image, or any likeness."** The fundamental law of gnosis is not to substitute imagery drawn from the human mind, or from Nature, for the reality of the living God. The encounter of the being of the soul with the being of God, the reality of God, the truth of God, is not possible through ordinary seeing or knowing. It happens in the reciprocal permeation of the love of God and of the love of the soul. This takes place beyond the level of ordinary images and ideas. It is the radiance of the reality of God—the truth of God—that permeates and envelops the soul of the human being.

## Week 7: The Third Commandment

**"Thou shalt not take the name of the Lord thy God in vain."** The fundamental law of sacred magic is to act in and through the name of the Divine, whilst guarding against making the name of the Divine an instrument of one's own will. This includes activity in the name of God without making use of His name in order to adorn one's self with it. The spoken name of God releases the summoning power contained in it, signifying a magical invocation. Herein lies the possible serious misuse of the holy name of God. If God becomes viewed as a kind of "religious superstructure" rather than the original divine ideal, the name of the Lord is misused.

## Week 8: The Fourth Commandment

**"Remember the Sabbath day, to keep it holy."** Meditation is "sanctified rest," where thought is turned towards that which is above. Meditation is the turning within of the soul that is devoted to the search for truth. Meditation is also a turning away from the outside world and its concerns, influences, after-effects, and memories thereof. Ideally, one seventh of the time ought to be consecrated to turning within, to rising up out of the stream of daily life. Meditation is the "hallowing of the Sabbath." It signifies the fulfillment of the command to turn within for inner reflection. Meditation, contemplation, and prayer all belong to inner reflection or "hallowing the Sabbath." Spiritualization is the goal and meaning of turning within. Turning within mirrors the divine work of creation and rest. The resting which follows the work of God's creation is a spiritualization of the preceding work of creation. Meditation first purifies its own source, the soul, from which it arises. The fundamental law of hermeticism is "as above, so below." And just as God rested on the seventh day, in contemplation and meditation, so—by way of analogy—are human beings also called to devote a certain amount of time to the "sanctified rest" of meditation.

## Week 9: The Fifth Commandment

**"Honor thy father and thy mother."** All progress presupposes continuity—coherence between the past, present, and future. One must abstain from all action that breaks continuity, cutting the current of life. It is the fundamental law of a constructive attitude, which is essential in spiritual life, and is the foundation of all tradition, all continuity in progress, growth, development, and evolution. To honor "father" and "mother" is the spirit and soul of tradition, of constructive continuation from the past to the present, of true progress across the ages, of the path of the life of humankind towards truth. It is the very essence of the life of the spirit and the soul. Interiorization in peace and quiet makes possible the becoming aware of father-love and mother-love as mirrors of divine love. It is the experience of honored paternal love that renders us capable of opening our hearts to the Divine, and honoring the Divine Father of Creation. It is the experience of honored maternal love that underlies our ability to recognize and hallow the Divine Mother of Creation. *Honor thy father and thy mother, as in heaven, so also upon the earth.*

## Week 10: The Sixth Commandment

**"Thou shalt not kill."** The fundamental law of a constructive attitude is essential in spiritual life. "Thou shalt not kill" encompasses all physical acts of destroying life, all negative or destructive thoughts, all negative or hurtful feelings, and all harmful or negatively motivated words and deeds. Thou shalt not kill also applies to the realm of knowledge. One who denies the life of symbols, kills them in his thought. To deny that which reveals means to kill that which lives in the domain of thought. To deny is to kill; to forget is to bury. To honor and appreciate is to preserve the living; to restore to memory is to recall to life. Evil or error cannot be overcome by killing or destruction. The only way to overcome error is by way of transformation—ennoblement through purification. Contemplation leads to an inner deepening—along the paths of tolerance, peaceful coexistence, and the open confrontation between error and truth, between what is useful and what is good, between what is impressive and what is nobly beautiful. In the realm of the spirit it is impossible to kill something living. What takes place is simply an inner transformation, an alchemical process of purification and interiorization or spiritualization, but no extinction.

## Week 11: The Seventh Commandment

**"Thou shalt not commit adultery."** Continuity—or tradition and life—implies faithfulness to the cause that is espoused, to the direction taken, to the ideal that one has as a guide, and to all alliances with entities above and with human beings below, for the sake of the continuity of life. There is carnal adultery, psychic adultery, and spiritual adultery. Unfaithfulness on the physical level is autonomy of carnal desire, which destroys the unity of body, soul, and spirit, shredding the etheric fabric of a marriage union. Psychic adultery constitutes an unfaithful soul life, where one allows one's feelings to become involved with another beyond the appropriate bounds prescribed by psychic loyalty to one's partner. Spiritual adultery is the exchange of a higher moral and spiritual value for a lower moral and spiritual value. Every living spiritual tradition ought to be faithful to its original impulse. Adultery is essentially a form of killing—of separating soul and body, whose union is the archetype of marriage. Our eternal covenant with God requires eternal loyalty. In the bond of marriage between man and woman is mirrored the marriage covenant of God with each human soul.

### Week 12: The Eighth Commandment

**"Thou shalt not steal."** Theft is the desire to obtain without effort or sacrifice that whose worth implies effort and sacrifice. Stealing of material goods, of another's feelings or ideas, stealing social, occupational, or spiritual gain: all constitute theft. All "tricks" of a technical nature, having as their aim the dispensing with the effort and sacrifice required for normal spiritual growth and development, fall under the heading of theft. You will harvest only after having tilled the earth, only after having sown, and only after having waited for the time when the fruit will be ripe for harvesting. All other gain is false.

### Week 13: The Ninth Commandment

**"Thou shalt not bear false witness against thy neighbor."** This commandment warns against the spirit of rivalry manifested as negative criticism. All action should be motivated by love for the cause and ideal rather than by a spirit of rivalry. Anyone who takes on himself the mission of judge can act only in the sense of destruction. Anyone who begins to criticize soon passes to censure and ends up condemning, which leads inevitably to division into hostile camps and to other forms of destruction. Criticism and polemicism are mortal enemies of the spiritual life. They signify the substitution of destructive electrical energy for constructive vital force. Slander—"false witness against your neighbor"—is a killing of the good reputation, respect, and trust of another human being; the extended soul life of another is distorted and destroyed. Slander is moral murder and robbery.

### Week 14: The Tenth Commandment

**"Thou shalt not covet thy neighbor's house."** This commandment expresses the spirit of rivalry manifesting as envy. The life, marriage, possessions, and honor of another human being are just as inviolable as they are for one's self. The physical body is a possession or extension of the human soul that allows the soul to live in the world as the place of the development of his or her consciousness. The portion of the outer world perceived as "possession," or property, is a kind of extended body, an extension of the field of action of the human soul. This is also the realm of the development of consciousness for each human soul. The house, yard, garden, and field of my neighbor is his or her "extended body," an extension of the field of action of the human soul. To desire thy neighbor's possessions is to violate his or her development. Coveting is a form of psychic murder and robbery.

## PART 3
## The Threefold Double

In exploring dimensions of the subconscious realm of the soul that manifest as the human double, it can be helpful to approach this as a threefold domain: 1) the realm sometimes referred to as the luciferic aspect of the double which includes patterns that arise out of egotism, self-delusion, anger, or irresponsibility; 2) the realm sometimes referred to as the ahrimanic aspect of the double which includes patterns that arise out of selfishness, fear, greed, or duty; 3) the realm referred to here as one's karmic double, which includes the patterns that arise out of one's own personal karmic history. The names Lucifer and Ahriman, used to identify different aspects of the double, arise out of the mythology of spiritual history, and were used by Rudolf Steiner in describing the "doppelgänger."

## Luciferic Double

Lucifer is a spiritual being, described in the Judeo-Christian tradition, who once dwelled in the heavens as the most light-filled spirit. Lucifer means "light-bearer." Egotism took seed in him and he disregarded the Word of God. He was cast out of heaven by the Archangel Michael in the battle with the spirits of darkness. The serpent in the Garden of Eden is a symbolic representation of Lucifer, who enticed humanity into the Fall through doubt, confusion, self-aggrandizement, and disobedience. The qualities of the luciferic double are archetypal for all of humanity. We all share these tendencies that reside in the human soul or astral body. Some of the aspects of the luciferic double are: pride, self-righteousness, deceit, self-delusion, false-beautification, anger, desire, self-aggrandizement, egotism, reckless abandon, irresponsibility, and excess of levity. Luciferic impulses and desires tend to overly excarnate and veil one from consciousness.

When the luciferic double is confronted, shame arises. In the biblical story of the Fall, after eating from the tree of the knowledge of good and evil, Adam and Eve felt shame and covered themselves with fig leaves. This symbolizes an attempt to cover over or hide one's misdeeds. The arising of shame is an innate response to deeds that are not in alignment with spiritual truth. This is the means by which one gains awareness and begins the work of the transformation of the luciferic double.

One must overcome the tendency to repress, deny, or avoid shame. If one allows one's self to feel shame when it occurs, to enter into it and perceive its beneficial purpose, it will reveal areas of the subconscious that need growth. This activates the recognition of behaviors and patterns that need transforming. When shame arises and is acknowledged, the luciferic aspect of one's soul recedes in the face of truth and righteousness, leading to reparation.

The luciferic double is overcome not only by means of shame, but through humility, selflessness, honesty, and renunciation of all lying.

## Ahrimanic Double

The being of Ahriman is introduced in the ancient Persian tradition of Zoroastrianism. Ahriman is the twin of Ahura-Mazda—Ahriman being the dark or evil twin and Ahura-Mazda being the light being of goodness or the Sun God. The Zoroastrian tradition depicts the polarity of good and evil. Ahriman wants nothing more than to entice all of humanity under his power, to disconnect humans from their spiritual consciousness and debilitate their inclination to love. In the same way that luciferic qualities are archetypal, so are the ahrimanic qualities of the double universally shared by all of humanity. Yet, while the luciferic characteristics reside in the human soul, the ahrimanic aspect of the double resides primarily in the etheric or chi realm of our being. Some aspects of the ahrimanic double are: fear, greed, selfishness, materialism, confusion, depersonalization, need to control, mechanization, doubt, cowardliness, hatred, gravity, and despair. Ahrimanic impulses and desires tend to overly incarnate and entrap one in the material world, disconnecting one from spiritual consciousness.

The ahrimanic double resides primarily in the etheric body. It affects a condition of weariness of life, heaviness, boredom, coldness, depression, loneliness; it is the deepest source of intemperance. Unlike in the luciferic double that, when confronted, precipitates shame which leads to transformation, when the ahrimanic double is revealed, hatred arises. This does not lead to transformation, but rather to a greater alienation. This aspect of our subconscious cannot be transformed as such, but must be brought into servitude, and eventually cast out. One must grant this aspect of the double no nourishment to sustain its power. By perceiving it and recognizing it, the ahrimanic double recoils. It must be overcome or dissolved through love, which can arise out of one's awareness of the presence of hatred. One cannot overcome ahrimanic impulses through force, just as one cannot fight the darkness. One can, however, light a candle that will dispel the darkness. Love is the power that can dispel ahrimanic forces.

## Karmic Double

The karmic double comprises the collective personal negative patterning of one's individual biography from the time of the Fall. It is part luciferic and part ahrimanic. It is an astral-etheric combination with a false balance, a "compromised heart." All inner compromises come from this double. The karmic double is influenced by circumstances that one formulates in the process of incarnating. Hereditary tendencies in one's constitution, temperament, and character relate to the karmic conditioning that provides a framework for the patterns of one's double to unfold. Upbringing, cultural background, and values influence the karmic double. The geographic forces where one is born and raised interface with the unfolding of one's karmic double. One's gender, male or female, also is related to the karmic tasks of a given incarnation. Also, undigested remnants of previous lives manifest in the karmic double of each individual. These factors all have significant purpose in the fulfillment of the karmic tasks undertaken in a given life that are residing within the individual karmic double.

The karmic double is unconscious until age seven; from ages seven to fourteen it is in a state of deep sleep; from ages fourteen to twenty-one it is in a dreamlike state; and at age twenty-one it is born and present throughout life. The karmic double is the most difficult to overcome because it is personal; it is our own individual legacy which we drag along from lifetime to lifetime. Unlike the luciferic double which can be freed through the growing inner love of truthfulness, and the ahrimanic double which must be cast out, the karmic double can eventually be expelled or shed much like the way a snake sheds its skin when it no longer needs it. Then it becomes perceptible and can be transformed and even trained to serve the good.

Near the time of death the karmic double is very present and then withdraws as the life forces diminish. Just prior to death, one is often in a very pure and almost blessed condition; this signifies the absence of the double.

One's karmic double is revealed when one dies. It is left in the Moon sphere after one's time in kamaloca. If one has overcome one's karmic double, and attained a purified astral body or Manas state, then after death the archetype of the collective misdeeds of humanity, the double of humanity, is revealed. It then becomes one's task to help redeem the karma of the Earth and humanity. This great task must also be accomplished in due course of time. The Ten Commandments present an evolutionary framework for the redemption of the double of humanity.

## Aspects of the Double

| **Luciferic** *in astral body* | **Ahrimanic** *in etheric body* | **Karmic** *astral-etheric combination* |
|---|---|---|
| pride | greed | heredity |
| deceit | materialism | constitution |
| egotism | calculated | temperament |
| anger | cold | character |
| self-aggrandizement | fear | culture |
| irresponsibility | doubt/confusion | gender |
| reckless abandon | hate | geographic location |
| self-delusion | controlling | climate |
| overly carefree | weariness | remnants from past |
| desire/lust | depression | lives |
| false beautification | boredom/restlessness | illness |
| arrogance | power-greed | rejection |
| denial | gravity | abandonment |
| cover over | source of intemperance | jealous |
| speculation | mechanistic | infidelity |
| presumption | impersonal | envy |
| power-egotism | loneliness | negativity |
| self-righteous | cowardliness | judgment/accusation |
| certainty | heaviness | victimized |
| Tower of Babel | long to destroy | resentment |
| disobedience | overly dutiful | rivalry |
| forcefulness | sloth, laziness/torpor | critical |
| insolence | amoral | distrusting |
| intolerance/aversion | calcified/hardened | ingratitude |
| irreverence | self-destruction | unforgiving |
| | | revenge |

## Meditation Exercise: Weeks 15–26

When sitting comfortably:

Inhale the breath of divine light outpouring from the Cosmos; exhale the breath of human love, streaming toward all of creation.

Find inner equilibrium. Become empty.

Read the passage for the noted aspect of the double.

Turn to the concentration for the day of the week: e.g., Saturday—Right Thought, Sunday—Right Resolve, etc.

Hold in meditation the aspect of the double in the light of the tenet of the eightfold path. At the close of the meditation, speak the words: "Within my heart let dwell the Cosmic Word. Within my will let work the Will of God."

Turn to the concentration on Right Contemplation. At the end of the meditation, speak the words: "Within my heart let dwell the Cosmic Word. Within my will let work the Will of God."

Repeat each day of the week with the corresponding tenet of the eightfold path.

### Week 15: Luciferic Double

Reread the passage regarding the luciferic double. Review the list of aspects of the luciferic double. Read the concentration for Saturday, Right Thought, etc. Enter into a meditation on the relationship between the luciferic double and Right Thought on Saturday, etc., following the meditation exercise above.

### Week 16: Ahrimanic Double

Reread the passage regarding the ahrimanic double. Review the list of aspects of the ahrimanic double. Read the concentration for Saturday, Right Thought, etc. Enter into a meditation on the relationship between the ahrimanic double and Right Thought on Saturday, etc., following the meditation exercise above.

### Week 17: Karmic Double

Reread the passage regarding the karmic double. Review the list of aspects of the karmic double. Read the concentration for Saturday, Right Thought, etc. Enter into a meditation on the relationship between the karmic double and Right Thought on Saturday, etc., following the meditation exercise above.

## PART 4
## The Threefold Luciferic Double

Lucifer erects three separating walls that breed isolation: 1) Lucifer separates human beings from the spiritual world; 2) Lucifer separates human beings from one another; 3) Lucifer separates one's consciousness from one's subconscious. The luciferic double can be thought of as having a threefold nature: luciferic thinking, luciferic feeling, and a luciferic will. Understanding these three aspects of the luciferic double can help one in dissolving these inner forces.

### Week 18: Luciferic Thinking

Luciferic thinking constructs a wall that separates one from the spiritual world. This is the stance: *I come in my own name, not in the name of the Father.* Lucifer is radiant and shines with his own light, but he does not let the light of the spiritual world shine through him. Forms of luciferic thinking include speculation and presumption taken as truth (lack of objectivity), and justification of one's own point of view.

The story of the Tower of Babel exemplifies luciferic thinking. The following story is an aggadah from a Midrash based on Genesis 11:1–9.

> Long, long ago, after the great flood, when all the people of the earth spoke one language, the descendants of Noah had been ravaged by many battles. To save their community, the people's council wanted to build a new city around a tall tower that would reach so high into the sky, it would touch the heavens. "We wish to become known throughout the world for our great tower," they said when they presented their

ideas to King Nimrod. "From the heights of the tower we will be able to see our enemies before they see us, destroy them with great force, and rule the earth." Nimrod was impressed and approved the plan.

And so representatives of the council journeyed to seek out the perfect place for their new city. After two years they came upon the land of Shinar, where they began to build their new city. Bricks were baked in giant ovens until they were harder than rocks. The tower grew so high that those carrying bricks and mortar up the giant ramps had to climb for a full year before they reached to top. Workers climbed day and night, day after day and night after night. The entire span of the growing tower was always filled with workers—some climbing up and some coming down.

The people's pride grew with each brick laid, as did their anticipation of the power they would possess once the tower was completed. Little by little, pride gave way to arrogance, and soon the people viewed themselves as greater and stronger than their Lord God in heaven. There were those who wanted to wage war with all who dwelt in heaven; those who wanted to place their own gods in heaven and do service only unto them; and others who wanted to smite the Lord Himself. The builders became obsessed with the growing tower. Nothing else mattered. When a coworker accidentally fell off the tower, there was less concern for his life than for any bricks that may have fallen with him.

And it came to pass that Abraham heard of the mighty tower being built, and so he traveled to the valley of Shinar. He saw how the tower had changed the people, how it had poisoned their hearts and minds. He tried to stop the building, but no one listened. Abraham prayed to the Lord: "God Almighty, stop the building of this tower and scatter these people throughout the world." The Lord summoned some of his trusted angels and sent them down to the new city to create confusion, and so they did.

Suddenly every builder spoke a different language, and no one on the tower could understand anyone else. When a man asked for a brick, his coworker handed him mortar. Frustration grew and soon workers were flinging bricks and mortar at one another, builders were falling from the tower, one after the other, and a great many died.

> Thus, the Lord punished all those who had rebelled against Him. The ones who had threatened heaven with arrows perished at the hands of their coworkers; those who had wanted to place their own gods in heaven were turned into wild animals; and those who had wanted to smite the Lord Himself were dispersed throughout the world. The rest of the people in the community were spared. They stopped work on the tower and left the land of Shinar forever.
>
> Fire fell from heaven and burned the top of the tower, and a great earthquake swallowed the bottom. The part of the tower that remained stands to this day, exposed to the winds of heaven, and casts a shadow that is many, many miles long.

One who comes in one's own name, or who builds a "tower" to replace a revelation from heaven by what one has fabricated oneself, will be blasted by a thunderbolt; he will undergo the humiliation of being reduced to his own subjectivity and to terrestrial reality.

> He who exalts himself will be abased, and he who humbles himself will be exalted (Luke 14:11).

In more subtle guises, when one forgets to recognize and honor the creator, one stands only for one's self. In order to counter this tendency, one seeks to remember God in every word and deed.

Humility is the transformative quality for luciferic thinking. One endeavors to bring the oscillation of thoughts to stillness and peace, to give up egotistical thinking, so that cosmic wisdom can enter and reveal truths that will illumine one's understanding. This is the process of silencing the ego in the realm of thinking, stilling the continuous rationale that validates and perpetuates one's luciferic patterns.

Take this into meditation throughout the week: on Saturday in relation to Right Thought, etc., following the meditation exercise above, seeking to identify and transform the luciferic impulses in one's self and in the circumstances of one's life.

## Week 19: Luciferic Feeling

Luciferic feeling constructs a wall that separates one from one's fellow human beings. Self-righteousness, self-assertion, the desire for power, and the assertion of self-interest by projecting one's self out into the world to gain or maintain personal power, exemplify luciferic feeling. This is often cloaked in the disguise of human rights: it is our "right" to do this.

This condition is depicted in the story from the Gospel of John:

> The scribes and the Pharisees brought before Jesus a woman who had been caught in adultery. They said to him, "This woman has been caught in the act of adultery. In the law, Moses commanded us to stone such. What do you say about her?" (John 8:3–11).

The scribes and Pharisees had the ulterior motive of wanting her silenced by death so she could not reveal any of the information she knew about them; for they, too, had enjoyed her company and shared their secrets with her. Their personal desire for covering over the truth and maintaining power was veiled by their claim that according to Moses this was the lawful punishment for her. It is our "right" to do so. They were asserting their own power under veiled pretenses. When Jesus bent down and wrote upon the Earth, he brought to consciousness the law of karma. When he arose and spoke: "Let him who is without sin among you, cast the first stone," he awakened their conscience through silence and questioning. Silence and questioning lead to an awakened conscience that can transform the desire for power to the longing for the well-being of all, and transform self-interest to magnanimity, greatness of heart. The self-righteous stance demanding personal rights becomes a truly righteous stance for the rights of all of humanity and the Earth.

Take this into meditation throughout the week: on Saturday in relation to Right Thought, etc., following the meditation exercise above, seeking to identify and transform the luciferic impulses in one's self and in the circumstances of one's life.

## Week 20: Luciferic Will

The luciferic will constructs a wall that separates consciousness from the subconscious. That which is above suppresses that which is below, or that which is below rules that which is above. This is the opposite orientation to "Thy will be done." Personal will supersedes divine will. There is a desire to hide what is true, to cover over the subconscious (covering over with the fig leaf in Paradise), a desire for self-beautification or false image—all of which are forms of deceit. First one lies about one's self, then one lies about others.

The story of King Saul and David in the first book of Samuel exemplifies the luciferic will. After David slew Goliath, his fame and reputation grew. It was said, "Saul has slain his thousands, and David his ten thousands" (1 Sam. 18:7).

Saul became jealous and sought David's death. When searching with his soldiers in the mountains of Engedi, Saul entered a cave to rest. Not knowing that David was already in the back of the cave hiding with his men, Saul slept. Thus, according to the promise of the Lord, David's enemy was delivered unto him. Instead of killing Saul, David cut the skirt off Saul's robe. In doing so he took away from Saul his dignity and importance in the affairs of men. A dignitary in a short skirt has little authority among his subjects. Saul can be seen here as representing the luciferic will which hunts human souls to possess them, in this case through jealousy. Saul strove to assert his will for personal power and glory. David did not kill him, but cut the skirt off his robe, depriving the luciferic will of its authority and power, exposing it in its true light, and subjugating it to a higher will, that of the Divine.

A more subtle example of luciferic will is portrayed in Peter's denial of Christ:

> Peter declared to him, "Though they all fall away because of you, I will never fall away." Jesus said to him, "Truly, I say to you, this very night, before the cock crows, you will deny me three times." Peter said to him, "Even if I must die with you, I will not deny you." And so said all the disciples.
>
> Then Jesus went with them to a place called Gethsemane, and he said to his disciples, "Sit here, while I go yonder and pray." And taking

with him Peter and the two sons of Zebedee, he began to be sorrowful and troubled. Then he said to them, "My soul is very sorrowful, even to death; remain here, and watch with me." And going a little farther he fell on his face and prayed, "My Father, if it be possible, let this cup pass from me; nevertheless, not as I will, but as thou wilt." And he came to the disciples and found them sleeping; and he said to Peter, "So could you not watch with me one hour? Watch and pray that you may not enter into temptation; the spirit indeed is willing, but the flesh is weak." Again, for the second time, he went away and prayed, "My Father, if this cannot pass unless I drink it, thy will be done." And again he came and found them sleeping, for their eyes were heavy. So leaving them again, he went away and prayed for the third time, saying the same words. Then he came to the disciples and said to them, "Are you still sleeping and taking your rest? Behold, the hour is at hand, and the Son of man is betrayed into the hands of sinners. Rise, let us be going; see, my betrayer is at hand."

While he was still speaking, Judas came, one of the twelve, and with him a great crowd with swords and clubs, from the chief priests and the elders of the people. Now the betrayer had given them a sign, saying, "The one I shall kiss is the man; seize him." And he came up to Jesus at once and said, "Hail Master!" And he kissed him. Jesus said to him, "Friend, why are you here?" Then they came up and laid hands on Jesus and seized him. And behold, one of those who were with Jesus stretched out his hand and drew his sword, and struck the slave of the high priest, and cut off his ear. Then Jesus said to him, "Put your sword back into its place; for all who take the sword will perish by the sword. Do you think that I cannot appeal to my Father, and he will at once send me more than twelve legions of angels? But how then should the scriptures be fulfilled, that it must be so?" At that hour Jesus said to the crowds, "Have you come out as against a robber, with swords and clubs to capture me? Day after day I sat in the temple teaching, and you did not seize me. But all this has taken place, that the scriptures of the prophets might be fulfilled." Then all the disciples forsook him and fled.

Then those who had seized Jesus led him to Caiaphas the high priest, where the scribes and the elders had gathered. But Peter followed him at a distance, as far as the courtyard of the high priest, and going inside he sat with the guards to see the end. Now the chief

> priests and the whole council sought false testimony against Jesus that they might put him to death, but they found none, though many false witnesses came forward. At last two came forward and said, "This fellow said, 'I am able to destroy the temple of God, and to build it in three days.'" And the high priest stood up and said, "Have you no answer to make? What is it that these men testify against you?" But Jesus was silent. And the high priest said to him, "I adjure you by the living God, tell us if you are the Christ, the Son of God." Jesus said to him, "You have said so. But I tell you, hereafter you will see the Son of man seated at the right hand of Power, and coming on the clouds of heaven." Then the high priest tore his robes, and said, "He has uttered blasphemy. Why do we still need witnesses? You have now heard his blasphemy. What is your judgment?" They answered, "He deserves death." Then they spat in his face, and struck him; and some slapped him, saying, "Prophesy to us, you Christ! Who is it that struck you?"
>
> Now Peter was sitting outside in the courtyard. And a maid came up to him, and said, "You also were with Jesus the Galilean." But he denied it before them all, saying, "I do not know what you mean." And when he went out to the porch, another maid saw him, and she said to the bystanders, "This man was with Jesus of Nazareth." And again he denied it with an oath, "I do not know the man." After a little while the bystanders came up and said to Peter, "Certainly you are also one of them, for your accent betrays you." Then he began to invoke a curse on himself and to swear, "I do not know the man." And immediately the cock crowed. And Peter remembered the saying of Jesus, "Before the cock crows, you will deny me three times." And he went out and wept bitterly (Matt. 26:33–75).

When shame uncovers what is false, deceit can be transformed into spiritual realism. In the ideal, one will transform the subconscious so that nothing needs to be hidden. Meditation creates the means for consciousness to penetrate the subconscious.

Take this into meditation throughout the week: on Saturday in relation to Right Thought, etc., following the meditation exercise above, seeking to identify and transform the luciferic impulses in one's self and in the circumstances of one's life.

## Aspects of the Luciferic Double in the Astral Body with the Counter-Balancing Virtues

| **Luciferic Aspects** | **Counter Impulses** |
|---|---|
| pride | humility |
| deceit | honesty |
| egotism | humility |
| anger | compassion |
| self-aggrandizement | interest in others |
| irresponsibility | responsibility |
| reckless abandon | caution/careful/thoughtful |
| self-delusion | honesty/self-awareness |
| overly carefree | responsible |
| desire/lust | purity/temperance |
| false beautification | acceptance of self |
| arrogance | tolerance |
| denial | willingness to look at truth |
| cover over | reveal truth |
| speculation | remain open-minded |
| presumption | non-judgmental |
| power-egotism | service |
| self-righteous | merciful/compassionate |
| certainty | open-mindedness |
| spiritual arrogance/Tower of Babel | foot-washing |
| rivalry | cooperation |
| disobedience | obedience |
| forcefulness | patience/respecting cycles of time |
| insolence | respect |
| intolerance/aversion | tolerance/non-judgmental |
| irreverence | reverent/respectful |

# PART 5
# The Threefold Ahrimanic Double

The ahrimanic double also has a threefold nature, that of thinking, feeling, and will. These three aspects of the ahrimanic double also erect barriers that lead to isolation and loneliness. Ahrimanic thinking separates our true thought nature from the spiritual world. Ahrimanic feeling separates our true soul nature from our fellow human beings. Ahrimanic will separates our conscious impulse to act in the world from the subconscious impulses. Having a clear understanding of these aspects of one's subconscious nature can reveal great possibilities for inner transformation.

## Week 21: Ahrimanic Thinking

Ahrimanic thinking is cold, mechanistic, calculating, heartless, and often filled with hatred. It precipitates fear and confusion. If, when one experiences this aspect of the double within one's self, one can identify it and be objective in relation to one's self, one has the possibility to turn one's thoughts to compassion, warmth, and love, which can dissolve and disempower ahrimanic thinking.

William Shakespeare portrays a vivid example of ahrimanic thinking in the character Iago in *Othello*. Iago, Othello's advisor, cunningly plots the demise of the Moor of Venice and his household, by falsely implicating Desdemona, Othello's wife, as unfaithful.

**Iago**
And what's he then that says I play the villain,
When this advice is free I give and honest, Probal to thinking, and indeed the course
To win the Moor again? For 'tis most easy
Th' inclining Desdemona to subdue
In any honest suit; she's framed as fruitful
As the free elements. And then for her
To win the Moor—were't to renounce his baptism, All seals and symbols of redeemed sin—
His soul is so enfettered to her love

> That she may make, unmake, do what she list, Even as her appetite shall play the god
> With his weak function. How am I then a villain
> To counsel Cassio to this parallel course, Directly to his good?
> Divinity of hell! When devils will the blackest sins put on,
> They do suggest at first with heavenly shows, As I do now. For whiles this honest fool Plies Desdemona to repair his fortunes,
> And she for him pleads strongly to the Moor, I'll pour this pestilence into his ear,
> That she repeals him for her body's lust;
> And by how much she strives to do him good, She shall undo her credit with the Moor.
> So will I turn her virtue into pitch,
> And out of her own goodness make the net
> That shall enmesh them all (act 2, scene 3, lines 336–362).

Another example of ahrimanic thinking can be seen in the rulers, soldiers, and the criminal to the right of Christ at the Crucifixion on Golgotha.

> Two others also, who were criminals, were led away to be put to death with him. And when they came to the place which is called The Skull, there they crucified him, and the criminals, one on the right, and one on the left. And Jesus said, "Father, forgive them; for they know not what they do." And they cast lots to divide his garments. And the people stood by, watching; but the rulers scoffed at him, saying, "He saved others; let him save himself, if he is the Christ of God, his Chosen One!" The soldiers also mocked him, coming up and offering him vinegar, and saying, "If you are the King of the Jews, save yourself!"... One of the criminals who were hanged railed at him, saying, "Are you not the Christ? Save yourself and us!" But the other rebuked him, saying, "Do you not fear God, since you are under the same sentence of condemnation? And we indeed justly; for we are receiving the due reward of our deeds; but this man has done nothing wrong." And he said, "Jesus, remember me when you come in your kingly power." And he said to him, "Truly, I say to you, today you will be with me in Paradise" (Luke 23:32–43).

The rulers, soldiers, and the criminal on the right challenged the power and omnipotence of Christ. The rulers expected power and super-human acts of intervention; the criminal on the right sought escape from true justice. Each portrayed aspects of ahrimanic thinking.

The criminal on the left understood that it was not omnipotence that was at stake, but it was love. The true impulse of love transcends all temptations, insults, and mockery. When mercy and compassion stream into one's thought life, Ahriman is defeated. Love is the power that can disarm Ahriman.

Take this into meditation throughout the week: on Saturday in relation to Right Thought, etc., following the meditation exercise above, seeking to identify and dissolve the ahrimanic impulses in one's self and in the circumstances of one's life.

## Week 22: Ahrimanic Feeling

When in the grips of ahrimanic feeling one can recognize a coldness of heart that turns inward upon one's self or outward toward others. It is marked by callousness, cut off from feelings. There is an absence of love. When turned inward or outward, it depletes life forces, severs human connections, breeds hatred, isolation, and distrust.

In Albert Camus's novel, *The Stranger*, the main character, Mersault, epitomizes ahrimanic feeling. He has murdered a man on the beach for no viable reason, and after he is condemned to die, he states, "I only wish a crowd to gather at my death and shout hatred at me." Mersault is completely cut off from the spiritual world; he has no faith in God or in his fellow human beings. He lives an existential life that has no meaning. Ahriman seeks for humanity to be cut off from the true meaning of life.

On a more subtle level, ahrimanic feelings are experienced whenever one is depressed, bored, greedy, covetous, critical, condemning, hopeless, sinister, cynical, alienated, controlling, fearful, lonely. To work consciously with these tendencies, one can continually be aware of others and consider them with warmth and compassion. To connect with others in truth, integrity, trust, cooperation, consideration, and care dissolves ahrimanic feelings, which otherwise lead to isolation and despair.

Take this into meditation throughout the week: on Saturday in relation to Right Thought, etc., following the meditation exercise above, seeking to identify and dissolve the ahrimanic impulses in one's self and in the circumstances of one's life.

### Week 23: Ahrimanic Will

Ahrimanic will is characterized by actions that have no conscience, that treat others or Nature as material objects, devoid of spiritual essence. One driven by ahrimanic will forces takes whatever actions suits his or her wishes without any regard for others. Often fear or the desire for personal gain motivate ahrimanic deeds. Examples might include: child pornography, the Nazi movement resulting in the holocaust, or sadomasochism. King Herod's slaughter of the innocents exemplifies ahrimanic will.

> Then Herod, when he saw that he had been tricked by the wise men, was in a furious rage, and he sent and killed all the male children in Bethlehem and in all that region who were two years old or under, according to the time which he had ascertained from the wise men (Matt. 2:16–17).

The means of overcoming ahrimanic will forces is to hold in consciousness the divine essence that indwells everyone and everything. When one acknowledges the divine nature of every aspect of creation, and acts with this consciousness, one's will forces will be immune to ahrimanic impulses.

Take this into meditation throughout the week: on Saturday in relation to Right Thought, etc., following the meditation exercise above, seeking to identify and dissolve the ahrimanic impulses in one's self and in the circumstances of one's life.

## Aspects of the Ahrimanic Double in the Etheric Body with the Counter-Balancing Virtues

| **Ahrimanic Aspects** | **Counter Impulses** |
|---|---|
| greed | generosity |
| materialistic | non-materialistic |
| calculating | concern for others |
| cold | warm |
| fear | love/inner peace |
| doubt/confusion | clarity |
| hate | love |
| controlling | faith in process |
| weariness | energetic |
| depression | joyful |
| boredom/restlessness | involved/productive |
| power/greed | service/generosity |
| gravity | inner balance |
| source of intemperance | temperance |
| mechanistic | humanistic |
| impersonal | personal/warm |
| loneliness | involved with others |
| cowardliness | courageous |
| heaviness | inner harmony |
| destructive | creative |
| overly dutiful | balance of joy and responsibility |
| sloth, laziness/torpor | efficient, productive |
| amoral | ethical, developed conscience |
| calcified/hardened | flexible/inner resilience |
| self-destruction | care of self |

## PART 6
## The Threefold Karmic Double

The karmic double can also be experienced as threefold in nature: including karmic thinking, karmic feeling, and karmic will. The karmic double is an amalgamation of luciferic and ahrimanic characteristics as they have manifested in each individual's biography. It is an astral-etheric combination consisting of three parts, with a false balance. Astrality, or unconscious desire patterns, enter the etheric sheath and create an etheric body full of astrality, a "thing-in-between." All inner compromises (when one feels a compromised heart) derive from the influence of this double. The karmic double arises in relationships that encompass issues such as betrayal, abandonment, jealousy, resentment, etc.: feelings that arise from interactions in relationships with others. The inner transformation required to redeem one's karmic double can only take place here on the Earth through ennobling human relationships.

The redemption of the karmic double begins with the transformation of karmic thinking, which allows the possibility for spiritual imagination to unfold. Then it is possible to address the realm of karmic feeling; when the karmic double is robbed of its intelligence, it will begin to follow the good, allowing spiritual inspiration to arise. Then the stage of spiritual intuition becomes possible as the karmic will becomes emptied of its own driving forces and able, like a vessel, to receive the grace of divine love as motivation for the will, thus uniting the human will with divine will.

### Week 24: Karmic Thinking

Karmic thinking results in easily finding fault with others, but has difficulty seeing one's own role of responsibility or culpability. With karmic thinking, one might imagine the human head as being astral. This is a picture of subconscious feelings ruling one's thoughts. There is no room for objectivity, creative forces, or freedom; the head consists of its own light. One's thoughts are governed by feelings that are clinging to maintain a karmic pattern. It thinks sultrily and passionately. The thought, *If only they would change*, represents karmic thinking. The blame or responsibility is placed on others. Karmic thinking can be transformed through courageously honest self-examination. Consider how it might be possible that you are fully responsible for the circumstances, although it is in no way evident. Try to imagine what could possibly have happened in a past life to make the current situation a perfect learning ground. Consider how *you* might change, rather than focusing on how the *other person* might change.

Read the short story "The Spark Neglected Burns the House," by Leo Tolstoy, which epitomizes karmic thinking. The old father, lying on the stove, portrays the inner voice that guides the transformation of karmic thinking. The Dalai Lama, in his position of non-blame toward the Chinese, exemplifies the eradication of karmic thinking.

**A Spark Neglected Burns The House** by Leo Tolstoy

*Then came Peter and said to him, "Lord, how oft shall my brother sin against me, and I forgive him? until seven times?" Jesus saith unto him, "I say not unto thee, until seven times; but, until seventy times seven. Therefore is the kingdom of heaven likened unto a certain king, which would make a reckoning with his servants. And when he had begun to reckon, one was brought unto him, which owed him ten thousand talents. But forasmuch as he had not wherewith to pay, his lord commanded him to be sold, and his wife, and children, and all that he had, and payment to be made. The servant therefore fell down and worshipped him, saying, 'Lord, have patience with me, and I will pay thee all.' And the lord of that servant, being moved with compassion, released him, and forgave him the debt. But that servant went out, and found one of his fellow servants, which owed him a hundred pence: and he laid hold on him, and took him by the throat saying, 'Pay what thou owest.' So his fellow servant fell down and besought him, saying, 'Have patience with me, and I will pay thee.' And he would not: but went and cast him into prison, till he should pay that which was due. So when his fellow servants saw what was done, they were exceeding sorry, and came and told unto their lord all that was done. Then his lord called him unto him, and saith to him, 'Thou wicked servant, I forgave thee all that debt, because thou besoughtest me: shouldest not thou also have had mercy on thy fellow servant, even as I had mercy on thee?' And his lord was wroth, and delivered him to the tormentors, till he should pay all that was due. So shall also my heavenly Father do unto you, if ye forgive not every one his brother from your hearts."*—Matthew 18:21–35

There once lived in a village a peasant named Iván Shcherbakóv. He was comfortably off, in the prime of life, the best worker in the village, and had three sons, all able to work. The eldest was married, the second about to marry, and the third was a big lad who could mind the horses and was already beginning to plow. Iván's wife was an able and thrifty woman, and they were fortunate in having a quiet, hardworking daughter-in-law. There was nothing to prevent Iván and his family from living happily. They had only one idle mouth to feed; that was Iván's old father, who suffered from asthma and had been lying ill on the top of the brick oven for seven years. Iván had all he needed: three horses and a colt, a cow with a calf, and fifteen sheep. The women made all the clothing for the family, besides helping in the fields, and the men tilled the land. They always had grain enough of their own to last over beyond the next harvest and sold enough oats to pay the taxes and meet their other needs. So Iván and his children might have lived quite comfortably had it not been for a feud between him and his next-door neighbor, Limping Gabriel, the son of Gordéy Ivánov.

As long as old Gordéy was alive and Iván's father was still alive to manage the household, the peasants lived as neighbors should. If the women of either house happened to want a sieve or a tub, or the men required a sack, or if a cart-wheel got broken and could not be mended at once, they used to send to the other house, and helped each other in neighborly fashion. When a calf strayed into the neighbor's thrashing-ground they would just drive it out, and only say, "Don't let it get in again; our grain is lying there." And such things as locking up the barns and outhouses, hiding things from one another, or backbiting were never thought of in those days.

That was in the fathers' time. When the sons came to be at the head of the families, everything changed.

It all began about a trifle.

Iván's daughter-in-law had a hen that began laying rather early in the season, and she started collecting its eggs for Easter. Every day she went to the cart shed, and found an egg in the cart; but one day the hen, probably frightened by the children, flew across the fence into the neighbor's yard and laid its egg there. The woman heard the cackling, but said to herself: "I have no time now; I must tidy up for Sunday. I'll fetch the egg later on." In the evening she went to the cart, but found no egg there. She went and asked her mother-in-law and brother-in-law whether they had taken the egg. "No," they had not; but her youngest brother-in-law, Tarás, said: "Your Biddy laid its egg in the neighbor's yard. It was there she was cackling, and she flew back across the fence from there."

The woman went and looked at the hen. There she was on the perch with the other birds, her eyes just closing ready to go to sleep. The woman wished she could have asked the hen and got an answer from her.

Then she went to the neighbor's, and Gabriel's mother came out to meet her.

"What do you want, young woman?"

"Why, Granny, you see, my hen flew across this morning. Did she not lay an egg here?"

"We never saw anything of it. The Lord be thanked, our own hens started laying long ago. We collect our own eggs and have no need of other people's! And we don't go looking for eggs in other people's yards, lass!"

The young woman was offended, and said more than she should have done. Her neighbor answered back with interest, and the women began abusing each other. Iván's wife, who had been to fetch water, happening to pass just then, joined in too. Gabriel's wife rushed out, and began reproaching the young woman with things that had really happened and with other things that never had happened at all. Then a general uproar commenced, all shouting at once, trying to get out two words at a time, and not choice words either.

"You're this!" and "You're that!" "You're a thief!" and "You're a slut!" and "You're starving your old father-in-law to death!" and "You're a good-for-nothing!" and so on.

"And you've made a hole in the sieve I lent you, you jade! And it's our yoke you're carrying your pails on—you just give hack our yoke!"

Then they caught hold of the yoke, and spilt the water, snatched off one another's shawls, and began fighting. Gabriel, returning from the fields, stopped to take his wife's part. Out rushed Iván and his son and joined in with the rest. Iván was a strong fellow, he scattered the whole lot of them, and pulled a handful of hair out of Gabriel's beard. People came to see what was the matter, and the fighters were separated with difficulty.

That was how it all began.

Gabriel wrapped the hair torn from his heard in a paper, and went to the District Court to have the law on Iván. "I didn't grow my heard," said he, "for pockmarked Iván to pull it out!" And his wife went bragging to the neighbors, saying they'd have Iván condemned and sent to Siberia. And so the feud grew.

The old man, from where he lay on the top of the oven, tried from the very first to persuade them to make peace, but they would not listen. He told them, "It's a stupid thing you are after, children, picking quarrels about such a paltry matter. Just think! The whole thing began about an egg. The children may have taken it—well, what matter? What's the value of one egg? God sends enough for all! And suppose your neighbor did say an unkind word—put it right; show her how to say a better one! If there has been a fight—well, such things will happen; we're all sinners, but make it up, and let there be an end of it! If you nurse your anger it will be worse for you yourselves."

But the younger folk would not listen to the old man. They thought his words were mere senseless dotage. Iván would not humble himself before his neighbor.

"I never pulled his beard," he said, "he pulled the hair out himself. But his son has burst all the fastenings on my shirt, and torn it.... Look at it!"

And Iván also went to law. They were tried by the Justice of the Peace and by the District Court. While all this was going on, the coupling-pin of Gabriel's cart disappeared. Gabriel's womenfolk accused Iván's son of having taken it. They said: "We saw him in the night go past our window, towards the cart; and a neighbor says he saw him at the pub, offering the pin to the landlord."

So they went to law about that. And at home not a day passed without a quarrel or even a fight. The children, too, abused one another, having learnt to do so from their elders; and when the women happened to meet by the riverside, where they went to rinse the clothes, their arms did not do as much wringing as their tongues did nagging, and every word was a bad one.

At first the peasants only slandered one another; but afterwards they began in real earnest to snatch anything that lay handy, and the children followed their example. Life became harder and harder for them. Iván Shcherbakov and Limping Gabriel kept suing one another at the Village Assembly, and at the District Court, and before the Justice of the Peace until all the judges were tired of them. Now Gabriel got Iván fined or imprisoned; then Iván did as much to Gabriel; and the more they spited each other the angrier they grew—like dogs that attack one another and get more and more furious the longer they fight. You strike one dog from behind, and it thinks it's the other dog biting him, and gets still fiercer. So these peasants: they went to law, and one or other of them was fined or locked up, but that only made them more and more angry with each other. "Wait a bit," they said, "and I'll make you pay for it." And so it went on for six years. Only the old man lying on the top of the oven kept telling them again and again: "Children, what are you doing? Stop all this paying back; keep to your work, and don't bear malice—it will be better for you. The more you bear malice, the worse it will be."

But they would not listen to him.

In the seventh year, at a wedding, Iván's daughter-in-law held Gabriel up to shame, accusing him of having been caught horse stealing. Gabriel was tipsy, and unable to contain his anger, gave the woman such a blow that she was laid up for a week; and she was pregnant at the time. Iván was delighted. He went to the magistrate to lodge a complaint. "Now I'll get rid of my neighbor! He won't escape imprisonment, or exile to Siberia." But Iván's wish was not fulfilled. The magistrate dismissed the case. The woman was examined, but she was up and about and showed no sign of any injury. Then Iván went to the Justice of the Peace, but he referred the business to the District Court. Iván bestirred himself: treated the clerk and the Elder of the District Court to a gallon of liquor and got Gabriel condemned to be flogged. The sentence was read out to Gabriel by the clerk: "The Court decrees that the peasant Gabriel Gordéev shall receive twenty lashes with a birch rod at the District Court."

Iván, too, heard the sentence read, and looked at Gabriel to see how he would take it. Gabriel grew as pale as a sheet, and turned round and went out into the passage. Iván followed him, meaning to see to the horse, and he overheard Gabriel say, "Very well! He will have my back flogged: that will make it burn; but something of his may burn worse than that!"

Hearing these words, Iván at once went back into the Court, and said: "Upright judges! He threatens to set my house on fire! Listen: he said it in the presence of witnesses!"

Gabriel was recalled. "Is it true that you said this?"

"I haven't said anything. Flog me, since you have the power. It seems that I alone am to suffer, and all for being in the right, while he is allowed to do as he likes."

Gabriel wished to say something more, but his lips and his cheeks quivered, and he turned towards the wall. Even the officials were frightened by his looks. "He may do some mischief to himself or to his neighbor," thought they.

Then the old Judge said: "Look here, my men; you'd better be reasonable and make it up. Was it right of you, friend Gabriel, to strike a pregnant woman? It was lucky it passed off so well, but think what might have happened! Was it right? You had better confess and beg his pardon, and he will forgive you, and we will alter the sentence."

The clerk heard these words, and remarked: "That's impossible under Statute 117. An agreement between the parties not having been arrived at, a decision of the Court has been pronounced and must be executed."

But the Judge would not listen to the clerk.

"Keep your tongue still, my friend," said he. "The first of all laws is to obey God, who loves peace." And the Judge began again to persuade the peasants, but could not succeed. Gabriel would not listen to him.

"I shall be fifty next year," said he, "and have a married son, and have never been flogged in my life, and now that pockmarked Iván has had me condemned to be flogged, and am I to go and ask his forgiveness? No; I've borne enough.... Iván shall have cause to remember me!"

Again Gabriel's voice quivered, and he could say no more, but turned round and went out.

It was seven miles from the Court to the village, and it was getting late when Iván reached home. He unharnessed his horse, put it up for the night, and entered the cottage. No one was there. The women had already gone to drive the cattle in, and the young fellows were not yet back from the fields. Iván went in, and sat down, thinking. He remembered how Gabriel had listened to the sentence, and how pale he had become, and how he had turned to the wall; and Iván's heart grew heavy. He thought how he himself would feel if he were sentenced, and he pitied Gabriel. Then he heard his old father up on the oven cough, and saw him sit up, lower his legs, and scramble down. The old man dragged himself slowly to a seat, and sat down. He was quite tired out with the exertion, and coughed a long time till he had cleared his throat. Then, leaning against the table, he said: "Well, has he been condemned?"

"Yes, to twenty strokes with the rods," answered Iván.

The old man shook his head.

"A bad business," said he. "You are doing wrong, Iván! Ah! It's very bad—not for him so much as for yourself!... Well, they'll flog him: but will that do you any good?"

"He'll not do it again," said Iván.

"What is it he'll not do again? What has he done worse than you?

"Why, think of the harm he has done me!" said Iván. "He nearly killed my son's wife, and now he's threatening to burn us up. Am I to thank him for it?"

The old man sighed, and said: "You go about the wide world, Iván, while I am lying on the oven all these years, so you think you see everything, and that I see nothing.... Ah, lad! It's you that don't see; malice blinds you. Others' sins are before your eyes, but your own are behind your back. 'He's acted badly!' What a thing to say! If he were the only one to act badly, how could strife exist? Is strife among men ever bred by one alone? Strife is always between two. His badness you see, but your own you don't. If he were bad, but you were good, there would be no strife. Who pulled the hair out of his beard? Who spoilt his haystack? Who dragged him to the law court? Yet you put it all on him! You live a bad life yourself, that's what is wrong! It's not the way I used to live, lad, and it's not the way I taught you. Is that the way his old father and I used to live? How did we live? Why, as neighbors should! If he happened to run out of flour, one of the women would come across: 'Uncle Trol, we want some flour.' 'Go to the barn, dear,' I'd say: 'take what you need.' If he'd no one to take his horses to pasture, 'Go, Iván,' I'd say, 'and look after his horses.' And if I was short of anything, I'd go to him. 'Uncle Gordéy,' I'd say, 'I want so-and-so!' 'Take it Uncle Trol!' That's how it was between us, and we had an easy time of it. But now?... That soldier the other day was telling us about the fight at Plevna. Why, there's war between you worse than at Plevna! Is that living?... What a sin it is! You are a man and master of the house; it's you who will have to answer. What are you teaching the women and the children? To snarl and snap? Why, the other day your Taráska—that greenhorn—was swearing at neighbor Irena, calling her names; and his mother listened and laughed. Is that right? It is you will have to answer. Think of your soul. Is this all as it should be? You throw a word at me, and I give you two in return; you give me a blow, and I give you two. No, lad! Christ, when He walked on earth, taught us fools something very different.... If you get a hard word from any one, keep silent, and his own conscience will accuse him. That is what our Lord taught. If you get a slap, turn the other cheek. 'Here, beat me, if that's what I deserve!' And his own conscience will rebuke him. He will soften, and will listen to you. That's the way He taught us, not to be proud!... Why don't you speak? Isn't it as I say?"

Iván sat silent and listened.

The old man coughed, and having with difficulty cleared his throat, began again: "You think Christ taught us wrong? Why, it's all for our own good. Just think of your earthly life; are you better off, or worse, since this Plevna began among you? Just reckon up what you've spent on all this law business—what the driving backwards and forwards and your food on the way have cost you! What fine fellows your sons have grown; you might live and get on well; but now your means are lessening. And why? All because of this folly; because of your pride. You ought to be plowing with your lads, and do the sowing yourself; but the fiend carries you off to the judge, or to some pettifogger or other. The plowing is not done in time, nor the sowing, and mother earth can't bear properly. Why did the oats fail this year? When did you sow them? When you came back from town! And what did you gain? A burden for your own shoulders.... Eh, lad, think of your own business! Work with your boys in the field and at home, and if someone offends you, forgive him, as God wished you to. Then life will be easy, and your heart will always be light."

Iván remained silent.

"Iván, my boy, hear your old father! Go and harness the roan, and go at once to the Government office; put an end to all this affair there;

and in the morning go and make it up with Gabriel in God's name, and invite him to your house for tomorrow's holiday (it was the eve of the Virgin's Nativity). Have tea ready, and get a bottle of vodka and put an end to this wicked business, so that there should not be any more of it in future, and tell the women and children to do the same."

Iván sighed, and thought, "What he says is true," and his heart grew lighter. Only he did not know how to begin to put matters right.

But again the old man began, as if he had guessed what was in Iván's mind.

"Go, Iván, don't put it off. Put out the fire before it spreads, or it will be too late."

The old man was going to say more, but before he could do so the women came in, chattering like magpies. The news that Gabriel was sentenced to be flogged, and of his threat to set fire to the house, had already reached them. They had heard all about it and added to it something of their own, and had again had a row, in the pasture, with the women of Gabriel's household. They began telling how Gabriel's daughter-in-law threatened a fresh action: Gabriel had got the right side of the examining magistrate, who would now turn the whole affair upside down; and the schoolmaster was writing out another petition, to the Tsar himself this time, about Iván; and everything was in the petition—all about the coupling-pin and the kitchen garden—so that half of Iván's homestead would be theirs soon. Iván heard what they were saying, and his heart grew cold again, and he gave up the thought of making peace with Gabriel.

In a farmstead there is always plenty for the master to do. Iván did not stop to talk to the women, but went out to the threshing floor and to the barn. By the time he had tidied up there, the sun had set and the young fellows had returned from the field. They had been plowing the field for the winter crops with two horses. Iván met them, questioned them about their work, helped to put everything in its place, set a torn horse collar aside to be mended, and was going to put away some stakes under the barn, but it had grown quite dusk, so he decided to leave them where they were till next day. Then he gave the cattle their food, opened the gate, let out the horses. Tarás was to take to pasture for the night, and again closed the gate and barred it. "Now," thought he, "I'll have my supper, and then to bed." He took the horse collar and entered the hut. By this time he had forgotten about Gabriel and about what his old father had been saying to him. But, just as he took hold of the door handle to enter the passage, he heard his neighbor on the other side of the fence cursing somebody in a hoarse voice: "What the devil is he good for?" Gabriel was saying. "He's only fit to be killed!" At these words all Iván's former bitterness towards his neighbor re-awoke. He stood listening while Gabriel scolded, and, when he stopped, Iván went into the hut.

There was a light inside; his daughter-in-law sat spinning, his wife was getting supper ready, his eldest son was making straps for bark shoes, his second sat near the table with a book, and Tarás was getting ready to go out to pasture the horses for the night. Everything in the hut would have been pleasant and bright, but for that plague—a bad neighbor!

Iván entered, sullen and cross; threw the cat down from the bench, and scolded the women for putting the slop pail in the wrong place. He felt despondent, and sat down, frowning, to mend the horse collar. Gabriel's words kept ringing in his ears: his threat at the law court, and what he had just been shouting in a hoarse voice about some one who was "only fit to be killed."

His wife gave Tarás his supper, and, having eaten it, Tarás put on an old sheepskin and another coat, tied a sash round his waist, took some bread with him, and went out to the horses. His eldest brother was going to see him off, but Iván himself rose instead, and went out into the porch. It had grown quite dark outside, clouds had gathered, and the wind had risen. Iván went down the steps, helped his boy to mount, started the foal after him, and stood listening while Tarás rode down the village and was there joined by other lads with their horses. Iván waited until they were all out of hearing. As he stood there by the gate he could not get Gabriel's words out of his head: "Mind that something of yours does not burn worse!"

"He is desperate," thought Iván. "Everything is dry, and it's windy weather besides. He'll come up at the back somewhere, set fire to something, and be off. He'll burn the place and escape scot free, the villain! There now, if one could but catch him in the act, he'd not get off then!" And the thought fixed itself so firmly in his mind that he did not go up the steps but went out into the street and round the corner. "I'll just walk round the buildings; who can tell what he's after?" And Iván, stepping softly, passed out of the gate. As soon as he reached the corner, he looked round along the fence, and seemed to see something suddenly move at the opposite corner, as if some one had come out and disappeared again. Iván stopped, and stood quietly, listening and looking. Everything was still; only the leaves of the willows fluttered in the wind, and the straws of the thatch rustled. At first it seemed pitch dark, but, when his eyes had grown used to the darkness, he could see the far corner, and a plow that lay there, and the eaves. He looked a while, but saw no one.

I suppose it was a mistake," thought Iván; "but still I will go round," and Iván went stealthily along by the shed. Iván stepped so softly in his bark shoes that he did not hear his own footsteps. As he reached the far corner, something seemed to flare up for a moment near the plow and to vanish again. Iván felt as if struck to the heart; and he stopped. Hardly had he stopped, when something flared up more brightly in the same place, and he clearly saw a man with a cap on his head, crouching down, with his hack towards him, lighting a bunch of straw he held in his hand. Iván's heart fluttered within him like a bird. Straining every nerve, he approached with great strides, hardly feeling his legs under him. "Ah," thought Iván, "now he won't escape! I'll catch him in the act!"

Iván was still some distance off, when suddenly he saw a bright light, but not in the same place as before, and not a small flame. The thatch had flared up at the eaves, the flames were reaching up to the roof, and, standing beneath it, Gabriel's whole figure was clearly visible.

Like a hawk swooping down on a lark, Iván rushed at Limping Gabriel. "Now I'll have him; he shan't escape me!" thought Iván. But Gabriel must have heard his steps, and (however he managed it) glancing round, he scuttled away past the barn like a hare.

"You shan't escape!" shouted Iván, darting after him.

Just as he was going to seize Gabriel, the latter dodged him; but Iván managed to catch the skirt of Gabriel's coat. It tore right off, and Iván fell down. He recovered his feet, and shouting, "Help! Seize him! Thieves! Murder!" ran on again. But meanwhile Gabriel had reached his own gate. There Iván overtook him and was about to seize him, when something struck Iván a stunning blow, as though a stone had hit his temple, quite deafening him. It was Gabriel who, seizing an oak wedge that lay near the gate, had struck out with all his might.

Iván was stunned; sparks flew before his eyes, then all grew dark and he staggered. When he came to his senses Gabriel was no longer there: it was as light as day, and from the side where his homestead was something roared and crackled like an engine at work. Iván turned round and saw that his back shed was all ablaze, and the side shed had also caught fire, and flames and smoke and bits of burning straw mixed with the smoke, were being driven towards his hut.

"What is this, friends?" cried Iván, lifting his arms and striking his thighs. "Why, all I had to do was just to snatch it out from under the eaves and trample on it! What is this, friends?" he kept repeating. He wished to shout, but his breath failed him; his voice was gone. He wanted to run, but his legs would not obey him, and got in each other's way. He moved slowly, but again staggered and again his breath failed. He stood still till he had regained breath, and then went on. Before he had got round the back shed to reach the fire, the side shed was also all ablaze; and the corner of the hut and the covered gateway had caught fire as well. The flames were leaping out of the hut, and it was impossible to get into the yard. A large crowd had collected, but nothing could be done. The neighbors were carrying their belongings out of their own houses, and driving the cattle out of their own sheds. After Iván's house, Gabriel's also caught fire, then, the wind rising, the flames spread to the other side of the street and half the village was burnt down.

At Iván's house they barely managed to save his old father; and the family escaped in what they had on; everything else, except the horses that had been driven out to pasture for the night, was lost; all the cattle, the fowls on their perches, the carts, plows, and harrows, the women's trunks with their clothes, and the grain in the granaries—all were burnt up!

At Gabriel's, the cattle were driven out, and a few things saved from his house.

The fire lasted all night. Iván stood in front of his homestead and kept repeating, "What is this? Friends! One need only have pulled it out and trampled on it!" But when the roof fell in, Iván rushed into the burning place, and seizing a charred beam, tried to drag it out. The women saw him, and called him back; but he pulled out the beam, and was going in again for another when he lost his footing and fell among the flames. Then his son made his way in after him and dragged him out. Iván had singed his hair and beard and burnt his clothes and scorched his hands, but he felt nothing. "His grief has stupefied him," said the people. The fire was burning itself out, but Iván still stood repeating: "Friends! What is this? One need only have pulled it out!"

In the morning the village Elder's son came to fetch Iván.

"Daddy Iván, your father is dying! He has sent for you to say good-bye."

Iván had forgotten about his father, and did not understand what was being said to him.

"What father?" he said. "Whom has he sent for?"

"He sent for you, to say good-bye; he is dying in our cottage! Come along, daddy Iván," said the Elder's son, pulling him by the arm; and Iván followed the lad.

When he was being carried out of the hut, some burning straw had fallen on to the old man and burnt him, and he had been taken to the village Elder's in the farther part of the village, which the fire did not reach.

When Iván came to his father, there was only the Elder's wife in the hut, besides some little children on the top of the oven. All the rest were still at the fire. The old man, who was lying on a bench holding a wax candle in his hand, kept turning his eyes towards the door. When his son entered, he moved a little. The old woman went up to him and told him that his son had come. He asked to have him brought nearer. Iván came closer.

"What did I tell you, Iván?" began the old man "Who has burnt down the village?"

"It was he, father!" Iván answered. "I caught him in the act. I saw him shove the firebrand into the thatch. I might have pulled away the burning straw and stamped it out, and then nothing would have happened."

"Iván," said the old man, "I am dying, and you in your turn will have to face death. Whose is the sin?"

Iván gazed at his father in silence, unable to utter a word.

"Now, before God, say whose is the sin? What did I tell you?"

Only then Iván came to his senses and understood it all. He sniffed and said, "Mine, father!" And he fell on his knees before his father, saying, "Forgive me, father; I am guilty before you and before God."

The old man moved his hands, changed the candle from his right hand to his left, and tried to lift his right hand to his forehead to cross himself, but could not do it, and stopped.

"Praise the Lord! Praise the Lord!" said he, and again he turned his eyes towards his son.

"Iván! I say, Iván!"

"What, father?"

"What must you do now?"

Iván was weeping.

"I don't know how we are to live now, father!" he said.

The old man closed his eyes, moved his lips as if to gather strength, and opening his eyes again, said: "You'll manage. If you obey God's will, you'll manage!" He paused, then smiled, and said: "Mind, Iván! Don't tell who started the fire! Hide another man's sin, and God will forgive two of yours!" And the old man took the candle in both hands and, folding them on his breast, sighed, stretched out, and died.

Iván did not say anything against Gabriel, and no one knew what had caused the fire.

And Iván's anger against Gabriel passed away, and Gabriel wondered that Iván did not tell anybody. At first Gabriel felt afraid, but after awhile he got used to it. The men left off quarrelling, and then their families left off also. While rebuilding their huts, both families lived in one house; and when the village was rebuilt and they might have moved farther apart, Iván and Gabriel built next to each other, and remained neighbors as before.

They lived as good neighbors should. Iván Shcherbakóv remembered his old father's command to obey God's law, and quench a fire at the first spark; and if any one does him an injury he now tries not to revenge himself, but rather to set matters right again; and if any one gives him a bad word, instead of giving a worse in return, he tries to teach the other not to use evil words; and so he teaches his womenfolk and children. And Iván Shcherbakóv has got on his feet again, and now lives better even than he did before.

Take this into meditation throughout the week: on Saturday in relation to Right Thought, etc., following the meditation exercise above, seeking to identify and transform one's karmic thoughts.

## Week 25: Karmic Feeling

The feelings that arise as a result of less than ideal interactions in relationships can reveal to one the karmic issues in one's life. These feelings can be turned inward toward the self, creating a sense of being a victim, or they can be turned outward toward another in confrontation. One can turn inward with feelings of betrayal, abandonment, jealousy, rejection, distrust. It is also common to project onto others feelings of accusation, criticism, judgment, vengeance, infidelity, emotional violence. Negative feelings that accompany emotional pain in relation to another are most often karmic and provide us with insights into the work of transformation that lies ahead.

The story of Cain and Abel is an archetype for karmic feeling.

> Now Adam knew Eve his wife, and she conceived and bore Cain, saying, "I have gotten a man with the help of the Lord." And again she bore his brother Abel. Now Abel was a keeper of sheep, and Cain a tiller of the ground. In the course of time Cain brought to the Lord an offering of the fruit of the ground, and Abel brought of the firstlings of his flock and of their fat portions. And the Lord had regard for Abel and his offering, but for Cain and his offering he had no regard. So Cain was very angry, and his countenance fell. The Lord said to Cain, "Why are you angry, and why has your countenance fallen: If you do well, will you not be accepted? And if you do not do well, sin is crouching at the door; its desire is for you, but you must master it." And Cain spoke with Abel his brother. And it came to pass when they were in the field, Cain rose up against his brother Abel, and killed him. Then the Lord said to Cain: Where is Abel your brother?" He said, "I do not know; am I my brother's keeper?" And the Lord said, "What have you done? The voice of your brother's blood is crying to me from the ground. And now you are cursed from the ground, which has opened its mouth to receive your brother's blood from your hand. When you till the ground, it shall no longer yield to you its strength; you shall be a fugitive and a wanderer on the earth." Cain said to the Lord, "My punishment is greater than I can bear. Behold, thou hast driven me this day away from the ground; and from thy face I shall be hidden; and I shall be a fugitive and a wanderer on the earth, and

> whoever finds me will slay me." Then the Lord said to him, "Not so! If any one slays Cain, vengeance shall be taken on him sevenfold." And the Lord put a mark on Cain, lest any who came upon him should kill him. Then Cain went away from the presence of the Lord, and dwelt in the land of Nod, east of Eden (Gen. 3:4–16).

Cain's fratricide is the seed and origin of all violence, war, and disharmony amongst humankind. The feelings that arise in relation to jealousy, betrayal, infidelity, etc., guide one to karmic issues that could be addressed and healed. The transformation of karmic feeling requires forgiveness. When Peter asked Jesus, "How many times must I forgive, seven times?" Jesus answered, "I do not say to you seven times, but seventy times seven times, for as you forgive one another, so shall you be forgiven by your Father in heaven."

Take this into meditation throughout the week: on Saturday in relation to Right Thought, etc., following the meditation exercise above, seeking to identify and transform one's karmic feelings.

### Week 26: Karmic Will

Deeds enacted in relation to another, as a result of subconscious thoughts and feelings, are most often expressions of karmic will. Often these deeds occur before one realizes the source of motivation or justification for them. One can feel driven to do certain things. It is as if one cannot do otherwise. One then must live with the consequences of one's actions. Karmic will forces can be overcome by constraining the desires to act out of a self-justified rationale. The personal will can be stilled to allow the light of higher consciousness to stream in and guide one's actions.

Judas's betrayal of Christ is an archetype of karmic will.

> When it was evening, he sat at table with the twelve disciples; and as they were eating, he said, "Truly, I say to you, one of you will betray me." And they were very sorrowful, and began to say to him one after another, "Is it I, Lord?" He answered, "He who has dipped his hand in the dish with me, will betray me. The Son of man goes as it is written

> of him, but woe to that man by whom the Son of man is betrayed! It would have been better for that man if he had not been born." Judas, who betrayed him, said, "Is it I, Master?" He said to him, "You have said so."...
>
> While he was still speaking, Judas came, one of the twelve, and with him a great crowd with swords and clubs, from the chief priests and the elders of the people. Now the betrayer had given them a sign, saying, "The one I shall kiss is the man; seize him." And he came up to Jesus at once and said, "Hail Master!" And he kissed him. Jesus said to him, "Friend, why are you here?" Then they came up and laid hands on Jesus and seized him....
>
> When Judas, his betrayer, saw that he was condemned, he repented and brought back the thirty pieces of silver to the chief priests and the elders, saying, "I have sinned in betraying innocent blood." They said, "What is that to us? See to it yourself." And throwing down the pieces of silver in the temple, he departed; and he went and hanged himself. But the chief priests, taking the pieces of silver, said, "It is not lawful to put them into the treasury, since they are blood money." So they took counsel, and bought with them the potter's field, to bury strangers in. Therefore that field has been called the Field of Blood to this day (Matt. 26:20–27:8).

Take this into meditation throughout the week: on Saturday in relation to Right Thought, etc., following the meditation exercise above, seeking to identify and transform one's karmic will.

Aspects of the Karmic Double:
An Astral-Etheric Combination with the Counter-Balancing Virtues

| **Karmic Aspects** | **Counter Impulses** |
|---|---|
| heredity | overcoming heredity, developing individual destiny |
| constitution | developing physical health |
| temperament | balancing temperament |
| character | cultivating virtues in one's character |
| culture | awareness of one's cultural home, developing world citizenship |
| gender | awareness of one's gender in fulfilling karmic challenges |
| geographic location | awareness of geography in karmic situations |
| climate | awareness of the effect of climate on one's life |
| remnants from past lives | sensitivity to echoes from the past |
| illness | conscious exploration of illness, transforming suffering into inner transformation |
| rejection | feeling compassion for the other |
| abandonment | cultivating a sense of self-worth from within |
| jealousy | contentment with self, acceptance of others |
| infidelity | faithful and honest |
| envy | celebrating others achievements |
| negativity | positivity |
| judgment/accusation | compassion, self-scrutiny |
| victimized | take responsibility for one's circumstances |
| resentment | love and compassion for the other |
| rivalry | consciousness of unity and inclusiveness |
| distrusting | trust in the divine plan and use discernment with others |
| ingratitude | gratitude toward the Divine and fellow humans |
| unforgiving | forgiving |
| revenge | acceptance and compassion, turn the other cheek |

## PART 7
## The Ten Commandments

Part seven of this meditation course returns to the Ten Commandments given by Moses. They were given to help the people of Israel (and in a deeper sense the whole world) in the struggle against the forces of the double. When understood and lived, the Ten Commandments can bring one into harmony with the purified astral body, with the Virgin Sophia.

The intention here is to inscribe these laws into one's being in order that they guide one in consciousness throughout one's life.

The meditations during the next ten weeks include concentration on one of the Ten Commandments in conjunction with the weekly cycle of the eightfold path, as in part 2. The intention is that after working through the first part of this course, this experience will be deepened. One seeks to take these moral laws into the fiber of one's soul, allowing them to permeate one's consciousness and imprint themselves upon the guiding force of one's will.

During the first week the focus of concentration will be on the first commandment: "Thou shalt have no other gods before me." On Saturday this concentration on the first commandment will be held in the light of Right Thought; on Sunday the first commandment will be held in the light of Right Resolve, etc. Following are short passages to help enter into the essence of each commandment.

It is recommended that one reads or rereads part 2 of Valentin Tomberg's *Covenant of the Heart* for a more in-depth commentary on each of the Ten Commandments.

### Week 27: The First Commandment

**"Thou shalt have no other gods before me."** Mysticism is the awakening of the soul to the presence of God. The first commandment calls upon us to acknowledge the God who transcends the self, the living God of Creation, and that no other gods be acknowledged as equal. This is the living God whose breath is the "vertical line" that supports increasing interiorization. This is the living God who guides our development from subjective conscience to the conscience of the world, from expansion of the individual self to its very own source from which all selves radiate out. "He who is" has a claim to undivided devotion from the center and essence of the whole consciousness of human beings. This is the God who "is more I than I myself am." "Other gods"—beings of the spiritual hierarchies who serve the living God—are of a lesser order than the living God. And beings of the sub-earthly spheres, who can enslave the self and block its path to true freedom, are not to be worshipped or considered as gods. *Love the Lord thy God with all thy heart, with all thy soul and with all thy might. Surrender to the living God.*

## Week 28: The Second Commandment

**"Thou shalt not make for thyself a graven image, or any likeness."** The fundamental law of gnosis is not to substitute imagery drawn from the human mind, or from Nature, for the reality of the living God. The encounter of the being of the soul with the being of God, the reality of God, the truth of God, is not possible through ordinary seeing or knowing. It happens in the reciprocal permeation of the love of God and of the love of the soul. This takes place beyond the level of ordinary images and ideas. It is the radiance of the reality of God—the truth of God—that permeates and envelops the soul of the human being.

## Week 29: The Third Commandment

**"Thou shalt not take the name of the Lord thy God in vain."** The fundamental law of sacred magic is to act in and through the name of the Divine, whilst guarding against making the name of the Divine an instrument of one's own will. This includes activity in the name of God without making use of His name in order to adorn one's self with it. The spoken name of God releases the summoning power contained in it, signifying a magical invocation. Herein lies the possible serious misuse of the holy name of God. If God becomes viewed as a kind of "religious superstructure" rather than the original divine ideal, the name of the Lord is misused.

## Week 30: The Fourth Commandment

**"Remember the Sabbath day, to keep it holy."** Meditation is "sanctified rest," where thought is turned towards that which is above. Meditation is the turning within of the soul that is devoted to the search for truth. Meditation is also a turning away from the outside world and its concerns, influences, after-effects, and memories thereof. Ideally, one seventh of the time ought to be consecrated to turning within, to rising up out of the stream of daily life. Meditation is the "hallowing of the Sabbath." It signifies the fulfillment of the command to turn within for inner reflection. Meditation, contemplation, and prayer all belong to inner reflection or "hallowing the Sabbath." Spiritualization is the goal and meaning of turning within. Turning within mirrors the divine work of creation and rest. The resting which follows the work of God's creation is a spiritualization of the preceding work of creation. Meditation first purifies its own source, the soul, from which it arises. The fundamental law of hermeticism is "as above, so below." And just as God rested on the seventh day, in contemplation and meditation, so—by way of analogy—are human beings also called to devote a certain amount of time to the "sanctified rest" of meditation.

## Week 31: The Fifth Commandment

**"Honor thy father and thy mother."** All progress presupposes continuity—coherence between the past, present, and future. One must abstain from all action that breaks continuity, cutting the current of life. It is the fundamental law of a constructive attitude, which is essential in spiritual life, and is the foundation of all tradition, all continuity in progress, growth, development, and evolution. To honor "father" and "mother" is the spirit and soul of tradition, of constructive continuation from the past to the present, of true progress across the ages, of the path of the life of humankind towards truth. It is the very essence of the life of the spirit and the soul. Interiorization in peace and quiet makes possible the becoming aware of father-love and mother-love as mirrors of divine love. It is the experience of honored paternal love that renders us capable of opening our hearts to the Divine, and honoring the

Divine Father of Creation. It is the experience of honored maternal love that underlies our ability to recognize and hallow the Divine Mother of Creation. *Honor thy father and thy mother, as in heaven, so also upon the earth.*

## Week 32: The Sixth Commandment

**"Thou shalt not kill."** The fundamental law of a constructive attitude is essential in spiritual life. "Thou shalt not kill" encompasses all physical acts of destroying life, all negative or destructive thoughts, all negative or hurtful feelings, and all harmful or negatively motivated words and deeds. Thou shalt not kill also applies to the realm of knowledge. One who denies the life of symbols, kills them in his thought. To deny that which reveals means to kill that which lives in the domain of thought. To deny is to kill; to forget is to bury. To honor and appreciate is to preserve the living; to restore to memory is to recall to life. Evil or error cannot be overcome by killing or destruction. The only way to overcome error is by way of transformation—ennoblement through purification. Contemplation leads to an inner deepening—along the paths of tolerance, peaceful coexistence, and the open confrontation between error and truth, between what is useful and what is good, between what is impressive and what is nobly beautiful. In the realm of the spirit it is impossible to kill something living. What takes place is simply an inner transformation, an alchemical process of purification and interiorization or spiritualization, but no extinction.

## Week 33: The Seventh Commandment

**"Thou shalt not commit adultery."** Continuity—or tradition and life—implies faithfulness to the cause that is espoused, to the direction taken, to the ideal that one has as a guide, and to all alliances with entities above and with human beings below, for the sake of the continuity of life. There is carnal adultery, psychic adultery, and spiritual adultery. Unfaithfulness on the physical level is autonomy of carnal desire, which destroys the unity of body, soul, and spirit, shredding the etheric fabric of a marriage union. Psychic adultery constitutes an unfaithful soul life, where one allows one's feelings to become involved with another beyond the appropriate bounds prescribed by psychic loyalty to one's partner. Spiritual adultery is the exchange of a higher moral and spiritual value for a lower moral and spiritual value. Every living spiritual tradition ought to be faithful to its original impulse. Adultery is essentially a form of killing—of separating soul and body, whose union is the archetype of marriage. Our eternal covenant with God requires eternal loyalty. In the bond of marriage between man and woman is mirrored the marriage covenant of God with each human soul.

## Week 34: The Eighth Commandment

**"Thou shalt not steal."** Theft is the desire to obtain without effort or sacrifice that whose worth implies effort and sacrifice. Stealing of material goods, of another's feelings or ideas, stealing social, occupational, or spiritual gain: all constitute theft. All "tricks" of a technical nature, having as their aim the dispensing with the effort and sacrifice required for normal spiritual growth and development, fall under the heading of theft. You will harvest only after having tilled the earth, only after having sown, and only after having waited for the time when the fruit will be ripe for harvesting. All other gain is false.

## Week 35: The Ninth Commandment

**"Thou shalt not bear false witness against thy neighbor."** This commandment warns against the spirit of rivalry manifested as negative criticism. All action should be motivated by love for the cause and ideal rather than by a spirit of rivalry. Anyone who takes on himself the mission of judge can act only in the sense of destruction. Anyone who begins to criticize soon passes to censure and ends up condemning, which leads inevitably to division into hostile camps and to other forms of destruction. Criticism and polemicism are mortal enemies of the spiritual life. They signify the substitution of destructive electrical energy for constructive vital force. Slander—"false witness against your neighbor"—is a killing of the good reputation, respect, and trust of another human being; the extended soul life of another is distorted and destroyed. Slander is moral murder and robbery.

### Week 36: The Tenth Commandment

**"Thou shalt not covet thy neighbor's house."** This commandment expresses the spirit of rivalry manifesting as envy. The life, marriage, possessions, and honor of another human being are just as inviolable as they are for one's self. The physical body is a possession or extension of the human soul that allows the soul to live in the world as the place of the development of his or her consciousness. The portion of the outer world perceived as "possession," or property, is a kind of extended body, an extension of the field of action of the human soul. This is also the realm of the development of consciousness for each human soul. The house, yard, garden, and field of my neighbor is his or her "extended body," an extension of the field of action of the human soul. To desire thy neighbor's possessions is to violate his or her development. Coveting is a form of psychic murder and robbery.

## PART 8
## The Five Currents Of The Will

The human being possesses five organs of action—the four limbs and the head in its function as a limb. These five organs of action are an expression of the five currents of the will, which can be expressions of *objective will* or of a subconscious origin here referred to as the five dark currents of the will. The five wounds of Christ correspond to the five currents of the future evolution of the human will, where each limb is dedicated to the will of God.

The five dark currents of the will, which are introduced in the fifth Arcanum of *Meditations on the Tarot*, are: 1) the desire for personal greatness, 2) to take, often at the expense of others, 3) to keep, often at the expense of others, 4) to advance at the expense of others, and 5) to maintain one's position at the expense of others—which correspond, in their turn, to the five limbs. The desire to take or get hold of things is bound to the right hand; the desire to retain or keep things belongs to the left hand; the desire to advance at the expense of others corresponds to the right foot; the desire to hold onto one's position at the expense of others to the left foot. The desire for personal greatness corresponds to the head, only in its function as a limb.

| Dark Currents of the Will | Light Currents of the Will |
|---|---|
| *Desire for personal greatness* | Humility, anonymity |
| *To take, often at the expense of others* | To give, to serve others selflessly at one's own expense |
| *To keep, often at the expense of others* | To share, to surrender control, to have faith in plentitude |
| *To advance at the expense of others* | To withdraw personal desire and serve the good of all |
| *To maintain one's position at the expense of others* | To surrender one's position if it will benefit others; to concern one's self with the good of all |

It is not the case concerning the desire for personal greatness that it corresponds to the head. The head does not bear the fifth wound, for two reasons: firstly, because it bears the "crown of thorns,"... which is borne, in principle, by every person capable of *objective* thought—the "crown of thorns" being given to the human being since the beginning of human history. It is that subtle organ which is designated for us in the Occident as the "eight-petalled lotus," and which is designated in India as the "thousand-petalled lotus" or *sahasrara* (crown center). This crown center is a "natural gift," as it were, to each human being and every normal person possesses it. The "thorns" of the crown center function as the "nails" of objectivity, which give conscience to thought. It is thanks to them that thought has not become wholly emancipated and as arbitrary, for example, as the imagination is. Thought *as such* is, in spite of all, the organ of truth, not of illusion.

Thus, it is not thought as such which allows the desire for personal greatness or the tendency towards megalomania, but rather *the will* which makes use of the head and which can take hold of thought and reduce it to the role of its instrument. And this constitutes the second reason as to why the fifth wound—that of *organic* humility, replacing the current of the will-to-greatness—is not found in the head, but rather in the heart, i.e., it reaches the heart, penetrating from the right-hand side. Because it is there that the will-to-greatness has its origin and it is there from whence it takes hold of the head and makes it its instrument. This is why many thinkers and scientists want to think "without the heart" in order to be objective—which is an illusion, because one can in no way think without the heart, the heart being the activating principle of thought; what one can do is to think with a humble and warm heart instead of with a pretentious and cold heart.

Thus, the fifth wound (which is the *first* in so far as its importance is concerned) is that of the heart instead of the head, the head being *from the point of view of the active will* an instrument or "limb" of the heart (Anonymous, 1991, p. 110).

**Head (as a Limb of the Heart)**

*The desire for personal greatness*

*Luciferic—egotism, megalomania*

Counter impulse: organic humility, anonymity

**Right Side (masculine)**
Reaches out to the world

**Right Arm/Hand**

*Taking at the expense of others*

*Ahrimanic—*
*greed, stealing*

Counter impulse:
giving, serving others selflessly at one's own expense

**Right Foot**

*Advancing at the expense of others*

*Luciferic and ahrimanic—*
*fear, egotism*

Counter impulse:
withdrawing personal desire, serving the good of all

**Left Side (feminine)**
Receptive

**Left Arm/Hand**

*Holding onto at the expense of others*

*Ahrimanic—*
*fear, control, impeding flow*

Counter impulse:
sharing, surrendering control, having faith in plentitude

**Left Foot**

*Maintaining one's position at the expense of others*

*Luciferic and ahrimanic—egotism, fame, arrogance, self-interest*

Counter impulse:
maintaining or surrendering one's position for the benefit of others, concern for the good of all

The immobilization of the subconscious forces of the human will can be seen in the image of Christ nailed to the cross. The wounds in his hands and feet represent the spiritualization of the human will. The fifth wound, the piercing of His side with the spear of Longinus, interiorizes the alliance with God to the depths of one's being. It addresses the human heart, the blood, and the holy water of our being. When each of us, as human beings, can dedicate our will, our deeds, our heart, our blood, and the water of our being to the divine will of the Universe, we will consecrate our lives to God. This is the condition of those beings who have received the stigmata.

### Week 37: Overcoming the Desire for Personal Greatness

**The transformation of the will as expressed in the head as a limb of the heart.** Turn your thoughts to the fifth wound of Christ, the piercing of His side by the spear of Longinus. From this wound poured forth water and blood upon the Earth for the healing of the Earth and humanity. Enter into a meditation on the relationship between the desire for personal greatness, the condition of humility, and the fifth wound of Christ—the wound of the Sacred Heart—remembering that the heart is the activating principle of thought. On Saturday meditate in relation to Right Thought, on Sunday in relation to Right Resolve, etc., following the meditation exercise above.

### Week 38: Overcoming Greed and Stealing

**The transformation of the will as expressed in the right hand.** Focus on the right hand, one's actions in the world. Consider your life's deeds in relation to taking at another's expense, stealing, greed, and the counter impulse of giving and serving others at your own expense. Reflect on the dark and light-filled currents of the right hand in relation to the nailing of Christ's right hand to the cross, the immobilization of the personal will for the manifestation of divine will. Read the concentration for Saturday, Right Thought; for Sunday, Right Resolve; etc. Enter into a meditation on the relationship between the right hand current of the will and Right Thought on Saturday, between the right hand current of the will and Right Resolve on Sunday, etc., following the meditation exercise above.

### Week 39: Overcoming Fear, Control, Hoarding

**The transformation of the will as expressed in the left hand.** Focus on the left hand, how it can express fear, control, hoarding, or faith, generosity, flexibility. Consider your life's deeds in relation to holding on to at another's expense, and the counter impulse of releasing and sharing with others with inner freedom. Reflect on the dark and light-filled currents of the left hand in relation to the nailing of Christ's left hand to the cross, the immobilization of the personal will for the manifestation of divine will. Read the concentration for Saturday, Right Thought, etc. Enter into a meditation on the relationship between the left hand current of the will and Right Thought on Saturday, etc., following the meditation exercise above.

### Week 40: Overcoming the Desire for Power, Fame, Position

**The transformation of the will as expressed in the right foot.** Focus on the right foot, one's position in the world. Consider your life's work in relation to advancing at others' expense, seeking power, fame, and position, and the counter impulse of withdrawing personal desire and serving the good of all. Reflect on the dark and light-filled currents of the right foot in relation to the nailing of Christ's right foot to the cross, the immobilization of the personal will for the manifestation of divine will. Read the concentration for Saturday, Right Thought, etc. Enter into a meditation on the relationship between the right foot current of the will and Right Thought on Saturday, etc., following the meditation exercise above.

### Week 41: Overcoming Self-Interest and Fear

**The transformation of the will as expressed in the left foot.** Focus on the left foot, how it can express fear, egotism, self-interest, or faith, interest in others, an inner disposition to serve. Consider your life's deeds in relation to maintaining your position at others' expense, and the counter impulse of maintaining or surrendering one's position for the good of all. Reflect on the dark and light-filled currents of the left foot in relation to the nailing of Christ's left foot to the cross, the immobilization of the personal will for the manifestation of divine will. Read the concentration for Saturday, Right Thought, etc. Enter into a meditation on the relationship between the left foot current of the will and Right Thought on Saturday, etc., following the meditation exercise above.

## Week 42: The Transformation of the Dark Currents of the Will

If we look closely at the five currents of the will starting from the head down to the feet, we see the progression of the infiltration first of luciferic impulses working in the head, which makes way for ahrimanic impulses to take hold in the hands. Then we have a collaboration of luciferic and ahrimanic influences in the feet. We can see here a common pattern whereby Ahriman patiently waits until Lucifer gets in and takes hold of one's thoughts as an expression of the subconscious will. Then the stage is set for ahrimanic forces to infiltrate one's actions. Once this is set in motion, an interweaving or collaboration of luciferic and ahrimanic impulses takes hold. The transformation of these will forces occurs in the same pattern. It begins in the heart and is expressed in the thinking, which, often through shame, can turn from arrogance to humility, concern for others, and loving service. The short story, "The Legend of Houghty Aggej," by W.M. Sarschim,* poignantly portrays the transformation of the dark currents of the will into light-filled currents selflessly serving the highest good.

Aggej, governor of a large district wherein he is respected for the order he imposes, but feared greatly for the power he wields, believes he is the most powerful ruler on earth. He defies the Bishop when one day in church the Bishop reads the scripture, "And the rich will become poor, and the poor will become rich." Aggej orders that the page upon which these words are written be torn from the Holy Book and the Bishop be thrown in prison. Soon thereafter when hunting, Aggej pursues a majestic stag to all extremes. He loses his horse and clothes, and when he returns naked, no one believes he is the governor, for God sent an angel in Aggej's likeness

* The complete story can be found in *To Grow and Become*, translated and collected by Rudolf Copple, published by The Association of Waldorf Schools of North America (AWSNA), 1994.

to rule his kingdom in his place. The new Aggej rules with kindness and compassion. Aggej seeks to kill his imposter, but in a moment of grace it is revealed to him that the new governor is an angel of God that was sent to punish him for his misdeeds. In his remorse Aggej wanders the countryside. He takes on the life of a beggar and eventually becomes a servant to the brotherhood of the blind. In service to the poor, he finally finds fulfillment and love. When, through the angel's invitation, Aggej is offered his governorship back, he refuses to accept his former position. He is unwilling to go back to the loneliness and isolation of his prior position of power, but rather dedicates himself to serving the blind brothers where he finds happiness and fulfillment in helping others.

Take this story into meditation throughout the week, reflecting on the progression of luciferic, ahrimanic, and luciferic-ahrimanic forces infiltrating the will, and being eradicated from the will first in the heart/head, then the hands, and then the feet: on Saturday in relation to Right Thought, etc., following the meditation exercise above. Seek to identify and transform the dark currents of the will in yourself and in the circumstances of your life.

## Week 43: The Cultivation of Objective Forces of the Will

When the five currents of the will give access to an *objective will,* the future organs of the will are in the process of formation. The passage below from the Gospel of Matthew illustrates the future condition of the human will, where each limb is dedicated to the will of God.

> Then cometh Jesus with them unto a place called Gethsemane, and saith unto the disciples, "Sit ye here while I go and pray yonder." And he took with him Peter and the two sons of Zebedee, and began to be sorrowful and very heavy. Then saith he unto them, "My soul is exceeding sorrowful, even unto death: tarry ye here, and watch with me." And he went a little farther, and fell on his face, and prayed, saying, "O my Father if it be possible, let this cup pass from me: nevertheless, not as I will, but as thou wilt." And he cometh unto the disciples, and findeth them asleep, and saith unto Peter, "What, could ye not

> watch with me one hour? Watch and pray, that ye enter not into temptation: the spirit indeed is willing, but the flesh is weak." He went away again the second time, and prayed, saying, "O my Father, if this cup may not pass away from me, except I drink it, thy will be done." And he came and found them asleep again: for their eyes were heavy. And he left them, and went away again, and prayed the third time, saying the same words. Then cometh he to his disciples, and saith unto them, "Sleep on now, and take your rest; behold, the hour is at hand, and the Son of man is betrayed into the hands of sinners" (Matt. 26:36–45).

Reflect on the unfolding of the objective will as the future organ for the manifestation of divine will. Read the concentration for Saturday, Right Thought, etc. Enter into a meditation on the relationship between objective will and Right Thought on Saturday, etc., following the meditation exercise above.

## PART 9
## The Zodiacalization of the Will

The human will can also be expressed in a twelvefold manner. These twelve currents stream from the twelve petals of the heart chakra, expressing the human will in its present condition of development. These twelve currents of will correspond to the twelve zodiacal aspects of our human nature. The energy currents or virtues that emanate from the great cosmic beings that inhabit the realms of the zodiac have a relationship to the currents that flow from the twelve petals of the heart chakra. The next twelve meditations relate to the twelve cosmic virtues that can be cultivated through the human will. These virtues, when integrated into one's will forces, bring one into harmony with cosmic laws, forming the organ of objective will. For further reading on the twelve virtues, Herbert Witzenmann's book, *The Virtues: The Seasons of the Soul*, is recommended.

## Week 44: Devotion ♈

**Blessed are the devoted for they shall have the power of self-sacrifice.** A cosmic outpouring of the heart-force of devotion streams toward humanity from the great beings of the First Hierarchy (Seraphim, Cherubim, and Thrones) known to us as the Ram or Aries. When, through love, one bears responsibility for other human beings, one feels the experience of devotion. True devotion becomes the inner power of sacrifice. In devotion to others, one offers one's self to them. Through love, devotion arises. Through devotion, deeds of self-sacrifice unfold as the fruit of spiritual love. One can experience images of this in Aggej's devotion to the brotherhood of the blind and Christ's devotion to the healing of humanity. Reflect on devotion and the power of sacrifice. Read the concentration for Saturday, Right Thought, etc. Enter into a meditation on the relationship between devotion, sacrifice, and Right Thought on Saturday, etc., following the meditation exercise above.

## Week 45: Balance ♉

**Blessed are the balanced for they shall make progress.** A cosmic outpouring of the capacity for balance streams toward humanity from the great being of the First Hierarchy known to us as the Bull or Taurus. Through the sacrificial force of devotion, one finds one's inner spirit essence, and its relationship with the spirit essence in the world outside one's self. Like a child who stands upright and learns to balance, one lives between the world of spirit and the Earth. Here is the challenge of balance, from which point one can decide to walk forward upon a path of progress, for balance leads to progress, a path of higher development. An image of balance becoming progress can be seen in Mary Magdalene who, in turning toward the teachings of Christ, brought her body, soul, and spirit into harmony. She found her inner spirit essence and its relationship with the spirit essence in the world outside of herself. This prepared the ground for the progress she underwent, enabling her to serve Christ and experience His resurrection. Reflect on balance and its relation to progress. Read the concentration for

Saturday, Right Thought, etc. Enter into a meditation on the relationship between balance, progress, and Right Thought on Saturday, etc., following the meditation exercise above.

### Week 46: Endurance ♊

**Blessed are those who endure, for they shall have faith.** A cosmic outpouring of the strength of endurance streams toward humanity from the great being of the First Hierarchy known to us as the Twins or Gemini. One who steadfastly progresses toward the unfolding of one's true essence demonstrates perseverance. In persevering, one is faithful to the mandate that one spiritually undertook when incarnating onto the Earth. By working ceaselessly to develop one's inner capacities in the service of others, one fulfills what one owes the world and the people linked with one by destiny. Thus one is faithful. An image of faith expressed through perseverance is that of Job, who endured unimaginable suffering and tragedy. His faith was steadfast throughout, which in the end was rewarded by the restoration of all of his losses. We can also imagine Adam and Eve as archetypes of humanity, who through doubt ate of the tree of the knowledge of good and evil and suffered the loss of union with God. Through toil, suffering, and death we are working to reestablish faith through perseverance or endurance. Reflect on enduring faith. Read the concentration for Saturday, Right Thought, etc. Enter into a meditation on the relationship between endurance, faith, and Right Thought on Saturday, etc., following the meditation exercise above.

### Week 47: Selflessness ♋

**Blessed are the selfless, for they shall undergo catharsis.** A cosmic outpouring of the attribute of selflessness streams toward humanity from the great being of the First Hierarchy known to us as the Crab or Cancer. Faithful endurance is selfless. Selflessness is the path to the human center. It is the path of purification which overcomes fear and greed and liberates one from the dependency of desire. Through consideration of others and self-denial, selflessness leads to catharsis or inner transformation. Catharsis is achieved by vanquishing and transforming the obstacles which threaten the human center of balance. An image of selflessness leading to catharsis is Aggej's selflessly serving the brotherhood of the blind, which led to an inner catharsis, guiding him to turn away from the chance to take back his position as governor. Reflect on selflessness which leads to catharsis. Read the concentration for Saturday, Right Thought, etc. Enter into a meditation on the relationship between selflessness, catharsis, and Right Thought on Saturday, etc., following the meditation exercise above.

## Week 48: Compassion ♌

**Blessed are the compassionate, for they shall be free.** A cosmic outpouring of the heart-force of compassion streams toward humanity from the great being of the First Hierarchy known to us as the Lion or Leo. Selflessness leads to compassion. True compassion experiences all suffering as its own. It is spiritual union. Through compassion for others, one unites spiritually with them and experiences their suffering while maintaining a sense of self and the faculty for objective judgment. Through compassion we release the higher aspect hidden within the other. Everyone for whom we do not feel compassion, who remains external to us, imposes an influence on us. This may be experienced as a desire for avoidance or to dominate, for example. Through the interweaving of compassion, these influences dissolve and freedom arises. True compassion frees one from the entanglements of negativity; it also frees the other whom it encompasses. An example of this is the Dalai Lama's compassion for the Chinese people. Though he does not condone the actions of the Chinese government, he holds a spiritual vision of those people who have harmed the Tibetan people. His heart is free from the bondage of resentment, hatred, or judgment. Compassion releases the heart from the prison of judgment and sets it free to fulfill its true task, which is love. Reflect on compassion which leads to freedom. Read the concentration for Saturday, Right Thought, etc. Enter into a meditation on the relationship between compassion, freedom, and Right Thought on Saturday, etc., following the meditation exercise above.

## Week 49: Courtesy ♍

**Blessed are the courteous, for they shall have tact of heart.** A cosmic outpouring of the will for acts of courtesy streams toward humanity from the great being of the First Hierarchy known to us as the Virgin or Virgo. Through the spiritual union of compassion, one can feel the dignity and true essence of courtesy. True courtesy honors the spiritual "I" of the other and in so doing, one experiences one's self in the other, thus showing esteem for the spirit within the other and within the self. Lack of courtesy is the absence of recognizing and honoring the spirit "I" of another and debases the human condition. One can feel a sense of self-humiliation in the discourteous person. Criticism that does not recognize the potential for development becomes a self-debasement of the critic. Through understanding, courtesy continuously completes and transforms the imperfect. Courtesy is the enactment of tact of heart. An example of this is Sir Gawain, the chivalrous Arthurian knight who, through courtesy and tact of heart, transformed the lower nature of Lady Orgeluse. Reflect on courtesy which leads to tact of heart. Read the concentration for Saturday, Right Thought, etc. Enter into a meditation on the relationship between courtesy, tact of heart, and Right Thought on Saturday, etc., following the meditation exercise above.

## Week 50: Contentment ♎

**Blessed are the contented, for they shall have equanimity.** A cosmic outpouring of the peace of contentment streams toward humanity from the great being of the First Hierarchy known to us as Michael holding the Scales or Libra. Courtesy desires nothing for itself. It only desires to help others in fulfilling their life purpose. If one is convinced that within all of creation dwells the predisposition to its own perfection, one accepts life, seeing the obstacles to one's unfolding as necessary conditions of progress and a spur to personal growth. If one does not recognize the hidden plan of the unfolding of one's evolution, but expects outer measures to effect essential changes, one experiences great frustration and dissatisfaction. Selfless tact of heart is the soil in which inner peace or contentment can grow. This inner peace is ever threatened by reflections on the political and social conditions of our world. The conviction of the ever-present help of the spiritual world, pure faith in the goodness of creation with no security from outer life, is the demand of our time. This will lead to inner peace or contentment which becomes equanimity. An example is Aggej's contentment to serve the brotherhood of the blind. He found equanimity, an inner peace in his soul, no longer desiring the things he didn't possess or fearing the absence of outer security. Reflect on contentment which leads to equanimity. Read the concentration for Saturday, Right Thought, etc. Enter into a meditation on the relationship between contentment, equanimity, and Right Thought on Saturday, etc., following the meditation exercise above.

### Week 51: Patience ♏

**Blessed are the patient, for they shall be enlightened.** A cosmic outpouring of the temperance of patience streams toward humanity from the great being of the First Hierarchy known to us as the Eagle/Scorpion or Scorpio. Equanimity holds in its hand the scales of patience. Patience allows wisdom to unite with one's will forces, to facilitate the unfolding of the cosmic order. It allows our thoughts to mature. Impatience expresses resistance to the unfolding of the cosmic order, tempting one toward prejudice and haste. When one acts out of true patience, one brings to balance wisdom-filled cognition, and will forces that submit to spiritually active judgement, thus awakening insight or the faculty of discernment. Zoroaster sat for ten years in meditation on the mountaintop before Ahura-Mazda spoke to him, and the Buddha sat for days beneath the Boddhi tree awaiting enlightenment. Reflect on patience which leads to insight. Read the concentration for Saturday, Right Thought, etc. Enter into a meditation on the relationship between patience, insight or discernment, and Right Thought on Saturday, etc., following the meditation exercise above.

## Week 52: Control of Tongue ♐

**Blessed are the self-disciplined, for they shall know the truth.** A cosmic outpouring of the mastery of self-discipline streams toward humanity from the great being of the First Hierarchy known to us as the Archer or Sagittarius. Discerning patience controls the tongue and leads to self-discipline. Control of tongue allows one's spirit to awaken to an inner knowing of the truth in world phenomena. When one speaks and judges too precipitously one impairs the process which brings truth to consciousness and allows one's actions to grow out of one's understanding of the world. When one lacks control of tongue, one speaks out of personal opinion rather than out of spiritual truth. Truth is the spirit of things that comes to birth in our understanding. Words spoken with impatience blind us from the truth. Control of one's tongue not only gives the self an opportunity to perceive the truth, it also allows the other to become active in truth-filled perception. Through self-discipline, the other becomes inwardly active and perceives him or herself in his or her own veiled condition. Through control of tongue an interchange between the self and the world are felt and truth becomes known. In Leo Tolstoy's short story, "A Spark Neglected Burns the House," Iván does not tell the village that Gabriel was the one that set the roof of his house on fire. With his control of tongue he comes to realize his own responsibility in the situation and finds the truth of his own thoughts and deeds. Reflect on control of tongue which leads to knowing the truth. Read the concentration for Saturday, Right Thought, etc. Enter into a meditation on the relationship between control of tongue, knowing the truth, and Right Thought on Saturday, etc., following the meditation exercise above.

## Week 53: Courage ♑

**Blessed are the courageous, for they shall have the power to redeem.** A cosmic outpouring for the strength of courage streams toward humanity from the great being of the First Hierarchy known to us as the Goatfish or Capricorn. Knowing the truth leads to courage in the soul. True courage grows out of a soul experience that integrates the past and the future, for truth transcends time. One brings into earthly life the impulse to correct the consequences of one's deeds in a previous earthly life. Through the interpenetration of the spiritual seeds from the past and potential capability for the future, the present becomes the moment of courage. Courage is practiced in inner soul anticipation and exercised in the outer events of destiny. In the knowledge that in a past life the strength was developed that places the individual before a set of circumstances in a later life, the courage that has the power to redeem emerges. In an encounter with people with whom one is connected by destiny, this courage becomes the awakener of consciousness. Examples are the courage of Mahatma Gandhi and Martin Luther King Jr. awakening the resulting consciousness that is gradually working to help redeem the world. Another example is the courage of Sir Gawain to enter the castle of Marvels and face Klingsor, the Sorcerer of Darkness, for the redemption of the captive maidens and the tyrannization of humanity. We have the ultimate example in the courage of Christ, who, out of His love for humanity, endured the scourging, the crowning of thorns, carrying the cross, and the Crucifixion for the redemption of humanity and the whole Earth. Reflect on courage which leads to the power to redeem. Read the concentration for Saturday, Right Thought, etc. Enter into a meditation on the relationship between courage, the power to redeem, and Right Thought on Saturday, etc., following the meditation exercise above.

### Week 54: Discretion ♒

**Blessed are the discreet, for they shall have strength of mind.** A cosmic outpouring of the soul force of discretion streams toward humanity from the great being of the First Hierarchy known as the Water Bearer or Aquarius. When fear of mortality is overcome and one experiences the true essence of one's immortal self, discretion emerges in the soul life. Discretion is the force through which the soul takes hold of itself and experiences itself, not as an inhabitant of the sense-world, but of the spiritual world. The opposite of discretion is surrender to the senses. With genuine knowledge of spiritual essence one becomes reticent or discreet. A reversal of thinking arises which could be called repentance. Through repentance one becomes inwardly self-aware. Discretion in silence is a concentration of force, which is a sheath around the spirit in us. The ability to be silent becomes the protection that guards the spirit in us. Discretion honors the integration of the spiritual and human within. It becomes strength of mind or meditative force. An example of discretion lives in the story of King Saul and David in the first book of Samuel 18–24. After David slew Goliath, his fame and reputation grew. Saul became jealous and sought David's death. When searching with his soldiers in the mountains of Engedi, Saul entered a cave to rest. Not knowing that David was already in the back of the cave hiding with his men, Saul slept. Thus, according to the promise of the Lord, David's enemy was delivered unto him. In his discretion, David did not kill Saul, but cut the skirt off his robe, depriving King Saul of his authority and power, exposing it in its true light, and subjugating it to a higher will, that of the Divine. Although his mortal life was in danger, David acted in consideration of the spiritual reality of the situation.

Another example of this is Lazarus-John who, through discretion, upheld his devotion to Christ and refused to bow down before the emperor Domition, although it engendered a severe threat to his physical well-being (mortal self). Lazarus-John, through meditative strength and purity of heart, became a vessel for the Book of Revelation and the Gospel of John. Reflect on discretion and the development of strength of mind. Read the concentration for Saturday, Right Thought, etc. Enter into a meditation on the relationship between discretion, strength of mind, and Right Thought on Saturday, etc., following the meditation exercise above.

## Week 55: Magnanimity ♓

**Blessed are the magnanimous, for they shall be filled with love.** A cosmic outpouring of the heart-force of magnanimity streams toward humanity from the great being of the First Hierarchy known to us as the Fish or Pisces. In silence, the inner activity of the spirit awakens one's awareness of one's own true being, bringing to birth a sense of individuality. Through one's sense of individuality, one can meet the individuality of another.

Magnanimity is the generous capacity, full of interest and respect, that makes space within itself for every manifestation of being. Every individual is acknowledged as the inviolable signet of the spirit inmost in every human being. The heart-force of magnanimity feels responsible to every other individual, just as it is responsible to the spirit which is the common origin of individuals, from which they gain independence and are called on to fulfill together at the higher level of free community. This heart-force is love. An example of this is St. Francis, whose love for every creature and every person poured forth from his heart. His magnanimity embraced Brother Sun, Sister Moon, Brother Wind, Sister Earth, Brother Fire, Sister Water, every human soul, and all of creation. Reflect on magnanimity and the fullness of love. Read the concentration for Saturday, Right Thought, etc. Enter into a meditation on the relationship between magnanimity, love, and Right Thought on Saturday, etc., following the meditation exercise above.

## PART 10
## The Solarization of the Chakras

The zodiacalization of the will, or the cultivation of the virtues in the human will, corresponds to the activation of the twelve petals of the heart chakra. The work toward the solarization of all the chakras, the transfiguration of the chakras into the full radiance of their spiritual essence, places the heart in the center of all its work. Christ taught, "Love one another." We can see that the task of spiritual alchemy is the transmutation of the substances (metals) of the other chakras or lotuses into the substance of the heart (gold). Spiritual alchemy aims at the transformation of the seven lotuses or chakras into a system of seven hearts, i.e., to transform the human being entirely into heart forces. This means the true humanization of the whole human being becomes the transformation of the chakras into a system functioning by love and for love. The Transfiguration of Christ on Mt. Tabor offers a picture of the ultimate fulfillment of the solarization of the chakras.

> And after six days Jesus taketh with him Peter, and James, and John his brother, and bringeth them up into a high mountain apart: and he was transfigured before them; and his face did shine as the Sun, and his garments became white as the light. And behold, there appeared unto them Moses and Elijah talking with him. And Peter answered, and said unto Jesus, "Lord, it is good for us to be here, if thou wilt, I will make here three tabernacles; one for thee, and one for Moses, and one for Elijah." While he was yet speaking, behold, a bright cloud overshadowed them: and behold, a voice out of the cloud, saying, "This is my beloved Son, in whom I am well pleased; hear ye him." And when the disciples heard it, they fell on their face, and were sore afraid. And Jesus came and touched them and said, "Arise, and be not afraid." And lifting up their eyes, they saw no one, save Jesus only. And as they were coming down from the mountain, Jesus commanded them, saying, "Tell the vision to no man, until the Son of man be risen from the dead" (Matt. 17:1–9).

As Christ revealed his true nature to his three closest disciples, they beheld the Sun-radiance of His being, the fullness of the illumination of His astral body, each chakra streaming forth its radiant light. The darkness of midnight was illumined as if by the Sun at noon. The Christ Being, the Sun Spirit of the Universe, the Eternal Being of Love, came into earthly existence to be an example of divine love and to teach the way of love. The solarization of the chakras is the ultimate transformation of each chakra into a radiant heart center, an active source of divine love.

> The heart or twelve-petalled lotus is the only chakra that is not attached to the organism. It can go out of it and live by the exteriorisation of its "petals," which can be rayed outwards with and in others. When transformed, the heart will become a traveler, a visitor, and anonymous companion of those who are in prison, those who are in exile, and those who bear heavy loads of responsibility, traversing ways leading from one end of the Earth to the other, and also ways through spheres of the spiritual world—from purgatory to the very feet of the Father. Because no distance is insurmountable for love and no door can prevent it from entering—according to the promise which says:

> "and the gates of hell shall not prevail against it" (Matt. 16:18). It is the heart which is the marvelous organ called to serve love in its works. It is the structure of the heart—simultaneously human and divine, a structure of love—which by way of analogy can open our understanding to the words of the Master: "And lo, I am with you always, to the end of time" (Matt. 28:20). (Anonymous, 1991, p. 227)

The work of the transformation of the human being into a being of heart is accomplished in the inner life of the human being, the lotus flowers being only the field where the effects of this purely inner work are manifested. The meditations for the next ten weeks address the solarization or alchemical transformation of each chakra into a living Sun within our being.

## Week 56: The Solarization of the Chakras

In the context of the foregoing introduction, meditate on the Transfiguration of Christ on Mt. Tabor as a living image of the fulfillment of the solarization of the chakras. Meditative exercises for the solarization of each chakra are given below. Each chakra or lotus flower has a specific number of petals. The human condition since the Fall has suffered the disharmonization of the lotus petals. Through spiritual exercises infusing the chakras with divine love, the task of the human being now is to bring half the petals of each lotus flower into harmonious activity, and the other half will be restored to their vital spiritual capacity through divine grace. In understanding the disfiguration of each chakra, it is helpful to reflect on the Paradise story from the Book of Genesis. The story of the Fall can be understood in seven stages, each one corresponding to the disfiguration of one of the chakras. In the same way that the seven stages of the Fall correspond to the disfiguring of each of the chakras, the seven healing miracles of Christ described in the Gospel of John offer the healing principles for each of the chakras. Although the healing miracles were performed on individuals (e.g., the healing of the man born blind), the healing principles are for all human beings. In the following weeks, each meditation addresses one chakra in relation to its spiritual function, the corresponding stage of the Fall or the cause of disfiguration, and the means of healing or transfiguring it to its condition of radiance. The healing of the lotus petals in conjunction with the infusion of divine love into each chakra is the work of the solarization of the chakras.

## Week 57: The Solarization of the Root Chakra ☽

The root chakra, the four-petalled lotus flower, corresponding to the Moon, is the center of the creative force within the human organism, the coiled kundalini energy. It is the portal to the Divine Mother. The root chakra houses the negative karma of one's entire past existence. Thus, Adam and Eve placed fig leaves over their root chakras to hide the knowledge of their disobedience from God. The root chakra embodies the numerical principles of four, and half of four—two. In the four-petalled lotus flower, two of the petals suffering from disharmony need transfiguring through human effort. The apostle Peter was given two keys to the kingdom. He is depicted holding the two keys crossed over his root chakra. What are the two keys to the kingdom? In the Book of Revelation, the Son of Man is described: "And he had in his right hand seven stars: and out of his mouth came a sharp two-edged sword." What is the meaning of the sharp two-edged sword? The dualism of good and evil taught by Zoroaster helps us understand the two keys to the kingdom given to Peter, and the sharp two-edged sword protruding from the mouth of the Son of Man. To heal the four-petalled lotus flower, one must know what is good and what is evil. One edge of the sword cuts through to reveal the truth, the other overcomes evil. We must work in two directions: to stand for the true, the beautiful, and the good; and to stand against evil. Then the two keys to the kingdom will be attained.

The area of vulnerability here is *doubt*, the uncertainty or confusion of what is good and what is evil. This is portrayed by Eve in the Paradise story when the serpent tells her that she will not die if she eats the apple. This contraindicates what God told her. She becomes confused and doubts God's word. Doubt is the first stage of the Fall which corresponds with the root chakra. The meditation for this week addresses the undermining power of doubt, in relation to its counterpart—faith.

The miracle of changing water into wine at the wedding in Cana (John 2:1–11) provides the mystical teaching to heal the root chakra. Mary told the servants, "Do whatever He tells you." These words of Mary give the clear instruction to heal the root chakra. If one follows the teachings of Christ one will know the "good" and align with it, and know "evil" and work to transform it, and one's faith in God will be central to one's existence. Christ infused the water with divine love. As the guests drank the water—changed into wine—they became transformed into living vessels of divine love. Through divine love one acts for the "good" and acts to transform "evil." The solarization of the root chakra is its ultimate transformation into a radiant heart center, an active source of divine love.

Here one can enter into a meditation on the relationship between doubt and its counterpart—faith—in relation to Right Thought on Saturday, etc., following the meditation exercise above with the imagination of the solarization of the root chakra. One may consider, for example: What is doubt? How does it arise? What is its consequence? How is doubt overcome or transfigured? The solarization of the root chakra is a manifestation of knowing what is good and what is evil, fully aligning one's self with the good and against evil, and experiencing unshakable faith in God. When the root chakra is fully transfigured, this center will be an inexhaustible source of élan vital, the Force that transforms all gross and subtle things. *Deliver us from evil.*

## Week 58: The Solarization of the Second Chakra ♀

The second chakra, the six-petalled lotus, in the region of the abdomen and corresponding to the planet Venus, is the center of harmony and health. It is the center of the life force or etheric flow in the human organism. The seal of Solomon, the hexagram, indicates the form of the six petals. The second chakra embodies the numerical principles of six, and half of six—three. In the six-petalled lotus flower, three petals suffering from disharmony need transfiguring by the human being. The three vows of poverty, chastity, and obedience lead to the healing of the second chakra. Poverty is the condition of non-attachment to the material world. It is the condition of not being governed by desire. It also constitutes the condition of spiritual emptiness, longing for the spirit: *blessed are the poor in spirit.* Chastity is the condition of purity. One who is chaste practices fidelity in body, soul, and spirit. Obedience constitutes adherence to the spiritual law, serving the will of God. Christ spoke the words: "I am the Way, the Truth, and the Life." This is the threefold path of Christ.

The area of vulnerability related to the second chakra is the temptation to yield to personal *desire.* This disturbs the harmony of body, soul, and spirit. In the Paradise story, Eve succumbs to this temptation for she desires to attain the knowledge of good and evil so as to become like God. Personal desire brings one into horizontal consciousness. It disconnects one from vertical alignment with the Divine. The second stage of the Fall is succumbing to personal desire, corresponding to the second chakra. The meditation for this week addresses the disunifying power of personal desire and its counterpart—poverty, chastity, and obedience: the desire to serve God.

The miracle of the healing of the nobleman's son (John 4:46–54) provides the mystical teaching to heal the second chakra. The nobleman suffered from the personal desire to please his master. He did not have the vertical alignment to act in harmony with divine truth, and consequently he gave his son over to be raised by his master. Finally when his son was dying, the nobleman went to Jesus and implored Him, saying, "Sir, come down ere my child die." Jesus answered him, saying, "Go thy way; thy son liveth." An inner transformation took place within the nobleman, whereby he overcame his focus on pleasing his master, and arising into his own Egohood, he took responsibility for his son. This brought about a balance of body, soul, and spirit within the nobleman. This healed his son also, for "the sins of the fathers are visited upon the sons." The solarization of the second chakra is its ultimate transformation into a radiant heart center, an active source of divine love.

Here one can enter into a meditation on the relationship between personal desire and its counterpart—poverty, chastity, and obedience: the desire to serve God—in relation to Right Thought on Saturday, etc., following the meditation exercise above, with the imagination of the solarization of the second chakra. One may consider, for example: What is personal desire? How does it arise? What is its consequence? How is it overcome or transfigured? When the second chakra is fully transfigured, this center becomes a center of holiness, of harmony between the body, soul, and spirit. *Lead us not into temptation.*

## Week 59: The Solarization of the Third Chakra ☿

The third chakra, the ten-petalled lotus, in the region of the solar plexus and corresponding to the planet Mercury, is the center of movement and thought. It is the chakra that governs the astral forces within the human body. It is the door to the sense world, the seat of the origin of science. Through one's senses one perceives the world and enters into relationship with it. One reaches out to experience what is outside one's self. Out of desire one can grasp at experiences or take at the expense of others, often governed by subconscious impulses. As the portals of the senses allow one to come into relation with all that is outside one's self, they also present one with a panorama of temptation. Christ spoke the words: "I am the door, the entrance, and the exit." These words reveal the true meaning of the spiritualized senses. When one's eyes see with the eyes of the spirit, when one's ears hear the Divine Word, when one's hands touch with the power of healing, etc., then the sense portals of one's being become spiritualized.

The third chakra embodies the numerical principles of ten, and half of ten—five. In the ten-petalled lotus flower, five of the petals suffering from disharmony need transfiguring by the human being. These five petals correspond to the five dark currents of the will. The ten commandments given by Moses address the transfiguring of the ten-petalled lotus flower.

Thou shalt have no other gods before me.
Thou shalt not make for thyself a graven image, or any likeness.
Thou shalt not take the name of the Lord thy God in vain.
Remember the Sabbath day, to keep it holy.
Honor thy father and thy mother.
Thou shalt not kill.
Thou shalt not commit adultery.

Thou shalt not steal.
Thou shalt not bear false witness against thy neighbor.
Thou shalt not covet thy neighbor's house.

The vulnerability of the third chakra relates to the right hand of the five dark currents of the will. The right hand grasps, taking often at the expense of others. In the Paradise story, Eve enacts this when she takes the apple. In taking the apple the soul is grasping to fulfill personal desire. Grasping or taking is the third stage of the Fall corresponding to the third chakra. The meditation for this week addresses the temptation of grasping in order to fulfill personal desires, and its counterpart—to give at one's own expense, to serve God and one's neighbors selflessly.

The miracle of the healing of the paralyzed man at the pool in Bethesda (John 5:1–15) provides the mystical teaching to heal the third chakra. This miracle teaches the healing of human karma. Karma is incurred through actions that are motivated by selfish desire, or any action that is not motivated by selfless love. The paralyzed man was immobilized because his past was driven by selfish greed, lacking consideration for anyone else. As a result, he lay for 38 years beside the pool in Bethesda, awaiting healing. Because he was paralyzed, it was necessary for someone to help him into the pool when the angel stirred the waters. No one had interest in helping him, for he had not displayed interest or concern for others. When Christ asked him if he wanted to be made whole, the paralyzed man answered saying, "I have no one, when the water is troubled, to put me into the pool." Then Christ said unto him, "Rise, take up thy bed, and walk." Immediately the man was made whole and took up his bed and walked. He brought his karma (his bed) into verticality, into alignment with spiritual law. Christ later saw him in the temple and said unto him, "Behold, thou art made whole: sin no more, lest a worse thing come unto thee." When one fully aligns one's actions with spiritual law, one's conscience guides one to act out of selflessness, out of love for God and one's neighbor. The solarization of the third chakra is its ultimate transformation into a radiant heart center, an active source of divine love.

Enter into a meditation on the relationship between taking or grasping in order to fulfill personal desires, and its counterpart—to give at one's own expense, to serve God and one's neighbors selflessly—in relation to Right Thought on Saturday, etc., following the meditation exercise above, with the imagination of the solarization of the third chakra. One may consider, for example: What is grasping? How does it arise? What is its consequence? How is it overcome or transfigured? When the third chakra is fully transfigured, this center—that is so significant for scientific thinking—becomes a center of conscience, guiding one to become a servant of God and one's neighbors. *Forgive us our trespasses as we forgive those who trespass against us.*

### Week 60: The Solarization of the Heart Chakra ☉

The fourth chakra, the twelve-petalled lotus, in the heart region and corresponding to the Sun in our solar system, is the center of love in the human being. The heart governs the circulation of the blood in the human organism, the blood being the physical vessel for the Ego or higher Self. The heart also guides human thought. If thinking is heartless, it is cold and lacks compassion. If thinking is heart-filled, it radiates warmth and wisdom. As it is the domain of love, it is through the heart chakra that one can experience communion with the Divine. The heart is at the center of all human works. The true humanization of the whole human being requires the transformation of the human being entirely into heart, functioning by love and for love.

The heart chakra embodies the numerical principles of twelve, and also half of twelve—six. In the twelve-petalled lotus flower, six of the petals suffering from disharmony need to be transfigured by the human being. The work of healing the heart chakra can be taken up with the six subsidiary exercises given by Rudolf Steiner in *Guidance in Esoteric Training*. The book *Enlivening the Chakra of the Heart* by Florin Lowndes guides one through these exercises. The spiritualizing of the twelve-petalled lotus also corresponds to the integration of the twelve virtues addressed above in part 9.

Blessed are the devoted, for they shall have the power
of self-sacrifice.
Blessed are the balanced, for they shall make progress.
Blessed are those who endure, for they shall have faith.
Blessed are the selfless, for they shall undergo catharsis.
Blessed are the compassionate, for they shall be free.
Blessed are the courteous, for they shall have tact of heart.
Blessed are the contented, for they shall have equanimity.
Blessed are the patient, for they shall be enlightened.
Blessed are the self-disciplined, for they shall know the truth.
Blessed are the courageous, for they shall have the power to redeem.
Blessed are the discreet, for they shall have strength of mind.
Blessed are the magnanimous, for they shall be filled with love.

With the integration of these virtues, the heart chakra will become radiant and guide one's being in the service of divine love.

The heart chakra is the central lotus flower. It is the balance point between the three upper chakras or centers of wisdom, and the three lower chakras or centers of revelation. This central organ governs the Ego development or the flowering of the higher Self. The temptation regarding the twelve-petalled lotus is that of egotism, the desire for personal greatness, or false love of self. It is a matter of whether the heart is turned inward toward one's self in egotism or turned outward toward the world in love. In the Paradise story, Adam and Eve eat the apple. In so doing they ingest spiritual sustenance that was meant to remain external to the human being and stream its forces for the benefit of all of creation. That which is divinely intended to ray out from the human heart is taken into the self for self-serving purposes. This is false communion, the fourth stage of the Fall corresponding to the fourth chakra. The meditation for this week addresses the temptation of egotism and its counterpart—humility, the practice of which leads to selfless love for all of creation.

The miracle of the feeding of the five thousand (John 6:1–14) provides the mystical teaching to heal the fourth chakra. During the Sermon on the Mount, Christ could see that the multitudes were hungry. They suffered an emptiness, a spiritual hunger, which is a constant condition when one lives in a state of egotism. Christ realized the need to transform egotism into selflessness. With five small barley loaves and two fish offered by a young boy, Christ nourished the five thousand with the light of the Father (which draws the grain forth from its seed) and the life force of the Mother (which quivers through the element of water). Within the multitudes gathered there, an inner light began to shine. When everyone had eaten their fill, the remains were gathered that nothing be lost, filling twelve baskets. These symbolize the twelve seed forces of spiritual nourishment for the twelve petals of the heart chakra. Christ spoke the words: "For the bread of God is he that cometh down from heaven, and giveth life unto the world." Then said they unto him, "Lord, evermore give us this bread." And Jesus said unto them, "I am the bread of life: he that cometh to me shall never hunger; and he that believeth in me shall never thirst" (John 6:33–35).

> The heart or twelve-petalled lotus is the only chakra that is not attached to the organism. It can go out of it and live by the exteriorisation of its "petals," which can be rayed outwards with and in others. When transformed, the heart will become a traveler, a visitor, and anonymous companion of those who are in prison, those who are in exile, and those who bear heavy loads of responsibility, traversing ways leading from one end of the earth to the other, and also ways through spheres of the spiritual world—from purgatory to the very feet of the Father. Because no distance is insurmountable for love and no door can prevent it from entering—according to the promise which says: "and the gates of hell shall not prevail against it" (Matt. 16:18). It is the heart which is the marvelous organ called to serve love in its works. It is the structure of the heart—simultaneously human and divine, a structure of love—which by way of analogy can open our understanding to the words of the Master: "And lo, I am with you always, to the end of time" (Matt. 28:20). (Anonymous, 1991, p. 227)

Here one can enter into a meditation on the relationship between egotism, self-centeredness, and self-aggrandizement, and its counterpart—humility (and the practice of selfless love for all of creation)—in relation to Right Thought on Saturday, etc., following the meditation exercise above, with the imagination of the solarization of the fourth chakra. One may consider, for example: What is egotism? How does it arise? What is its consequence? How is it overcome or transfigured? When the fourth chakra is fully transfigured, the boundless source of love flowing within the heart will turn toward the world. The heart will become a traveler to serve love in its works. The solarization of the fourth chakra is its ultimate transformation into an unfathomable source of divine love which serves the world. *Give us this day our daily bread.*

## Week 61: The Solarization of the Fifth Chakra ♂

The fifth chakra, the sixteen-petalled lotus, in the larynx region and corresponding to the planet Mars, is the center of creative speech. This is the center through which our spiritual will can be realized. It is the center from which vibration or sound issues forth. Through God's will and the Logos, creation came into existence. The fifth chakra is the creative will center which manifests in human speech, and can be transformed into the center for the healing power of the Word, the Logos center in the human being.

The throat chakra embodies the numerical principles of sixteen, and half of sixteen—eight. In the sixteen-petalled lotus flower, eight petals suffering from disharmony and needing transfiguring are to be worked upon by the human being. The work of healing the larynx chakra is fulfilled through the embodiment of the eightfold path of the Buddha, the moral transformation of the soul, achieving the state of Manas, that of the purified astral body. One then has a pure or virgin soul, as was the case with the Virgin Mary and St. Francis of Assisi.

Right Thought
Right Resolve
Right Word
Right Action
Right Livelihood
Right Endeavor
Right Memory
Right Contemplation

The disfiguration of the throat chakra is caused by fear. Fear arises when one feels unsafe in relation to outer circumstances or in relation to one's self. This is portrayed in the Paradise story when, after eating the apple, Adam and Eve ran and hid from God. They knew they had transgressed and felt the destabilizing force of being disconnected to God. Fear arises when one is cut off from God. Fear is the fifth stage of the Fall corresponding to the fifth chakra. The meditation for this week addresses the debilitating power of fear, in relation to its counterpart—courage to transform one's self through love.

The miracle of walking on water (John 6:16–21) provides the mystical teaching to heal the fifth chakra. At evening, after the feeding of the five thousand on the hill where the Sermon on the Mount took place, the disciples set sail across the Sea of Galilee to Capernaum. Jesus was not with them. A great storm arose on the sea. The cosmic winds of the Father and the rising tides of the Mother tossed the boat upon the sea. The disciples saw a figure walking toward them across the water, one who was in perfect harmony with the Father and the Mother so as not to be affected by the storm. They were afraid. But Jesus said unto them, "It is I; be not afraid." Then they received him into the ship and immediately the ship was at the land whither they went. Why were the disciples afraid? They beheld something that was supernatural. They were raised into another level of perception that was unfamiliar and resulted in fear. Christ comforted them with his speech: "Fear not, it is I." The ability to overcome fear requires the presence of Christ, the I AM within one's self. It requires the ability to face the unknown in faith that Christ is present and is so to heal and guide and bring one safely to shore. One can become fearless when one has no need of any support on Earth. To go forward—not in fear, but in love and courage—to transform one's self, knowing Christ is present always, even unto the end of time, is the work of the sixteen-petalled lotus flower.

Christ spoke the words: "I am the good shepherd." This I AM saying corresponds to the throat chakra. The sheep know their shepherd through the sound of his voice, through hearing his creative speech, the Divine Word expressed through him.

Here one can enter into a meditation on the relationship between fear and its counterpart—courage to transform one's self through love in God's presence—in relation to Right Thought on Saturday, etc., following the meditation exercise above, with the imagination of the solarization of the fifth chakra. One may consider, for example: What is fear? How does it arise? What is its consequence? How is it overcome or transfigured? When the fifth chakra is fully transfigured, the creative center of speech becomes magical: illumining, consoling, and healing. The solarization of the fifth chakra is its ultimate transformation into a radiant heart center, an active source of divine love, healing humanity through the power of the Word. *Thy will be done on earth as it is in heaven.*

## Week 62: The Solarization of the Sixth Chakra ♃

The sixth chakra, the two-petalled lotus, in the region of the third eye and corresponding to the planet Jupiter, is the center of intellectual initiative, spiritual thinking, and spiritual seeing. The sixth chakra is the Divine I AM center of one's being. It is the center of wisdom, from whence one knows the truth. Moses had a highly developed, two-petalled lotus flower. The third eye chakra embodies the numerical principles of two, and also half of two—one. In the two-petalled lotus flower, one petal suffering from disharmony and needing transfiguring is to be worked on by the human being. The work of healing the third eye chakra is fulfilled through developing the capacity of concentration that will bring one to the center of divine consciousness. The fulfillment of healing this chakra will result in the purification of the life forces, achieving the state of Buddhi, that of the purified etheric body.

The disfiguration of the third eye chakra is caused by deceit or falsehood that arises through shame. Shame arises when one feels an awareness of transgressing spiritual law and, subsequently, there commonly arises cunning deception to hide the truth. This is portrayed in the Paradise story when, after eating the apple, Adam and Eve's eyes were opened and they saw that they were naked and covered themselves with fig leaves. They knew they had transgressed and sought to hide the truth. In the arising of shame, one's awareness is alerted to the condition of transgression. Shame is a natural result of misdeeds. If one is responsive to shame, one can be guided to correct one's actions. If one seeks to cover up the truth, one will live in fear and uncertainty; life will be a lie. Deceit arising from shame is the sixth stage of the Fall corresponding to the sixth chakra. Deceit leads to spiritual blindness. The meditation for this week addresses the decaying power of deceit, which leads to blindness, in relation to its counterpart—truthfulness, which leads to spiritual sight and healing.

The miracle of the healing of the man born blind (John 9:1–41) provides the mystical teaching to heal the sixth chakra. The man born blind was not blind because he had sinned, nor because his parents had sinned, but rather that the works of God should be made manifest in him. To heal this man's sight, Jesus spat on the ground and made clay with the earth and the spittle. He anointed the eyes of the blind man with the clay and told him to go and wash his eyes in the pool of Siloam. When the man had washed his eyes, he could see. Three ingredients were used to heal the blind man's eyes: saliva—the residual working of the Word; earth—the substance of the Mother in the depths; and spring water—the purest impulse from the depths of life. Christ spoke the words: "I am the light of the world." The purest light from the heights of the Father and the purest water from the depths of the Mother commingled with Christ's saliva and the earth, unifying the healing agents of the Father and Mother through Him. When asked by the accusers if he had truly been blind and who had healed him, the man spoke the truth with no impulse to deceive the accusers. The healing of the man born blind signified for the blind man the bestowal of physical vision. Applied to humanity as a whole, it has the significance of the restoration of spiritual seeing.

Here one may enter into a meditation on the relationship between deceit arising from shame, and its counterpart—truthfulness arising from the courage to see—in relation to Right Thought on Saturday, etc., following the meditation exercise above, with the imagination of the solarization of the sixth chakra. One may consider, for example: What is deceit? How does it arise? What is its consequence? How is it overcome or transfigured? When the sixth chakra is fully transfigured, intellectual initiative becomes compassion-filled insight into the world. The solarization of the sixth chakra is its ultimate transformation into a radiant heart center, an active source of divine love, an awakened I AM. *Thy kingdom come.*

## Week 63: The Solarization of the Seventh Chakra ♄

The seventh chakra, the eight-petalled lotus, in the region of the crown and corresponding to the planet Saturn, is the center of revelation of wisdom, and the place of one's spiritual name. The seventh chakra is the portal to the Father. It houses the memory of all of one's positive karma throughout existence. It weaves one's relationship between consciousness and death and is the human portal to death. The crown chakra embodies the numerical principles of eight, and also half of eight—four. In the eight-petalled lotus flower, four petals suffering from disharmony and needing transfiguring are to be worked upon by the human being. The work of healing the crown chakra is fulfilled through the embodiment of the beatitudes taught by Christ during the Sermon on the Mount. The fulfillment of healing this chakra will result in the purification of the physical body—achieving the state of Atma.

> Blessed are the seekers of the spirit, for theirs is the kingdom of heaven.
>
> Blessed are those who bear suffering, for they shall be comforted.
>
> Blessed are the meek, for they shall inherit the Earth.
>
> Blessed are those who hunger and thirst after righteousness, for they shall be satisfied.
>
> Blessed are the merciful, for they shall receive mercy.
>
> Blessed are the pure in heart, for they shall see God.
>
> Blessed are the peacemakers, for they shall be called children of God.
>
> Blessed are those who are persecuted for righteousness' sake, for theirs is the kingdom of heaven.
>
> Blessed are ye when men revile you and persecute you and say all manner of evil against you falsely on my account, rejoice and be exceedingly glad, for great is your reward in heaven.

The disfiguration of the crown chakra is caused by a separation of life and consciousness which arises from doubt, and leads to death. This separation impedes one from reaching the Father.

Doubt results from the simultaneous working of two streams: that of light streaming into the crown from the spirit realm, and that of darkness streaming into the human subconscious from the material Earth realm. When one experiences this divisive condition, doubt arises and one is faced with a choice between the light of the spirit and the darkness of the material world. In the Paradise story, Adam and Eve chose to eat the apple, following the enticement of the serpent. They chose the stream of darkness from the material Earth realm. This resulted in toil, suffering, and death. When one chooses the stream of spiritless matter, one's life becomes separated from one's consciousness, resulting in death. Death arising from the separation of life and consciousness is the seventh stage of the Fall, corresponding to the seventh chakra. The meditation for this week addresses the condition of death, resulting from the separation of life and consciousness, in relation to its counterpart—uniting consciousness and life.

The miracle of the raising of Lazarus (John 11:1–45) provides the mystical teaching to heal the seventh chakra. Jesus's beloved friend, Lazarus, chose the way of light to the degree that he lost his relationship to the Earth. His life forces became weakened to the point of physical death. When one chooses the way of light, a refining process takes place that separates one from the Earth. Those who choose the way of darkness experience a coarsening process. Lazarus faded out of physical life because his compassion was focused entirely on the spirit realm. When one's conscience is fully awakened, one has compassion for both the spirit realm and the earthly realm, for incarnated and also non-incarnated beings. When Christ called out, "Lazarus, come forth," He called upon Lazarus's compassion for the incarnated beings of the Earth, that he might serve them and fulfill his mission for humanity in that incarnation. Lazarus was able to unite his consciousness with life, and through his resurrection he was able to serve humanity for over sixty years longer, writing the Book of Revelation and the Gospel of John. Christ spoke the words: "I am the resurrection and the life." Christ is the embodiment of the force that fully unites life and consciousness—Atma, the state of the purified physical body.

Here one can enter into a meditation on the relationship between doubt which separates life from consciousness, and its counterpart—uniting consciousness and life—in relation to Right Thought on Saturday, etc., following the meditation exercise above, with the imagination of the solarization of the seventh chakra. One may consider, for example: What is the separation of life and consciousness? How does it arise? What is its consequence? How is it overcome or transfigured? When the seventh chakra is fully transfigured, one becomes full of warmth as the fire of Pentecost. One ceases to be abstract and transcendent, but rather illumined with light and warmth. The solarization of the seventh chakra is its ultimate transformation into a radiant heart center, an active source of divine love, uniting one with the Father. *Hallowed be Thy name.*

## Week 64: The Solarization of the Chakras

During this week the meditation considers the seven stages of the Fall in relation to the base metals that correspond to the planets. Here one can meditate on the alchemical transformation of base metals into gold. One may consider the qualities of each of the base metals and what is required to transform them into gold, in relation to the inner transformation required to heal each of the chakras. One may deeply consider the characteristics of each base metal in relation to the stage of the Fall (e.g., lead: poisonous, dense, heavy, etc., in relation to death.) Then one might turn one's thoughts to the qualities of gold in relation to unifying life and consciousness. It is suggested to begin with lead in relation to death on Saturday; gold in relation to egotism on Sunday; silver in relation to doubt on Monday; iron in relation to fear on Tuesday; mercury (quicksilver) in relation to grasping on Wednesday; tin in relation to deceit on Thursday; and copper in relation to personal desire on Friday, in correspondence with the chart below.

**Figure 15**

## The Alchemical Transformation of the Chakras

| | Chakra | Lotus Petals | Planet | Metal | Alchemical Transformation |
|---|---|---|---|---|---|
| Saturday | crown | 8 | ♄ | lead into Gold | death into unifying life and consciousness |
| Thursday | third eye | 2 | ♃ | tin into Gold | deceit into truthfulness |
| Tuesday | larynx | 16 | ♂ | iron into Gold | fear into courage to transform one's self through love |
| Sunday | heart | 12 | ☉ | gold into Gold | egotism into love |
| Wednesday | solar plexus | 10 | ☿ | mercury into Gold | grasping into giving |
| Friday | abdomen | 6 | ♀ | copper into Gold | personal desire into serving God and one's neighbor |
| Monday | root | 4 | ☽ | silver into Gold | doubt into faith in God |

## Week 65: The Solarization of the Chakras

Each day this week the meditation focuses on one lotus flower, illuming its radiant potential, the inner condition that hinders its fulfillment, and the healing miracle and enzyme offered to work on one's own healing, using the charts below. It is suggested to begin with the root chakra in relation to doubt and the healing miracle at the Wedding at Cana on Saturday, working one's way up the chakras throughout the week.

**Figure 16**

The Stages of the Fall Related to the Chakras

| Chakra | Lotus Petals | Planet | Stage of the Fall | The Consequence |
|---|---|---|---|---|
| crown | 8 | ♄ | separation of life and consciousness | *Prevents the purification of the physical body—anti-Atma. Hinders the ability to reunite the physical body with the Divine.* |
| third eye | 2 | ♃ | deceit | *Prevents the purification of the etheric body—anti-Buddhi. Hinders the ability to reunite the etheric body with the Divine.* |
| larynx | 16 | ♂ | fear | *Prevents the purification of the astral body—anti-Manas. Hinders the ability to reunite the astral body with the Divine.* |
| heart | 12 | ☉ | egotism | *The separation of the physical body from the Divine.* |
| solar plexus | 10 | ☿ | grasping | *The beginning of the separation of the etheric body from the Divine.* |
| abdomen | 6 | ♀ | desire | *The beginning of the separation of the astral body from the Divine.* |
| root | 4 | ☽ | doubt | *The beginning of the disintegration of the Ego—oneness with God.* |

**Figure 17**

| The Solarization of the Chakras | | | | | |
|---|---|---|---|---|---|
| Chakra | Lotus Petals | Planet Metal | Capacity | Alchemical Transformation | Healing Miracle "I AM" Saying |
| crown | 8 | ♄ lead | revelation of wisdom | *Becomes full of warmth as fire of Pentecost; thinking ceases to be abstract and transcendent.* | *Raising of Lazaras. I AM the resurrection and the life.* |
| third eye | 2 | ♃ tin | intellectual initiative | *Becomes compassion-filled insight into the world.* | *Healing of man born blind. I AM the light of the world.* |
| larynx | 16 | ♂ iron | creative word | *Becomes magical: illumining, consoling, and healing.* | *Walking on water. I AM the good shepherd.* |
| heart | 12 | ☉ gold | love | *Becomes radiant to serve love in its works.* | *Feeding of the five thousand. I AM the bread of life.* |
| solar plexus | 10 | ☿ mercury | science | *Becomes conscience, to become a servant of God and neighbor.* | *Healing of paralyzed man. I AM the door.* |
| abdomen | 6 | ♀ copper | harmony and health | *Becomes a center of holiness: harmony between spirit, soul, and body.* | *Healing of nobleman's son. I AM the way, the truth, and the life.* |
| root | 4 | ☽ silver | creative force | *Becomes source of energy and inexhaustible élan.* | *Changing water into wine at the wedding in Cana. I AM the true vine.* |

Suggested closing words each day:
*Within my heart let dwell the Cosmic Word.*
*Within my will let work the Will of God.*

# Bibliography

Abelard, P., Heloise (1901). *The Love Letters of Abelard and Heloise.* (unknown translator). I. Gollanz, H. Morten (Eds.). Retrieved from http://www.sacred- texts.com/chr/aah/index.htm.

Adbelkader, R. (2011). *Congo Violence Fueled By Common Material In Cell Phones, Laptops.* Retrieved from http://www.huffingtonpost.com/nycity-news-service/congo-violence-fueled-by_b_184192.html.

Aivanhov, M. (1976). *The Second Birth.* Los Angeles, CA: Prosveta U.S.A. Edition.

Algis, V. (2006). The Agony of Atomic Genius. *The New Atlantis*, Number 14, 94.

Anonymous. (1991). *Meditations on the Tarot.* Rockport, MA: Element Books.

Aquinas, T. (2005). *Summa Contra Gentiles.* (J. Rickaby, S.J. Joseph, Trans.) London: Burns & Oates B. Herder.

Aurobindo, S. (2003). *The Future Evolution of Man: The Divine Life Upon Earth.* Twin Lakes, WI: Lotus Press.

*Bhagavad Gita.* (1962). Trans. Mascaro, J. New York: Penguin Books.

Bird, K. and Sherwin, M. (2009). *American Prometheus: The Triumph and Tragedy of J. Robert Oppenheimer.* Pennsylvania: Atlantic Books.

Bishop, D. Forgiveness in Religious Thought. *Studies in Comparative Religion* (Vol. 2, No. 1). World Wisdom, Inc. Retrieved from http://www.studiesincomparativereligion.com/public/articles/Forgiveness_in_Religious_Thought-by_Donald_H_Bishop.aspx

Blavatsky, H.P. (1971). Thoughts on Ormuzd and Ahriman. *Sunrise magazine*, Theosophical University Press. Retrieved from http://www.theosophy-nw.org/theosnw/world/mideast/mi-hpb.htm.

Bock, E. (2009). *Studies in the Gospels* (Vol. 1). Edinburgh: Floris Books.

Boyce, M. (1990). *Textual Sources for the Study of Zoroastrianism.* Chicago: University of Chicago Press.

Brown, T. (2000). *The Quest.* Berkeley: Berkeley Trade.

Brownmiller, S. (1975). *Against Our Will: Men, Women, and Rape.* New York: Simon and Schuster.

Bulgakov, S. (1997). *The Holy Grail and the Eucharist.* New York: Lindisfarne Books.

Campbell, J. (1991). *The Masks of God, Vol. 4: Creative Mythology.* New York: Penguin Books.

Camus, A. (1989). *The Stranger.* (M. Ward, Trans.). New York: Vintage Books.

Carter, J. (July, 1977). Presidential Medal of Freedom Remarks on Presenting the Medal to Dr. Jonas E. Salk and to Martin Luther King, Jr. *The American Presidency Project.*

Cousineau, P. (2011). *Beyond Forgiveness: Reflections on Atonement.* San Francisco, CA: Jossey-Bass.

Dalai Lama and Hopkins, J. (2003). *How to Practice: The Way to a Meaningful Life.* New York: Atria Books.

De Vendômois, J.S., Roullier, F., Cellier, D., Séralini, G-E. (2009). A Comparison of the Effects of Three GM Corn Varieties on Mammalian Health. *Institute of Biological Science,* 5(7): 706-726. Also retrieved from http://www.biolsci.org/v05p0706.htm.

Easwaran, E. (2007). *The Dhammapada.* Tomales, CA: Nilgiri Press.

———. (2011). *Ghandhi, the Man.* Tomales, CA: Nilgiri Press.

Emmerich, A. (1954). *The Life of Jesus Christ* (Vol. 1). Rockford, IL: Tan Books.

Engdahl, F. (2007). *Seeds of Destruction: The Hidden Agenda of Genetic Manipulation.* Montreal, Canada: Global Research.

Francke, S. and Cawthorne, T. (1996). *The Tree of Life and the Holy Grail.* London: Temple Lodge.

Freud, F. (1989). *Introductory Lectures on Psychoanalysis.* New York: Liveright Publishers.

Ghose, A. and McDermott, R. (1988). *Essential Aurobindo.* New York: Lindisfarne Books.

Griffiths, B. (2001). *River of Compassion.* Springfield, IL: Templegate Publishers.

Grimal, P. (1965). *Larousse World Mythology.* Secaucus, NJ: Chartwell Books.

Hadot, P. (1995). *Philosophy as a Way of Life*. Malden, MA: Blackwell Publishing.

Hammarskjöld, D. (1964). *Markings*. (L. Sjöberg & W.H. Auden, Trans.). New York: Alfred A. Knopf.

Haskins, S. (1993). *Mary Magdalen: Myth and Metaphor*. New York: Harcourt, Brace, & Company.

Hillman, J. (1997). *The Soul's Code*. New York: Grand Central Publishing.

Hoddeson, L.; Henriksen, P.; Meade, R.; Westfall, C. (1993). *Critical Assembly: A Technical History of Los Alamos During the Oppenheimer Years, 1943–1945*. New York: Cambridge University Press.

Issacson, E. (2012). *Through the Eyes of Mary Madgalene*. New Mexico: Logosophia Press.

James, W. (1984). *The Essential Writings*. New York: State University of New York Press.

Josephus, F. (94 CE). *Antiquities of the Jews*. Retrieved from http://www.creationism.org/books/josephus/JosephusAntiq01.htm#NoteJosephusAntiq01.Babel.

Jung, C.G. (1959). *The Archetypes and the Collective Unconscious* (R.F.C. Hull, Trans). In H. Read, M. Fordham, G. Adler, W. McGuire (Series Eds.), *The Collected Works of C. G. Jung* (Vol. 9). Princeton, NJ: Princeton University Press.

———. (1970). *Civilization in Transition* (R.F.C. Hull, Trans). In H. Read, M. Fordham, G. Adler, W. McGuire (Series Eds.), *The Collected Works of C. G. Jung* (Vol. 10). Princeton, NJ: Princeton University Press.

———. (1973). *C.G. Jung, Letters 1: 1906–1950*, ed. G. Adler, A. Jaffé, trans. R.F.C. Hull. London: Routledge & Kegan Paul.

———. (1975). *Psychology and Religion: West and East*. Princeton, NJ: Princeton University Press.

———. (1976). *The Portable Jung*. New York: Penguin Classics.

———. (1981). *The Archetypes and the Collective Unconscious*. Princeton, NJ: Princeton University Press.

———. (2001). *Psychology of the Unconscious*. Princeton, NJ: Princeton University Press.

Jung, E. and Franz, M. (1998). *The Grail Legend*. Princeton, NJ: Princeton University Press.

La Croix, M. (1981). *The Remnant.* New York: Avon Books.

Lee, H. (1993). *To Kill a Mockingbird.* New York: Harper Collins.

Lemke, U. (2000). *Das Kreuz als Lebensmotiv.* Stuttgart: Urachhaus Verlag.

Lendman, S. (2008, Feb-March). Review of *Seeds of Deception* by Jeffrey Smith. *Nexus magazine* (Vol. 15, No. 2).

Lowndes, F. (1998). *Enlivening the Chakra of the Heart.* London: Sophia Books, Rudolf Steiner Press.

*The Mahābhārata.* (2009). (Smith, J., Trans.) New York: Penguin Classics.

Maslow, A. (2011). *Toward a Psychology of Being.* Eastford, CT: Martino Fine Books.

Matthews, J. (1997). *Sources of the Grail.* New York: Lindesfarne Press.

McDermott, R. (2007). *The New Essential Steiner.* New York: Lindisfarne Books.

McGinnis, M. (2004). *Buddhist Animal Wisdom Stories.* Trumbull, CT: Weatherhill, Inc.

Miller, A. (1976). *The Crucible.* New York: Penguin.

Montefiore, S. (2006). *Speeches that Changed the World: The Stories and Transcripts of the Moments that Made History.* London: Quercus.

Nietzsche, F. (1974). *The Gay Science.* New York: Vintage.

Pearce, J. (2002). *The Biology of Transcendence, a Blueprint of the Human Spirit.* Vermont: Park Street Press.

Plato. (1952).*The Dialogues of Plato.* Trans. Jowett, B. Chicago: William Benton.

Prokofiev, S. (1995). *The Occult Significance of Forgiveness.* London: Temple Lodge.

Powell, R. (1996). *Chronicle of the Living Christ.* New York: Anthroposophic Press.

———. (2008). *The Mystery, Biography, and Destiny of Mary Magdalene.* Great Barrington, MA: Lindisfarne Books.

Prosecutor v. Furundzija (1995) Case no. IT-95-17/1 (International Criminal Tribunal for the former Yugoslavia, Trial Chamber).

Prosecutor v. Jean Paul Akayesu (1996) Case No. ICTR-96-4-T (International Criminal Tribunal for Rwanda, Trial Chamber).

Purucker, G. de. (2000). *Questions We All Ask* (Series 2, No. 27). Pasadena, CA: Theosophical University Press. Retrieved from http://wn.rsarchive.org/Lectures/OrigSuff/19061122p01.html

Ritchie, G. (2007). *Return from Tomorrow.* Grand Rapids, MI: Chosen Books.

Rosen, E. (1998). *Experiencing The Soul Before Birth, During Life, After Death.* New York: Hay House.

Ryce, M. (2013). Enlightenment, a Work in Progress as Found in The Khaburis Codex, Selected Passages From The Aramaic Testament. Retrieved from http://www.whyagain.org/index.php/en/khabouris-manuscript-aramaic/enlightenment-introduction

Sardello, R. (2001). *Freeing the Soul from Fear.* New York: Riverhead Trade.

Satprem. (1975). *Sri Aurobindo or The Adventure of Consciousness.* Pondicherry, India: Sri Aurobindo Ashram Press.

Schnurr, M. and Swatuk, L. (2010). Critical Environmental Security: Rethinking the Links Between Natural Resources and Political Violence. Center for Foreign Policy Studies: Dalhousie University.

Seddon, R. (2002). *The Future of Humanity and The Earth As Foreseen by Rudolf Steiner.* East Sussex, England: Temple Lodge Publishing.

Shakespeare, W. (2001). *The Tragedy of Othello, the Moor of Venice.* New York: Penguin Books.

Soloviev, V. (1995). *Lectures on Divine Humanity.* New York: Lindesfarne Press.

Steiner, R. (1905, October). *Foundations of Esotericism.* Lecture VIII: Berlin. Retrieved from http://wn.rsarchive.org/Lectures/FoundEsoter/19051003p01.html

———. (1906, November). The Origin of Evil. Lecture: Berlin. Retrieved from http://wn.rsarchive.org/Lectures/OrigSuff/19061122p01.html

———. (1909, March). The Deed of Christ and the Opposing Spiritual Powers, Lucifer, Ahriman, Asuras. Lecture. Retrieved from http://wn.rsarchive.org/Lectures/Dates/19090322p01.html

———. (1909, April). The Spiritual Bells of Easter. Lecture. Retrieved from http://wn.rsarchive.org/Lectures/Dates/19090410p01.html

———. (1915, June). Preparing for the Sixth Epoch. Lecture: Düsseldorf. Retrieved from http://wn.rsarchive.org/Lectures/19150615p01.html

———. (1919, December). Memory, After-Image and the Etheric Body. Lecture: Dornach. Retrieved from http://www.sheridanhill.com/memory.html.

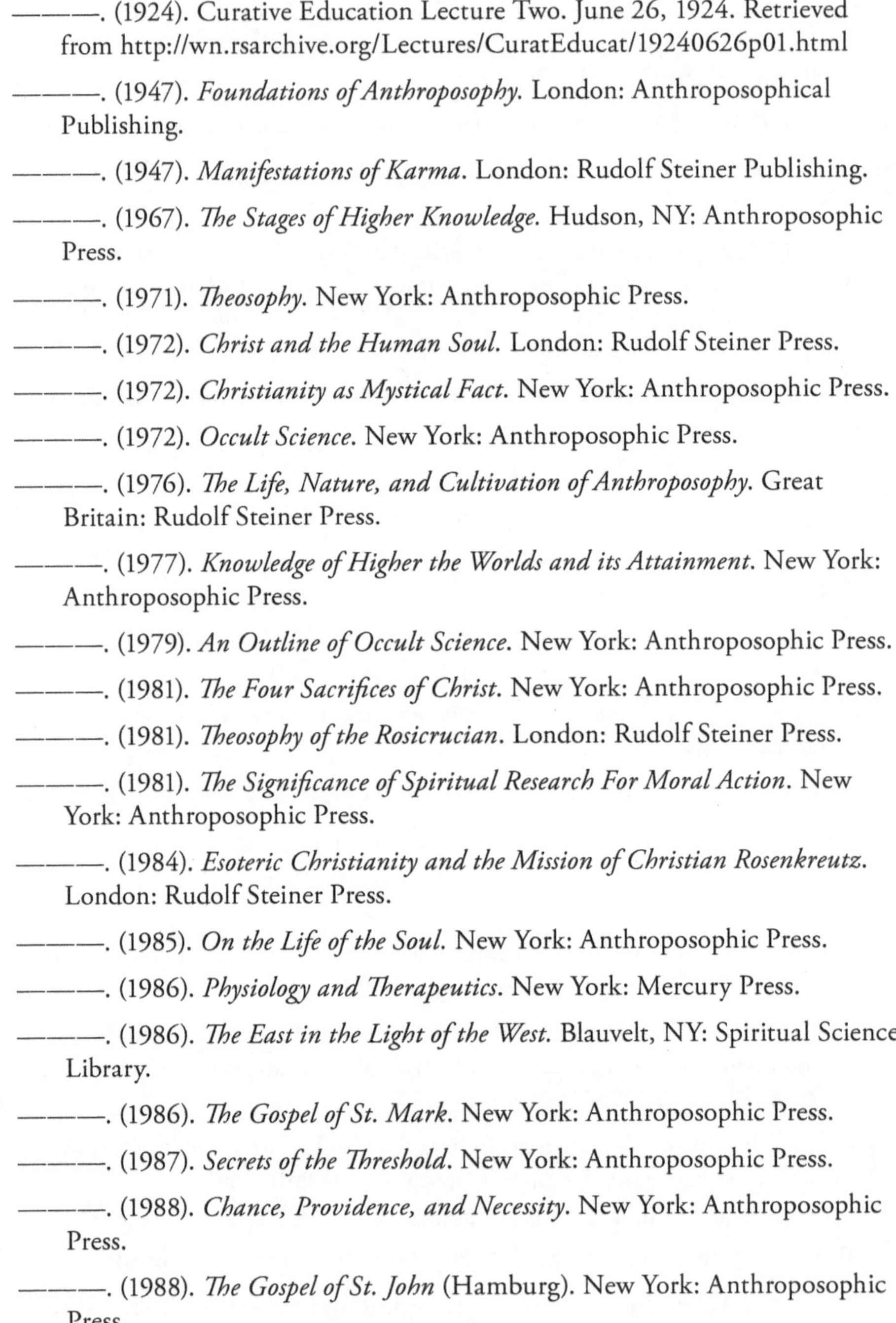

———. (1924). Curative Education Lecture Two. June 26, 1924. Retrieved from http://wn.rsarchive.org/Lectures/CuratEducat/19240626p01.html

———. (1947). *Foundations of Anthroposophy.* London: Anthroposophical Publishing.

———. (1947). *Manifestations of Karma.* London: Rudolf Steiner Publishing.

———. (1967). *The Stages of Higher Knowledge.* Hudson, NY: Anthroposophic Press.

———. (1971). *Theosophy.* New York: Anthroposophic Press.

———. (1972). *Christ and the Human Soul.* London: Rudolf Steiner Press.

———. (1972). *Christianity as Mystical Fact.* New York: Anthroposophic Press.

———. (1972). *Occult Science.* New York: Anthroposophic Press.

———. (1976). *The Life, Nature, and Cultivation of Anthroposophy.* Great Britain: Rudolf Steiner Press.

———. (1977). *Knowledge of Higher the Worlds and its Attainment.* New York: Anthroposophic Press.

———. (1979). *An Outline of Occult Science.* New York: Anthroposophic Press.

———. (1981). *The Four Sacrifices of Christ.* New York: Anthroposophic Press.

———. (1981). *Theosophy of the Rosicrucian.* London: Rudolf Steiner Press.

———. (1981). *The Significance of Spiritual Research For Moral Action.* New York: Anthroposophic Press.

———. (1984). *Esoteric Christianity and the Mission of Christian Rosenkreutz.* London: Rudolf Steiner Press.

———. (1985). *On the Life of the Soul.* New York: Anthroposophic Press.

———. (1986). *Physiology and Therapeutics.* New York: Mercury Press.

———. (1986). *The East in the Light of the West.* Blauvelt, NY: Spiritual Science Library.

———. (1986). *The Gospel of St. Mark.* New York: Anthroposophic Press.

———. (1987). *Secrets of the Threshold.* New York: Anthroposophic Press.

———. (1988). *Chance, Providence, and Necessity.* New York: Anthroposophic Press.

———. (1988). *The Gospel of St. John* (Hamburg). New York: Anthroposophic Press.

———. (1989). *The Karma of Untruthfulness* (Vol. 1). 12 Lectures. New York: Anthroposophic Press.

———. (1990). *Psychoanalysis and Spiritual Psychology*. New York: Rudolf Steiner Press.

———. (1991). *From Jesus to Christ*. Sussex, England: Rudolf Steiner Press.

———. (1993). *Understanding the Human Being: Selected Writings of Rudolf Steiner*. Bristol, England: Rudolf Steiner Press.

———. (1995). *Intuitive Thinking as a Spiritual Path*. New York: Anthroposophic Press.

———. (1995). *Self-Transformation*. London: Rudolf Steiner Press.

———. (1997). *An Outline of Esoteric Science*. New York: Steiner Books.

———. (1997). *The Effects of Esoteric Development*. Hudson, NY: Anthroposophic Press.

———. (1998). *Guidance in Esoteric Training*. London: Rudolf Steiner Press.

———. (1998). *Love and Its Meaning in the World*. Hudson, NY: Anthroposophic Press.

———. (1999). *A Psychology of Body, Soul, and Spirit*. Forest Row, England: Rudolf Steiner Press.

———. (1999). *First Steps in Inner Development*. Hudson, NY: Anthroposophic Press.

———. (2003). *Evil*. Forest Row, England: Rudolf Steiner Press. Lecture (January 15, 1914).

———. (2004). *Secret Brotherhoods and the Mystery of the Human Double*. Forest Row, England: Rudolf Steiner Press.

———. (2007). *Freemasonry and Ritual Work: The Misraim Service*. (J. Wood, Trans.) from The Collected Works of Rudolf Steiner. Great Barrington, MA: Steiner Books.

———. (2008). *Esoteric Cosmology*. Radford, VA: Wilder Publications.

Strong's Greek Lexicon. http://www.blueletterbible.org/lang/lexicon/lexicon.cfm?Strongs=G863

Strong's Hebrew Lexicon. http://bibleapps.com/hebrew/5375.htm

Suzuki, S. (2011). *Zen Mind, Beginner's Mind*. Boston, MA: Shambhala Publications, Inc.

Tidball, C. (2005). *Jesus, Lazarus, and the Messiah*. Great Barrington, MA: Steiner Books.

Tolstoy, L. (1967). *Twenty-Three Tales*. London: Oxford University Press.

Tomberg, V. (1941). *Lord's Prayer Course*. San Francisco, CA: Sophia Foundation publication.

———. (1941). *Our Mother Course*. San Francisco, CA: Sophia Foundation publication.

———. (1983). *Inner Development*. New York: Candeur Manuscripts.

———. (1985). *Anthroposophical Studies of the New Testament*. Spring Valley, NY: Candeur Manuscripts.

———. (1992). *Covenant of the Heart*. Massachusetts: Element Books.

———. (2006). *Christ and Sophia*. Great Barrington, MA: Steiner Books.

Trungpa, C. (2003). *The Collected Works of Chögyam Trungpa*. Boston, MA: Shambhala Publications, Inc.

Tucker, L. (2003). *Mystery of the White Lions: Children of the Sun God*. South Africa: Npenvu Press.

Tutu, D. (1999). *No Future Without Forgiveness*. New York: Doubleday.

(2008). Unknown author. SEC v. Madoff and BMIS LLC, *U.S. Securities and Exchange Commission*. Retrieved from http://www.sec.gov/litigation/complaints/2008/comp-madoff121108.pdf.

(2011). Unknown author. Madoff Says He Is Happier in Prison Than Free. *The New York Times*. Retrieved from http://www.nytimes.com/reuters/2011/10/27/business/business-us-madoff-interview.html?_r=1.

(2013). Unknown author. Forgiveness versus Might and Anger. *Hinduism.com.za*. Retrieved from http://www.hinduism.co.za/forgiven.htm#Forgiveness%20is%20a%20great%20power

United Nations Security Council (1999) Fourth Annual Report of the International Criminal Tribunal for Rwanda to the General Assembly. Retrieved from http://69.94.11.53/ENGLISH/annualreports/a54/9925571e.htm.

Valiunas, A. "The Agony of Atomic Genius," *The New Atlantis* (No. 14, Fall 2006).

Van der Post, L. (1978). The Other Side of Silence. Article in *Voices of the Wilderness*. South Africa: Jonathan Ball.

Vann, Joseph, ed. (1954). *Lives of the Saints*. New York: John J. Crawley & Co.

Vaughan-Lee, L. (1994). *In the Company of Friends*. Point Reyes Station, CA: The Golden Sufi Center.

Vitale, J. (2007). *Zero Limits*. Hoboken, NJ: John Wiley and Sons.

Voragine, J. de (1993). *Legenda Aurea* (The Golden Legend). Princeton, NJ: Princeton University Press.

Voreacos, D. (2009). "Madoff Criminal Charges: Summary of the 11 Counts Against Him." Bloomberg.com News. Retreived from http://www.bloomberg.com/apps/news?pid=newsarchive&sid=a6Osnj.SoYdM

Vyasa, V. (1962). *Bhagavad Gita*. (J. Mascaro, Trans.). New York: Penguin Books.

Waite, A. (1909). *The Hidden Church of the Holy Graal*. London: Rebman Limited.

Weber Linn, J. and Firor Scott, A. (2000). *Jane Addams: A Biography*. Illinois: University of Illinois Press.

Welchman, K. (2000). *Erik Erikson: His Life, Work, and Significance*. Berkshire, England: Open University Press.

Witzenmann, H. (1990). *The Virtues: The Seasons of the Soul*. Dornach: Spicker Books.

Zajonc, A. (2009). *Meditation as Contemplative Inquiry*. Great Barrington, MA: Lindisfarne Books.

Zimmer, H. (1973). *The King and the Corpse: Tales of the Soul's Conquest of Evil*. Princeton, NJ: Princeton University Press.

www.ingramcontent.com/pod-product-compliance
Lightning Source LLC
LaVergne TN
LVHW041114080826
845145LV00007B/1804